TOMMASO LECCISOTTI

Monte Cassino

Edited and translated into English by
ARMAND O. CITARELLA

ABBEY OF MONTE CASSINO

1987

TO

ABBOT DESIDERIUS

ON THE NINTH CENTENARY
OF HIS DEATH
(1087-1987)

FOREWORD TO THE ENGLISH EDITION

The English edition of Tommaso Leccisotti's Monte Cassino, *is based on the tenth Italian edition which appeared in January 1983 on the first anniversary of the author's death which occurred on January 3, 1982. A foremost scholar of Cassinese history, d. Tommaso Leccisotti presided for many years over the great Archives of the abbey of Monte Cassino, one of the richest collections of medieval manuscripts and documentary material in the world. When the present Archivist of Monte Cassino, d. Faustino Avagliano, O.S.B., asked me to prepare an English edition of the abbey's history written by his predecessor, I felt greatly honored and challenged. That classic work and other writings of d. Tommaso had long been familiar to me as a student of the social and economic history of southern Italy in the Middle Ages. In the Archives of Monte Cassino I had met and conversed with the former Archivist and had come to admire him greatly both as a person of great charm and exquisite courtesy and as a highly distinguished scholar with a remarkably long list of writings to his credit, spread over a period of sixty years *.*

The demanding task of translation was therefore gladly undertaken because I realized the value of having this masterpiece, with its vast sweep of Cassinese history, reach a still wider public.

This volume of popularization, or rather, to use the author's own definition, "of synthetic information about the history and life of Monte Cassino", has been a great success both with the public and the scholars ever since the first edition appeared in 1947 only three years after the fourth destruction of the abbey. It has since gone through ten editions, from the 1947 to the 1983 one

---

* *See the complete bibliography of his published works in* Tommaso Leccisotti Monaco e Scrittore (1895-1982), *edit, by F. Avagliano in* Miscellanea Cassinese n. 49, *Monte Cassino 1983.*

on which this translation is based. The eminent Cassinese scholar G. Falco expressed the critical consensus in these words: "I admire both his self-assurance and his felicity of expression. I myself could never have realized such a book. It is a beautiful work and a good one. It was necessary to say what Monte Cassino was and is today, in its lost beauty and its eternal meaning".

Two simple features have helped to give to Monte Cassino the great popularity it has enjoyed for almost forty years. Part I contains the chronological survey from the time of St. Benedict to the present. Part II, The Works, is a series of loving essays on the spiritual and intellectual life as well as the artistic and literary activity at the abbey through the centuries. From the first edition onward the publication has been furnished with an increasing number of admirable and historical illustrations, many of them in color as in the present volume. They help to bring life and a sense of reality to the abbey's long and noble history.

There is little that one can add except to beg the reader's understanding for the decision to make the narrative as readable as possible and let the main interest focus on the series of stirring events of this breathless cavalcade through fifteen centuries of Cassinese history. The artistic skill and the graceful style of the author, rich in evocative phraseology, classical allusions and the full array of the rhetorical devices of the Cassinese "cursus", would sound remote and anachronistic in current English. It was thus with much regret that a more direct but alas plainer style was adopted in this translation. The substance of the work was not sacrificed to the exigencies of style so that the deeper spiritual message would remain as fresh and clear as in the original.

Armand O. Citarella

St. Michael's College of Vermont
October 28, 1985

PART I

The days

I.

THE BEGINNINGS

«Haec erat terra tibi destinata» *.
(Hymn. Clun.)

1. THE CENTURIES-OLD MISSION OF MONTE CASSINO.

«Quel monte a cui Cassino è nella costa» [1] has fulfilled for almost thirty centuries its lofty mission as a center of spiritual life. This noble form of life has been present since prehistoric times. Besides the numerous fossil remains, one can find there the more remarkable signs of primitive human activity confirmed and, in fact, increased by the last and most recent excavations [2]. Among these remains which go at least as far as the iron age, there are numerous votive offerings and even a primitive altar. However, through the successive occupations of various peoples, the mountain also came to acquire great military importance. Thus the top became an acropolis. This, surrounded by enormous walls, formed a defensive system independent from that of the town below. Eventually, religious practice found its way back within these walls.

The Romans, who transformed old *Casinum* into a prosperous and noble town, had found that the acropolis of *Casinum* had a religious as well as a military function, although their conquest made unnecessary the maintenance of the ancient fortifications. Only later, when the power of the empire began to weaken, did prudence dictate the rehabilitation of the defensive system of the acropolis of Cassino. The extreme point of the fastness was used, as well as it could be, by connecting walls and reinforcing towers, but in the sixth century this defensive line had already

---

* This was the land destined to you. (Cluniac Hymn.)

been abandoned and thus St. Benedict was able to choose one of these towers as his abode.

It had been reserved to him to triumphantly plant the Cross on the stronghold, a place still favored by idolatrous practices even after the town had received the message of the Gospel. It was also his role to definitely convert to Christianity the whole surrounding region which, due to the ruins and destructions caused by the barbarian invasions, had experienced a dangerous return to paganism:

> «E quel sono io che su vi portai prima
> lo nome di colui che in terra addusse
> la verità che tanto ci sublima *»[3].

Since then that mountain, seat of a new and truer life, has assumed in the history of the Church and European culture, a well-determined role and position. In the life of Italy, especially in some centuries, it has had such an important function that it well justifies its definition by Urban II: «non tantum nobis, qui prope sumus, sed universae Italiae opportunus et necessarius **»[4].

2. THE SITE.

Providentially, the geographical position favored its mission. That large circle of mountains whose smooth curves seem to embrace and caress the vast fertile valley, gives to the site, according to an expression used by Montalembert, «a greatness and uncomparable majesty»[5]. Against this background the mountain rises rapidly to seventeen hundred feet as a gigantic platform prepared by the work of the ages to support an altar praying for harmony between heaven and earth.

The mountain is only the last and most advanced ramification of a whole range which from the north links up again with the

---

* «And I am the one who first brought up there, the name of him who brought that truth that so exalts us.»

** Suitable and necessary not only to us, who are near, but to the whole of Italy.»

Apennines; it juts out from it almost isolate. It is this position
which gives it a particular value. A great look-out and solid bastion — in the thirteenth century it was defined as an enormous
fortress — its barren massif dominated the large valley of the Liri
river. From the Middle Ages until not too long ago, this was the
easiest approach to southern Italy, because the other roadways
have to cross the Pontine marshes or the impervious passes of the
mountains of the Abruzzi. It is easy to understand therefore why
Monte Cassino became such an important element in political
contests and military struggles: its possession meant control of the
way to Rome. As the poet of the eleventh century sang: «Hinc est
iter ad urbem apostolicam *», and like Rome, Monte Cassino was
always the goal of pilgrims, visitors of all sorts from all places and
epochs; like the eternal city one of the most important historical
place on earth.

3. THE WORK OF ST. BENEDICT.

The importance of Monte Cassino, which was indeed
favored by its topography as well as human activity, derived principally from the work of Benedict of Norcia. The mountain was
the place predestined to him not only to chase away and for all
time the darkness of paganism but, above all, to give the world
the light of Benedict's Rule.

The spirit of God had drawn him, still young, from the corruption of Rome. Horrified by the sight of the dangers which
brought ruin to innocent youth, Benedict, followed by his trusted
nurse, had run to find refuge in a small village, Affile, in the Simbruini mountains. Fear of an unwelcomed popularity drew him
even farther away, among the deserted ruins in the vicinity of the
lake of Nero at Subiaco. A horrible cave where «in conspectu
Superni Spectatoris habitavit secum **»[6] was for some years the

---

* «From here is the way to the apostolic city».
** «In sight of the supreme Spectator he led a solitary life».

witness of his heroic asceticism. The disciples who had gathered around him then drew him out of his beloved solitude. Forced thus to temper the idealism of his early youth and inspired less by the spiritual athletes of the Egyptian desert than by the hermits of the Castoriana valley in the vicinity of Norcia, he divided his disciples into twelve groups and assigned to each a leader, reserving for himself the overall supervision with the help of a few chosen disciples.

He did not, however, stop at the imitation of these models. He was chosen by God to give a definitive form to Western monasticism, to be the father of many peoples. It was therefore the will of God that kept giving wider breadth to his idealism and opening larger fields for his mission while busy in the practical experimentation of everyday living. Like Abraham, once more he had to leave his people to establish the model city for Western monasticism. On his horizon black zones could be seen, covered still by the shadows of death, and this further stimulated the zeal of his soul that sought closeness to Christ.

This was the twofold mission that, as acknowledged by all future generations, attracted him irresistibly toward the mountain of Cassino. The last and decisive cause for his departure from the Simbruini hills was the jealous wickedness of a priest who began to harass the holy Abbot and to lay snares for what was most dear to him, the immortal souls of his disciples. It was, however, a merely occasional cause; Benedict knew full well that «one does not change the enemy by a change of place»[7], and in fact he gave no consideration to returning there even when, soon after he left Subiaco, he learned of the sudden death of his persecutor.

The tradition, corrupted in the course of the centuries but still quite probable in its main lines, places at the base of the new foundation and the new plan a donation of lands to the Saint in the territory of Cassino by some powerful secular lords. Certainly Benedict, as St. Gregory tells us, was on good terms with the nobility of Rome, who entrusted their children to him. The oblation of children of noble families, according to the Rule, which codifies the custom followed by the lawgiver, was accompanied by offerings of goods. There is no evidence to support the story that the donor was Tertullus himself, the father of Placidus. The relative tradition, even when it preserves, as even the most uncompromising critics recognize, some element of truth, is totally corrupt, and it is impossible to determine the size of the lands donated or to establish if among them there was the acropolis [8].

Benedict went there in full control of his actions and encoutered no obstacle in his evangelizing mission from local people who, though illegally, still continued in their idolatrous practices. This was true for both the local civil and religious authorities. All this leads one to believe that the Abbot and Apostle came to Cassino with well-defined rights and with support from powerful people, perhaps even on a mission entrusted to him by the proper authorities.

The most accepted tradition has set the arrival of St. Benedict at Monte Cassino in the year 529. It was the same year in which Justinian closed the schools of philosophy in Athens, by this time become useless and dangerous fields for empty battles of words, and the year in which he promulgated his famous Code. This date, however, though current for over seven centuries, after so many vicissitudes cannot be accepted as final, but with a certain degree of latitude one might call it a limit *ad quem*. It can still remain, not to indicate with absolute historical certainty the year in which the new inhabitants took possession of the acropolis, but at least to establish the basic limits of this event of exceptional importance, namely the first settlement of the Cassinese monastery. The primitive organization of the inner life of the community as well as the original buildings certainly required a few years of work. Nothing prevents us from placing, hypothetically of course, this period of development between the two dates, one more traditional than the other, of 525 and 529 [9].

The preexisting buildings were certainly not sufficient and not all adaptable to Benedict's aims. This typical citadel of western monasticism was thus shaped out of the old buildings with new additions necessary because of the new way of life introduced on the summit.

It was the opening of a school, that is, an association of men in the service of God, living communally in the fullest sense, where any personal egoism was banned. Their life was organized around the divine liturgy, having as a foundation stone against any deviation always possible in the course of time, a new characteristic, stability. «... they planted their feet and held on with a firm heart» [10]. It was indeed the «*agmen validissimum* *»: in the monastery, with the Rule as the law, the Abbot as the guide, the brothers as helpers, the monks fought for the conquest of the kingdom of God.

Thus endowed with the discretion and self-control typical of the Roman people and based on a profound knowledge of the human heart, the Rule made its first appearance in the world from that ancient tower, which through it now became a «citadel of life which it had been once of death» [11]. It was the expression of the mature experience of the lawgiver, and modern historians are unanimous in conceding that in its definitive redaction it could only date from the last years of the author's life.

In his wise work of codification Benedict succeeded in giving unity to western monasticism, in freeing it from exaggerations, vanities, and from non-orthodox infiltrations, and in assigning to it a liturgical canon. His code, which gathered together the flower of the Catholic tradition, gradually became «the very Rule of the Roman Catholic Church, the *Regula Patrum,* the *Regula Sancta* par excellence» [12].

The most recent studies, which once seemed to undermine the originality of St. Benedict, have actually placed in better view the preeminent role of the Cassinese lawgiver. He was not at all the green palm tree in the desert, as a certain literary current, that one might call romantic, is pleased to call him. St. Benedict was a link, priceless and unreplaceable, in a long chain; he was the son and the product of his age.

At any rate, these studies, especially the comparison with the so-called *Regula Magistri,* have allowed us to evaluate «the enor-

---

* «The very strong line».

mous progress made by St. Benedict... He arrived at a conception all his own, in which, although elements drawn from other sources are still visible, a new spirit gives life to every prescription and order; above all a balanced and wise conception which makes more fruitful and rich the previous monastic experience.

St. Benedict's own temperament is etched out in the constitution of the monastery, and that solidity which would defy the ages was the result more of his meditative and orderly mind than of any influence of the Roman temper. The very literary form of the Rule confirms this. This presents itself as something really new, the confluence of the whole monastic tradition reshaped by a personality so vigorous that it transpires through every page and every prescription. It remains therefore as one of the most original works of the whole body of patristic and monastic literature and the immense offspring of medieval monasticism derives from it [13].

The second book of the *Dialogi* of St. Gregory, from the middle of chapter VIII to chapter XXXVII, allows us a look at the Cassinese community as it was during the lifetime of its Patriarch. Here we find a description of the exterior daily life of that early monastery, which even then, however, was richly endowed and furnished with all the necessities [14]. It was, on the other hand, mainly through the Rule, the codified description of the everyday life as it took place under the immediate direction of the lawgiver, that we gain access to the inner, spiritual life of the community. Thus that «company of monks, secure and protected by religion, who read, tilled the soil and exercised the arts in the midst of a great society that was coming apart through barbarism, was laying the seed of the future civilization and recomposition of the people» [15]; they were ensuring the future of Europe and the civilized world. Not too far from there, in that very same region, Plotinus had proposed to establish his ideal city, Platonopolis. There, where the previous experiment, — symbolic omen and providential preparation — of the pagan philosopher had failed, the Christian ascetic had succeeded in opening a spring of never-failing life.

All the enchantment of the early beginnings of that life supernaturally lived emanates from the narrative of St. Gregory, who at times rises to tones of epic greatness. The gates of the monastery opened to let out men with the task to evangelize, to spread the gospel, with others to work in the fields; but also to receive all kinds of souls: here comes the humble subdeacon asking for a little oil, or the unfortunate pressed by his creditors, or a farmer begging the return to life of his dead son. The holy Bishop Sabinus comes here from his far away Apulia, and even Totila, the King of those Goths who burdened the coutry with war and plunder, comes riding up the mountain. The Saint's charity abounds with aid through the horror of the famine. In the tempestuous and uncertain flow of human vicissitudes, his is the word of comfort, exhortation, or reproach. As a beacon on the mountain he spreads his light far and wide although he especially warms with his affection the members of the house and the neighbors. Changing from *dirum magistri* to *pium patris affectum* *, he reproaches, incites and encourages; he keeps within the cloister those tempted by instability, procures what is needed many times directly from Providence through unexpected ways and gives back life to a monk who died while he was working.

A particular spirit of sweet, supernatural poetry seems to envelop his relations with his sister Scholastica; the blood relationship is purified and cultivated in the highest realm of the spirit. Once every year the old man descends from the cloister to go and meet Scolastica, the virgin who had preceded him at a very young age into the service of God, to spend some time with her in happy spiritual conversation. His final visit lasted all night, against Benedict's will. The entreaties and the love of the sister were more powerful, and a sudden storm appeared in its violence as the sign of the divine will, forcing her to stay over until the following morning [16]. Three days later he saw from his tower that blessed soul ascending into heaven in the form of a white dove. He had her body taken to the tomb he had prepared for himself in

---

* «From the severity of the teacher, to the affection of a loving father».

the small shrine of St. John the Baptist on the mountaintop.

Later, from the same tower Benedict saw another soul fly up to heaven, that of the Bishop of Capua, St Germanus. In the miraculous vision, high above all creation, the Creator Himself appeared to him and the universe in Him. That shining vision of an October night, as celebrated through the centuries, has made even more vivid the parallelism between St. Benedict and Moses.

These happenings, however, which made more intimate the Saint's communion with heaven, were the prelude to the end of his earthly journey. Struck by disease, six days before his death he had his tomb opened: then, feeling that the end was near and following the example of St. Spe, one of the ascetics about whom he had heard in his native Norcia, he had himself taken into the oratory, there fortified with the body and blood of our Lord and praying, he gave up his spirit in the arms of his disciples (ca. 547). Thus Benedict's earthly life came to an end. His triumphal entrance in the heavenly Jerusalem through a luminously bright street strewn with carpets was revealed to two of his disciples at two different places.

The earthly life of the Father thus closed, but his work was not ended. It has continued through the centuries in his model creation, Monte Cassino, and in the vaster confines of the entire world, in the lives of the numberless phalanxes of his children, who will always salute him as the shining standard — bearer and leader of the sacred militia.

In fact, while the Patriarch was still alive the Sacred Rule as a life-giving river had begun to flow from the mountain of Cassino to enrich the furrows of the rising Christian civilization. Among the monasteries whose foundation was with certainty the work of St. Benedict, the narrative by St. Gregory mentions those of Monte Cassino and Terracina and those that preexisted at Subiaco.

The lawgiver's renown seems to add credence to the thesis which proposes the foundation, since the earlier days, of other Benedictine houses, especially in Rome. The lack, however, of reliable sources and the falsifications found in the tradition impose upon us a cautious reserve.

At any rate, a new and decisive impulse to the intense growth which for centuries gave the Church and Europe a prevalent Benedictine character, came from an event that from a human point of view should have marked the end of St. Benedict's work on the mountain of Monte Cassino.

The Founder had appeared on the human stage during one of the most difficult periods in western history. He never let, however, external circumstances distract him from the ideal he was pursuing. His example had indicated the true meaning of human existence.

The first experience of his teaching took place not too many years after his death, when what he had foreseen in tears and sorrow came to pass. A Lombard band, withdrawing beyond the Liri, decided to drive the monks out of the mountaintop to seize that natural fortress and fortify it as a defense against the Roman duchy. They broke into the cloister under cover of night and easily overwhelmed the defenseless brothers (577-589). Life did not cease, however, it merely moved elsewhere.

The monks, though surprised in their sleep, were all saved by the promise wrenched from God by their Founder. Most of them found shelter in Rome in the shadow of the Lateran palace, but along the harsh and bitter roads of their exile they were accompanied by the most precious remembrances of their Father: the Rule in the codex that «ille suis sanctis manibus exaravit *» [17], the measures for the bread and wine granted to the monks, a few of the many sacks of flour found at the monastery gate on a day of great famine, and whatever else they were able to salvage — «quidquid ex suppellectili subripere poterant **».

Indeed the destruction of Monte Cassino was not an isolated episode. Most of Italy came under the heel of the Lombards, the «most savage of the savage Germans», but in Rome it did not take long for the surviving flame of Benedictine monasticism to

---

* «Which he had written with his sacred hands».
** «Whatever they were able to salvage».

come back to life and to shine even more brightly. Through the narratives of his sons, the remembrance of Father Benedict remained alive and strongly attracted the sensitive soul of a young Gregory who later in the *Dialogi* consecrated the blessed memory of the Saint.

At the same time the Rule began its triumphal journey; and in this too the merit belonged principally to Gregory. Received and consecrated by the adoption and sanction from the Apostolic See, the Code, Roman in concept and structure, became a companion to and commentary on the Gospels in the conversion of the people. The history of the diffusion and the influence of the Rule has since then completely fused with that of the Church; every other piece of monastic legislation yielded to the Rule of Benedict, thus paving the way for «that practical unity of religious concepts which lies at the base of the new civilization» [19].

It was once again the manifestation of the Eternal Law: from death comes life.

NOTES

[1] DANTE, *Paradiso,* XXII, 37. It is the translation of the text of the *Dialogi* of St. Gregory the Great, c. 8: «Castrum namque quod Casinum dicitur, in excelsi montis latere situm est qui videlicet mons distenso sinu hoc idem castrum recipit, sed per tria milia in altum se subrigens, velut ad aera cacumen tendit».

[2] The various researches done about the prehistory and protohistory of Monte Cassino have been utilized and recapitulated by A. PANTONI, *L'Acropoli di Montecassino e il primitivo monastero di San Benedetto,* Monte Cassino, 1980 (Miscellanea Cassinese, 43).

[3] DANTE, loc. cit., 40-42.

[4] *Cum nuper, 1098, Nov. 3.*

[5] C. DE MONTALEMBERT, *I monaci d'occidente,* Ital. transl. by A. Carraresi, III, Florence, 1965.

[6] GREGORII MAGNI, *Dialogi,* II, 3.

[7] *Ibid.,* II, 8.

[8] One might call it ironical and, at the same, happy auspice, that of all the marble statues of the Benefactors, only the one of Tertullus was still in its place and emerged waist

high above the rubble of the cloister, after the last destruction.

[9] Only the adjective «traditional» seems to be enough to indicate that this was not a groundless hypothesis; the two dates are both supported by ancient evidence, some sources going back to the ninth century.

[10] DANTE, *Paradiso*, XXII, 51.

[11] MARCI POETAE, *Carmen de S. Benedicto*, 26, *Patr. Lat.*, LXXX, 184.

[12] I. SCHUSTER, *Discorso per l'inaugurazione della cripta di S. Benedetto*, Cesena, 1913, 18.

[13] G. PENCO, *Storia del monachesimo*, 63-64. Also SALVATORELLI in *Dizionario Biografico degli Italiani*, 8, 286, stated that the difference of the Rule of St. Benedict from «the RM is so great that only the hypothesis that RM belongs to B, or at least a preceding familiarity and adoption, can make it comprehensible (once the precedence of RM is recognized) that B. had done alla that work of textual alteration, reduction, transformation, instead of writing it directly and integrally *ex novo*».

[14] The monastery then is large not so much for the number of monks, which apparently was of several groups of ten, but it was completely furnished with everything that was necessary. We have moved far from the experience of Subiacum, therefore Monte Cassino is not the thirteenth monastery, as some have claimed, but it represents something quite new and different, not from the point of view of ascetic teaching but from that of the organization. One cannot say that this unity of the new coenobium was suggested and determined by the topography of the area because even on the mountain of Cassino it would have been possible to scatter the disciples in various houses, and certainly there was quite a number of them hastening to the school of the well known Saint. This unitary character was maintained also in the establishment of Terracina. It was obviously a design carefully determined and forcefully carried out. Besides one must note that St. Benedict did not leave Monte Cassino again, although he must have followed the progress of the other monasteries. Monte Cassino then remained by desire and willed choice, the definitive and proper residence for St. Benedict, who for it, and only for it expressed the utmost concern.

[15] L. TOSTI, *Storia, I, 12. «Without any doubts, St. Benedict never intended to form a religious order in the current sense of the word. He laid down, however, principles which were used as basis of action by his posterity, gathering and synthesizing the preceding experiences. In a sense, we could ascribe to Benedictine monasticism also, what a noted writer observes: «The religious reforms destined to the greatest successes and the most successful survivals are precisely those that begin from the premise that they are only a link in a long chain, and that they bring to the world only the integral fulfillment of preexisting traditions», E. BUONAIUTI, Storia del Cristianesimo, II, M. E. Milan, 1943.*

[16] The ancient little church on the western slope of the mountain, which marked the yearly meeting place, has also been rebuilt after its destruction in the last war, in the same tenth-twelfth century style on designs provided by d. Angelo Pantoni with a beautiful apsidal mosaic executed on sketches provided by d. Francesco Vignarelli. It was solemnly consecrated by abbot Rea on Feb. 7, 1963. The same A. PANTONI has then defendeded its ancient tradition in his «Sulla locazione del convegno annuale di S. Benedetto e S. Scolastica, e sul monastero di Piumarola», in *Benedictina*, 15 (1968), 206-228.

[17] PAULI DIACONI *Epistola ad Carolum regem* in Albers, *Consuetudines*, III, 52, new edition with the name of Theodimar, in *Corpus Consuetudinum Monasticarum*, I, (see, infra p. 45) 157-175.

[18] PAULI DIACONI, *Historia Langobardorum*, IV, 15.

[19] I. Schuster, *L'imperiale abbazia di Farfa,* Rome, Vaticana, 1921, 19.

BIBLIOGRAPHY

Concerning the habitat at Monte Cassino, the main works are: G. De Marco, *Flora di Montecassino,* Montecassino 1887: Idem, Montecassino illustrato nei tre regni della natura, Naples, 1888; G. Sacchetti, *Storia geologica di Montecassino,* Cava dei Tirreni, 1920.

On ancient Cassino the most authoritative study, which quotes and examines the preceding bibliography, was done by G. F. Carettoni, *Casinum,* Rome, Istituto di Studi Romani, 1940 («Italia Romana» ser. I, vol. II).

For the Acropolis, in particular, and the Tower of St. Benedict the fundamental work now is the one by Pantoni, already mentioned.

Of the *Dialogi* of St. Gregory the Great, the second book of which is, together with the Rule, the main source for learning about life at Monte Cassino in its early years, to the edition of U. Moricca, Rome, Istituto Storico Italiano, 1924 (Fonti per la storia d'Italia, 57), it has been added recently the edition done by A. De Vogüé, with a French translation by P. Antin in the collection Sources Chrétiennes, nn. 251, 260, 265, for 1979-1980.

One must take into account its results in evaluating the previous biographies of St. Benedict, of which we wish to remember only for several points of view, those of L. Salvatorelli, *S. Benedetto e l'Italia del suo tempo,* Bari, Laterza, 1929 and I. Schuster, *La storia di S. Benedetto e dei suoi tempi*[4], Viboldone, 1963. At Monte Cassino then on the occurrence of the fifteenth centenary, the work of B. Fiore has been published, *San Benedetto, Vita e dottrina,* richly illustrated and reflecting local traditions.

For the circumstances and the probable hypotheses about the coming of St. Benedict to Monte Cassino, cfr. T. Leccisotti, *La venuta di S. Benedetto a Montecassino,* in «Atti del 7° Congresso internazionale di studi sull'alto medioevo, Norcia-Subiaco-Cassino-Montecassino, 29 settembre-5 ottobre 1980, Spoleto, Centro italiano di studi sull'alto medioevo, 1982, 685-696.

On the destruction of Monte Cassino see, S. Brechter, *Monte Cassinos erste Zerstörung...,* in «Studien und Mitteilungen zur Geschichte des Benediktiner-Ordens und seiner Zweige», 1938, 109-150. The author places the event in 577 without however reaching unquestionable certainty. Cfr. T. Leccisotti, *Rileggendo il libro II dei Dialoghi di S. Gregorio,* in «Benedictina», 28 (1981), 223-228.

For the monastic tradition in which the figure of St. Benedict must be placed, as well as for all the developments of monasticism to wich the history of Monte Cassino is tied, see G. Penco, *Storia del Monachesimo in Italia dalle origini alla fine del Medio Evo,* Ediz. Paoline, I (1961). In particular, for the Norcia monasticism which must have exercised profound influence on the mind of Benedict as a young boy see, P. Pirri, *L'abbazia di Sant'Eutizio in Val Castoriana presso Norcia e le chiese dipendenti,* Rome, 1960 (Studia Anselmiana, 45). For the relations between the Rule of St. Benedict and the monastic tradition, cfr. G. Turbessi, *Recenti indagini intorno alla Regola di San Benedetto e ai suoi rapporti con la precedente e coeva legislazioe monastica,* in *La Scuola Cattolica,* 1973, 479-510. For knowledge of the Rule, one should be familiar above all with the current recent volumes of A. de Vogüé, with the collaboration of J. Neufville, which appear also in che collection Sources Chrétiennes, nn. 181-186, 1971-1972, besides a seventh volume out of the series of 1977. For a more practical use, however, the second edition of A. LEN-TINI, *Montecassino,* 1980, which to the text and the Italian translation adds a clear and competent comment, is clearly unsurpassed.

The questions connected with the personality and the work of the second successor of St. Benedict, have been reexamined in a recent study by N. HUYGHEBAERT, *Simplicius, propagateur de la Règle bénédictine. Légende ou tradition?* in «Revue d'Histoire Ecclésiastique», 73 (1978), 45-54.

II.

THE RECOVERY

«... *Through the lands that had been Rome's, a*
new breath of Roman renaissance was felt... The
Rule advanced through Europe side by side with the
law of Rome... As Rome, so Monte Cassino par-
ticipated in the task to restore order to a society so
deeply troubled by the recent convulsions...»
*(*C. CALISSE, in *Convegno Storico di*
Montecassino, Rome, 1932, XXXIV).

1. EARLY SIGNS.

«The rebirth of Montecassino at the beginnings of the eighth
century is one of the events most pregnant with results in the
history of the papacy and southern Italy in the Middle Ages» [1].

It was, however, not an isolated case. A large area of Italy
had found itself helpless under the weight of Lombard occupation, and although the peninsula remained divided for centuries,
contacts with Roman civilization and the warmth of the Catholic
faith soon won over that fierce people, and «those that praying
Theodolinda brought at peace with God» [2] quickly made amends
for the violent past with a generosity never seen again.
Throughout Italy there was a splendid growth of flourishing churches, monasteries and other pious institutions. And like
everywhere else, it was so at Monte Cassino: the monastery rose
from death to life, and to life all the more vigorous and luxuriant
because of the richness of the soil.

As a matter of fact, the heights at Cassino had never — except only briefly — remained completely abandoned. From the
sources one can infer that there were custodians and that there
was no lack of visitors to the holy place, especially among
pilgrims going to Rome or going through on their way to the Holy
Land. The wide circulation of the Rule and the veneration of St.

Benedict were a strong incentive for coming to pray at his tomb.

Considering how strong an attraction St. Benedict exercised even beyond the Alps, it would be hard to believe that his own monks, now living in Rome, would take no interest. Too many concerns, especially moral ones, drew them there, particularly after the early fury of destruction which accompanied the Lombard invasion subsided. Some even like to see in Onoratus (whom a late tradition has made a ninth century abbot of Subiaco) a superior at Monte Cassino over a community that had been reestablished at the time of St. Gregory's writing. The existence, however, of a few monks, or better, hermits, on the deserted mountain amongst the ruin of the destroyed abbey, could hardly take away from the place the dominant aspect of a vast solitude.

It was the withdrawal from the site which indeed made possible the transfer by French pilgrims of the bodies of St. Benedict and his sister St. Scholastica across the Alps to Fleury, from where the body of St. Scholastica was then taken to Le Mans. The narration, full of the visions, prayers, and fastings usually found in such narratives, presents episodes so hard to believe and so full of contradictions that one must think it is false. Nevertheless, it gained credence in the eighth and ninth centuries when so many other tall tales were told and written about similar transfers from Italy. According to such stories, Rome also furnished bodies of saints to various places, as the bodies of St. Sebastian and St. Gregory to Soissons. The relics of these Saints, of course, are still in our days venerated in Rome.

Monte Cassino also persisted in the local veneration. In 759, in fact, Abbot Optatus of Monte Cassino, following the request of King Desiderius, sent a colony of monks with relics of St. Benedict to Leno near Brescia. These later were brought to Brescia and from there back to Monte Cassino in 1878 [4].

Other relics took other roads [5]. There was such a wealth that Monte Cassino distributed them without even keeping a record. Even if there had been adequate records kept of the collection, the greater part might have been lost anyway in the many misfortunes that eventually befell Monte Cassino.

Belief in the possession of these relics is made obvious by the language used over and over by the writers of this period whose documents have come down to us. The words *requiescit, corpus, pignora, sepulchrum,* and *confessio beati patris* convey an obvious meaning that the Greek hymn writers Joseph (ninth century) and Nilus (tenth century) confirm, celebrating with clear expressions the glorious sepulcher of Benedict.

And as at various times during the course of the centuries, Monte Cassino has again revealed in our days its precious deposit to our ecstatic and moved eyes. What, however, was not possible to our fathers could be done now — a complete scientific examination of all the relics and their exact determination.

Many years had to pass then, in the eighth century, before life was fully reawakened around the revered tombs. Undoubtedly the recovery took place gradually, but it was noticed only when it had made some significant progress. Its central figure was Petronax. He had come on a pilgrimage from his native Brescia to Rome and from there intended to continue on to the Holy Land. Gregory II, however, entreated him earnestly to go to Monte Cassino (ca. 717).

There he found some residents already under the leadership of Ciprianus; perhaps these men, who lived very simply, had been joined, as some later traditions relate, by some of the monks from Rome, where the monastery of the monks from Cassino was by this time «without any monastic observance». Petronax was chosen as abbot, the buildings that still existed were restored, and life became normal again, thanks also to the help of the monks of S. Vincenzo al Volturno, which had been recently founded. The arrival not long afterwards, in 729, of the Anglo-Saxon Willibald served to increase the enthusiasm within the new community when he put an end to his decade-long peregrination through all the sanctuaries of the world. From then on, he moved from Monte Cassino only by command of Gregory III, who in 740 sent him to Germany as a companion to St. Boniface who during his stay at Monte Cassino had served as dean and door keeper, first in the monastery above and then in the one below on the river Rapido.

The number of monks had been increasing so much that finally a division was necessary. People came from every corner of Europe to Monte Cassino, which had resumed its place as capital of western monasticism and the purest spring of religious life. The abbey, in the words of Mabillon became «an hostel of princes and even kings... and a convenient shelter from the storms of life». In fact, during this first century of the renewed life at the abbey, in the cloisters of Cassino the humble and the ignorant were joined by the powerful and the learned to serve the same Lord. Sturmi, the founder of Fulda and German monasticism was sent by St. Boniface to learn there the system of monastic life and to transplant it into those regions recently converted. St. Liudgerius, later bishop of Münster and apostle of Westphalia, stopped there for two years, and Charlemagne's uncle, Adalhardus, a refugee from the monastery of Corbie, found hospitality there. St. Anselm, the founder of the abbey of Nonantola, found shelter there against King Desiderius' persecution: Paul the Deacon, the historian of the Lombards, retired there and continued his literary activity. Even two kings, Carloman and Ratchis, representing two people who were traditional enemies, the Franks and the Lombards, now united fraternally in the humble anonymity of monastic ranks, and left behind the care of their kingdoms for that of fields and cattles, coming perhaps «to forget in the silence of the cloister the drama of their defeat and to convert their humiliation into victory» [8].

These and the many others who were flocking to the mountain of St. Benedict to ask for the habit came from among the Romans, Franks, and Byzantines. One must remember that at Monte Cassino the office was conducted in Greek and Latin for many years and there were important Greek liturgical observances. As these people coming from so diverse backgrounds brought with them distinctive tendencies and influences, the cloister acted as a melting pot where differences fused into new and more sensible communal experiences, which eventually went to enrich the life of the whole monastic world of Europe. In fact, it was not only the Cassinese way of life which was transplanted to the various regions of Italy, Germany, and France but also its literary and scientific aspects.

Monte Cassino thus became «a center of political activities where met and clashed the interests of popes, of Frankish rulers, of Lombard kings and dukes... an international center opened to influences from every corner of the Catholic world, an element not to be disregarded in the political arena. At Monte Cassino one does not breathe the air of the province» [9]. One can, in fact, say that it was just at that time that one begins to notice the traces of the close correspondence between the history of Monte Cassino and that of Italy. The struggle against the iconoclasts and the close allinace between the Popes and the Beneventans against Liutprand were determining factors in the recovery of Monte Cassino, and at the same time, a close bond of solidarity between Monte Cassino and Rome developed which was to last for centuries.

Besides sending Petronax, the Roman pontiffs continued to keep a vigilant eye on and to support the reborn community on the mountain of Cassino. To the name of Gregory II one must add that of Gregory III and, above all, of Zachary, to whom was credited for a long time the Greek translation of the *Dialogi* of St. Gregory, which as we now know was the work of the monk John. He gave substantial aid to the monastery and in the end returned to it the autograph copy of the Rule written by St. Benedict himself, a clear recognition of the abbey as the capital of western monasticism. According to some historians it was Zachary who granted the monastery its first and far reaching concession of privileges. The consecration of the basilica as well as the discovery of the sacred remains of St. Benedict and St. Scholastica have also been attributed to him. The relevant documents are, however, obvious falsifications, though it is possible that an authentic but incomplete source did exist, which the falsifier used as a base for his amplifications: some modern historians concur in this opinion.

The Lombard rulers vied with the popes in granting privileges and lands to the abbey. Gisulf II, Duke of Benevento, strengthened the position of Monte Cassino, donating large possessions and sanctioning her autonomy from minor local authorities. At a later time, king Desiderius also granted a privilege, which also has come down to us altered. These donations were part of a wide plan of political and religious renewal that the Lombard rulers had undertaken after the early fury of the conquest had abated. The monasteries, situated in strategic positions, were in the van of the conquerors' progress and vigilant sentinels of their safety. Thus, following a similar course at Monte Cassino, the pricipality of Benevento drew close to itself the major monastic institution of southern Italy.

The example of the rulers was followed by the people. Offerings from private sources became numerous and frequent, and though at times they were the result of some practical intent, they were on the whole principally inspired from religious motives. In fact, there is something that none of these converging elements would be capable of explaining, and that is «the miracle of a cloister that in a few decades becomes a model of monastic life for the faithful of the most distant regions, a fervid center of monastic expansion, a goal for pilgrims from the whole Catholic world, a place of refuge and of penance, a prison to princes deluded, repentant or overthrown. This miracle cannot be understood without considering the renown of the Saint that Gregory the Great had immortalized in his *Dialogi,* and the prodigious Benedictine spirit of purity and love, a spark of which animated the Beneventans, Willibald and Petronax making of Monte Cassino an island of peace in a very stormy world. All this cannot be understood without considering that almost thaumaturgic virtue that flowed from the Rule and the Saint's tomb to the people.

2. The imperial abbey.

Petronax died May 6, 750 happy in the certainty that he had assured the future of his community. Successors continued his work while the political horizon was undergoing changes.

Catastrophe was approaching for the Lombard kingdom and triumph for the Franks.

The two kings, who had both sought the peace of Monte Cassino, were forced by the course of events to return briefly to the world stage. Carloman was prevailed upon to return to France and try to moderate the course of royal policy: he died there a year later. Ratchis, on the other hand, even reassumed the throne in 756. At the death of his brother Aistulf, who had been a fierce proponent of continuing the struggle against the Romans, Ratchis resumed the rule of his people, fearing that the old *comes stabuli*, Desiderius, would persist in a policy which, according to his previsions, would lead to ruin. Ratchis did not, however, take the royal title; his condition of *famulus Cristi* prevented that, so he ruled but did not reign. His competitor, however, made an accord with the Pope and the obedient monk returned to the cloister in 757. His judgement was not wrong, and from the quiet summit of Cassino where once again he humbly tended the vineyard, he looked at the large plain below where his ancestors had ridden as proud conquerors; sadly and fearfully he followed the fatal course of events which later (744) would lead to the ruin of his people.

King Ratchis, a pious benefactor, had founded many monasteries, famous among them the one of Monte Amiata; he had also built many churches and altars, some still existing, and his memory on the mountaun of Cassino was linked with the oratory of St. Peter. Built at his own expense on the site where later the sacristy was, it became during the Carolingian period one of the three main churches of Monte Cassino and an important element in the old local liturgy. It was there that some processions started, that the palms were blessed and the dedication ceremonies were held on June 27.

Not far from Monte Cassino, in Piumarola, the wife of Ratchis, Tasia, with the advice and help of Petronax, had built a convent for nuns, where (together with her daughter, Rattruda) she lived out the rest of her saintly life.

St. Benedict seemed to gather under his wings the last relics of the Lombard people. Many went to the cloisters to hide their pain, waiting for a better day. It was also at this time perhaps that Ratchis' trusted friend Paul the Deacon came to the shelter of Cassino, as already mentioned. Paul was to gather in all the history of his people and pass it over to posterity.

Not many years after the fall of the Lombard kingdom, the conqueror himself, Charlemagne, came to the abbey (787) and bestowed many privileges on the community. Under the influence of Charles, the abbey was no longer just the pure source of benedictine religion, the guardian of the Rule, to which pious people from all the Christian world came; she became also a center for monastic expansion... «Following the steps of Paul the Deacon, answering royal requests, monks from Cassino cross the Alps many times» [11]. Indeed, Charlemagne requested from the Abbot of Monte Cassino an exact copy of the Rule, the measures for bread and wine and the description of all customs, in short, the theoretical and practical norms of monastic living.

At that time the abbot was Theodimar (778-797). He was born in Frisia or some part of France and was a relative of Liudger. In the very century of the restoration he represents the period that politically can be called Carolingian or Frankish, which remains important above all for the holiness of the spiritual life and the splendor of its literary achievements.

Theodimar was succeeded by Gisulf (797-817) who had already been assisting him for a few months before his death. With the new abbot, who belonged to the Beneventan ducal family, the range of activities at Monte Cassino was confined to the duchy, and Gisulf's management stressed practical goals. The sharp increase in economic resources made possible the beginning of an organization of the landed property, while the building program increased dramatically. As will be seen in the second part of this work, Gisulf arrived at a decisive and permanent solution of the housing problem and organized an administrative system. There was, however, no change in management by all the successors of Petronax, including Theodimar and Gisulf. Even while emphasizing one characteristic or another, the only goal was the prosperity of the monastery.

Granted immunity by Charlemagne and received in the imperial *defensio,* Monte Cassino had become an important link in the Carolingian chain. As a small state, it lived within the limits of the empire, fulfilling the tasks demanded by its high position and using the protection of the empire to find safety from the violence so prevalent at that time. At the same time the abbey had become one of the most notable cultural centers in Christendom.

3. THE SECOND DESTRUCTION.

The restoration of the empire in the West, in the Frankish nation, had brought to a close the era of the great invasions and ushered in an age of greater calm and normalcy. The renewed unity of the West, however, was only superficial; time and men of great talent were needed to cement it. As these were not forthcoming, the glorious inheritace of the great Charles in the hands of weak successors gradually broke into pieces. Adding to the misery, new invaders from the outside broke through the borders while within the central authority steadily lost its power to the emerging feudal forces. All this led to a state of deplorable anarchy.

Even at Monte Cassino the consequences of this new state of affairs were felt. Forced exactions by nearby feudal lords gradually impoverished the treasury, and a holy abbot, Deusdedit, in 834 died a victim of the abuses and torture of the prince of Benevento, Sicard. His successor began to disengage the abbey from the ties with Benevento, following an active policy of support for the empire. Bassaccius and Bertharius finally allied themselves with Capua.

Much more serious wounds, however, came as a result of the Arab invasion. This caused in southern Italy not only an acceleration of the process of political break-up and local divisions, but because of the struggle between the Arabs and the opposing forces the region became a theatre of continuing war between the

West and the East. The rivalries among the rulers of the area made the task of the invaders easier because in the never-ending wars for the possession of territory the local princelings did not hesitate to enlist the infidels who from Sicily, already in the first half of the ninth century, had been able to gain control of some towns in Apulia. Thus, Benevento itself had a regular Islamic garrison which, bellicose by nature, when not engaged in regular warfare roamed the nearby territories searching for booty. One of these plundering bands in 846 penetrated into the higher valley of the Volturno river and, not much later, attacked also a dependency of Monte Cassino, the monastery of S. Maria in Cingla in the vicinity of Alife, which became a victim of their violence.

A more serious threat appeared on the other coast of Italy. Arab marauders sailed from Palermo, and made several landings along the coast of the duchy of Naples, then continued north and advanced to the very gates of Rome, plundering and destroying the basilicas of St. Peter and of St. Paul, which were outside the walls. But as they were unable to force their entry into the city, they pushed along the Appian way to the valley of the Liri river, where they sacked and destroyed Fondi and then took position in front of Gaeta.

From there with their raids they terrorized the countryside, and after robbing and burning two dependencies of Monte Cassino, S. Andrea and S. Appollinare, coveting a much greater prey, they prepared to attack Monte Cassino itself. The cenobites, dismayed, gathered suppliantly with bare feet and ashes over their heads to sing litanies around St. Benedict's tomb. The apparition of the holy Abbot Apollinaris to his successor Bassaccius with the promise of help, at last, reheartened them. Divine help and the Neapolitan fleet, which suddenly appeared in the waters of Gaeta, saved, for the time at least, the land of St. Benedict from further and more complete ruin. The Arabs were forced to beat a hasty retreat to Africa.

In such a state of agitation and anguish and at the prospect of a worse future, the wretched populations turned to their natural patron, the emperor, beseeching him to undertake their defense. One of the embassies was led by Bassaccius, the abbot of Monte Cassino, and James, the abbot of San Vincenzo al Volturno. Once again, however, the expedition against Bari, organized and led by the emperor in answer to their pleas, did not succeed. The rage of Sawdan, the Arab emir of Bari, was so violent that for fourteen years he spared no corner of the Duchy of Benevento from devastations.

Not long after Bassaccius, in 856, Bertharius followed as abbot; he proved a faithful disciple and follower, especially as a supporter of learning and other cultural activities. Probably of a Lombard family, as the original form of his name, Berthari, seems to indicate, he was thought by some authors, even recent ones, to have come from a noble family, probably related to the Frankish kings. Although he may have come to Monte Cassino while still quite young, Bertharius was to become a complete man, wearing a double crown of holiness and learning. We know that he was the author of many works, some of which have come down to us: theological tracts, sermons, verses to his friends and in praise of the saints, grammar and medical studies. During his tenure he followed two main policies: opposition to the ever-increasing threat from the Arabs and providing for a solid organization of the important patrimony of St. Benedict, so that it would be more attuned to the times and ready to meet political exigencies.

In this first intent he gave valid support to the efforts of Louis II, to whom, accompanied by the Empress Engleberga, he gave splendid hospitality at Monte Cassino. A more famous meeting with Bertharius gathered together in the monastery of S. Salvator Pope Hadrian II, the empress, and her brother-in-law, King Lothair. This latter had vainly tried to obtain approval of his divorce from his legal wife Teutberga while maintaining illicit relations with his lover Valdrada. In this meeting, «the unhappy man, like a novel Juda, simulating good conscience with imprudent behavior», finally through perjury succeded in deceiving the good faith of the old pontiff and was thus allowed to take part again in the celebration of the sacred mysteries (July 1, 869). Not much time had elapsed, however, when the news of a terrible epilogue to this strange affair spread among the terrified people. While Lothair was at Lucca on his way back, he was seized by a violent fever which had previously begun to decimate his followers. At Piacenza the king took a turn for the worse until he lost his speech and became unconscious. In this condition, he died on August 8, 869. A similar fate befell all his company, and only a few survivors were left to bury the king in a monastery near the city. It had been barely a month since the meeting at Cassino, so the impression that this episode left behind was deep and terrible. Contemporaries saw it as a just punishment.

Always attempting to create a barrier to the Arab threat, Bertharius proposed a league among the various political entities of southern Italy, he also tried to keep peace among them. With Anastasius the archivist, who represented the Pope, and himself as the trusted representative of the empire, he tried to reestablish order in Naples, where Bishop Athanasius had been expelled by his own nephew, Sergius II, a loyal ally of the Arabs. When the mission bore no results, the bishop from his exile in Sorrento decided to take shelter with the Emperor Louis II. Athanasius was in the retinue of the emperor when he died July 15, 872 not far from the oratory of S. Quirico, about twelve miles from Monte Cassino. His body was transported to Monte Cassino amidst great manifestations of sorrow and was buried by Bertharius in «a dignified and most proper way» in the Church of St. Peter, the one founded by king Ratchis. Some time later, the abbot had to turn over the sacred remains against his will to an embassy sent from Naples, which claimed them back with great insistence.

It was perhaps because of the diversity of political views in this work of conciliation and attempted league, at a very critical time, that Bertharius found himself at times in conflict with John VIII, a determined proponent of concord and a vigorous fighter [12]. It was, however, John VIII himself who came to appreciate Bertharius' efforts and who granted to the abbot a little before his death (882), a long list of exemptions and privileges which came to represent the crowning achievement of the goal that the abbot of Cassino had vigorously pursued, the great work of reorganization of the patrimony of Monte Cassino.

While, in fact, Bertharius promoted learning and scientific pursuits and embellished the monastery with artistic works, while he enriched the collection of precious chalices, gospels, and various vestments, of which the listings by the chroniclers have preserved the memory for us, the Abbot was proceeding to a complete reorganization of the patrimony of the abbey. A proof of it is his «*Commemoratorium*», a list of all the possessions of Monte Cassino in Abruzzi, which remains even today the oldest and most trustworthy listing of the possessions of Monte Cassino.

Faced by the dangers already threatening at the time of his predecessor, Bertharius resolved to act from the very beginning of his rule and make ready for any emergency. Thus while using diplomacy, by sending envoys and gold to the marauding bands, he also hastened to fortify the territory entrusted to his care.

He began first of all to put in defensive readiness the very heart of the land of St. Benedict, Monte Cassino. He completely surrounded it by a wall with powerful towers so that it became a fortified castle. This, naturally, was not enough. While Monte Cassino remained, of course, the heart and the spring of life for the large domain of St. Benedict, the administrative center, one might say the brain of the organization, had been located for some time on the plain below. Here at the monastery of the Saviour, seat of the *curtis major,* all communications arrived and from here all directives were sent. Thus, it was necessary to make ready not only a stronghold for defense, but to protect also, as far as possible, the central organs necessary to the normal course of living. To the far-seeing Bertharius the nucleus of buildings erected by his predecessors looked suitable to form the center of a new community which could be easily defended from the mountain and which stood close to an important highway crossing. The inhabitants, gathered in a populated center, could find there more of life's comforts and security: at the same time they would have strengthened the position of the abbey's main administration. It is true that the old town of Cassino still survived; in fact, it continued its meager existence until the fifteenth century, but because of the distance and the poor conditions into which it had fallen, it would not have fulfilled the intent of the abbot.

Thus a new city arose in the vicinity of the monastery of S. Salvatore to which the founder gave the Greek name of *Eulogimenopolis,* that is, «the city of St. Benedict». Eulogimenopolis changed its name to S. Germano when Louis II, leaving the region for the last time after his dream of victory over the Arabs was shattered by the attitude of the local princes, donated to the town a finger of the Saint, whose remains he was taking with him from Capua. This change in name was favored not only by the devotion to the Saint but also by the difficulty of pronouncing Eulogimenopolis and because of the designs of the princes of Capua who, during the ensuing exile of the monks wanted to confirm their rights to the city.

For all that, after the departure and consequent death (Brescia 875) of the emperor and the ensuing anarchy created by the local lords, the hostile forces once again gained the upper hand. In 881 an Islamic band, ensconced in the Samnitic Appenines, destroyed the abbey of S. Vincenzo al Volturno. Other Arabs, who had been forced out of the bay of Naples, had found a shelter in Agropoli, on the coast a few miles south of Salerno. From there the anger and desire for vengeance of Docibile, the ruler of Gaeta, drew them to the right bank of the Garigliano river, from where for forty years they spread terror and desolation throughout the surrounding region. One of their first obiectives was the conquest of Monte Cassino; they were drawn to it not only by the reports of its great wealth and the strategic importance of its position but also by hatred for the firmness with which Bertharius opposed their activities.

Probably by preestablished plan, the first assault was launched against the monastery on the top of the mountain, which with its strong defensive works might have turned into a refuge or a fortress in support of the town and the monastery below. After Monte Cassino was invaded, destroyed, and burned on September 4, 883, every escape route to the mountain was cut for all those remaining on the plain. The monastery of S. Salvatore now was swarming with people because the regular residents, who by this time formed the majority of the Cassinese community, had been joined by refugees from the smaller houses and dependencies closest to the terrible danger. Bertharius, unwilling to risk the ruin of the whole community, sent a good part of them to Teano, where Monte Cassino had a house which was under the care of the vicar Angelarius.

The abbot, with a group of brave men, remained on the battlefield, awaiting the turn of events and eager to fulfill the will of God. It did not take long; on October 22 of that same year the Arabs swarmed over S. Salvatore and destroyed and burned it. As soon as Bertharius became aware that the enemies were breaking into the monastery, took his place in church and waited for them in prayer. Reached by the barbarians near the altar of St. Martin, he was cut down as were all those standing with him. The Arabs, after trying to set the splendid basilica on fire, withdrew beyond the river Garigliano, happy, triumphant, and loaded with booty. It was then possible to give proper burial to those remains which the flames had spared, and the body of the abbot was taken to the mountain and laid to rest in the chapter, next to his teacher and predecessor, Bassacius.

Thus perished the man who for many years had been the only opponent to the advance of Arab forces into those regions which from Rome had received civilization and faith. His work, even if for the time being violently cut off, in the long run did not remain without fruits.

The town, established by him and where his blood was shed, resumed living and prospered into our own days [13]. The monks of Monte Cassino, who were his trusted collaborators in carrying on the work of St. Benedict, had to wait long years before returning to their place of origin, but its survival had been ensured by Bertharius at the very time of his supreme sacrifice, and their return was to be crowned by long success and lasting vitality. The Crescent did indeed triumph over the Cross; the names still in use for several villages and areas serve to remind us of the Moslem domination over the «land of St. Benedict». Still the courageous abbot through his sacrifice had barred their march at the very limit of the venerable house of St. Benedict and denied them the final victory. A few years after, the local Christian princes, learning from the painful experience of the past, stirred from their long inertia. Setting aside for once their jealousies and mutual suspicions, they found the unity necessary to rid Italy of these fearsome and ruinous enemies at the battle of the Garigliano River (915).

The memory of Bertharius and the painful and at the same time glorious events connected with his name remained always alive at Monte Cassino. His relics were always honored through public worship until the time when the splendid chapel built by the pious don Ippolito Saltarelli (1650) was completely restored and when on October 20, 1938, the abbot don Gregorio Diamare most solemnly consecrated his altar.

NOTES

[1] G. FALCO, op. cit., 457.

[2] G. CARDUCCI, La chiesa di Polenta. The continuity of the ancient Italian monasticism, in spite of the Lombard invasion, has been supported by this author, against the current opinion, since 1952, see: Aspetti e problemi del monachesimo in Italia, in «Settimane di studio del Centro Italiano di studi sull'alto medioevo», IV, Spoleto 1957, 319 ff. The same thesis is supported by P. PIRRI, L'abbazia di Sant'Eutizio, op. cit., 16.

[3] See on this A. PANTONI, Un quesito su Onorato discepolo e testimone di S. Benedetto, in «Benedictina», 17 (1970), 327-338.

[4] P. GUERRINI, op. cit.

[5] Cfr. Il sepolcro di S. Benedetto, op. cit.

[6] It is the expression in the text examined by J. WINANDY in Corpus Consuetudinum, op. cit., 134, n. 21: «... apud beati patris confessionem diligentiam facimus». The ceremony, the liturgical washing of feet, appears to have been the same as the one still in use for the confession of St. Peter in Rome. Cfr. also E. JOSI, Cerimonie papali a S. Pietro in Vaticano nel secolo IX in «Roma», 1926, 1-2.

[7] For a competent author, G. P. BOGNETTI in Santa Maria di Castelseprio, Milan, Fondazione Treccani, 1948, p. 329: «The event of Petronax could be one aspect of that successive reflux toward the South of the missionary current... Only that for Petronax the

very suggestion of the Cassinese memories, the encouragement of the Pope and the maturity of the times, in a sense, led to a decisive return to the Benedictine tradition».

Besides, «it appears that Petronax, who belonged to a suffragan diocese of Milan, before the "Gallican" reform, may have brought a rite which had many contacts with the rite of Milan, and at the same time shows Greek characteristics, for which one doubts that they were the result of the nearby Neapolitan or Beneventan environment but belong instead to a liturgical background that he brought with him from Northern Italy, where, for the phenomenon, that this volume brings to light, the eastern contribution had been direct and fecund».

This study by the leading authority in the religious history of the Lombards and the other, also belonging to him, on *La continuità delle sedi episcopali e l'azione di Roma nel Regno longobardo* in *La chiesa nei regni dell'Europa occidentale e i loro rapporti con Roma sino all'800*, in «Settimana di Studio del Centro Italiano sull'alto medioevo», 8, Spoleto, 1960, 415-545, make even more suspect the position of the modern historians of monasticism, who, in the revival of Benedictine life in the eighth century, see a prevalence of Frankish and Anglosaxon influences. For Monte Cassino in particular, this author does not believe that one should insist so much on the action of Willibald, as decisive for the restoration, as especially J. CHAPMAN, *op. cit.,* has insisted. Undoubtedly, Willibald brought to the reviving community the fruits of his wide experience, but he also learned much that later he put to work across the Alps. At Monte Cassino he must have learned especially the fundamental concept of Benedictine stability, which later made him, a wanderer, reluctant to leave the cloister, even by papal command. Besides the monks of S. Vincenzo al Volturno had given their help to the restoration of Petronax before the coming of Willibald.

[8] G. FALCO, *op. cit.,* 565.

[9] *Ibid.,* 463-465.

[10] *Ibid.,* 462-463. Could we assume that the famous palimpsest of the Codex 271, which contained a Gregorian sacramentary, was one of the books donated by pope Zacharias? Or can we even assume that it was used by that group of monks, who lived on the mountain before the arrival of Petronax?

[11] *Ibid.,* 480.

[12] On the two letters and their value, see D. LOHRMANN, *Das Register Papst Johannes' VIII,* Tübingen, Niemeyer, 1968 (Bibliothek des Deutschen Instituts in Rom, 20), 247, 282.

[13] S. Germano then assumed the name of Cassino, after the formation of the kingdom of Italy (decree of July 26, 1863).

BIBLIOGRAPHY

This whole period is masterfully brought to life, in a so far unsurpassed manner, in the work of G. FALCO, *Lineamenti di storia cassinese,* in *Casinensia,* 457-548, Montecassino, 1929. A new edition of the same work in *Rivista Storica Italiana,* 16 (1929) was published again in *Albori d'Europa,* Rome 1947, 173-263. Here we make reference only to the Cassinese edition, because more easily accessible. In these pages the various problems are examined, especially the fundamental one of the first restoration. Of course, after so many years some conclusions need revision. One must also remember J. CHAPMAN, *La restauration du Mont-Cassin par l'abbé Petronax,* in «Revue Bénédictine», 21

(1904), 74-80, whose positions, however, must be at least partially corrected and B. PAR-INGER, *Le ms. de Saint-Gall 914 représente-t-il le latin original de la règle de S. Benoît?*, in «Revue Bénédictine», 61, (1951), 81-140, which is even less acceptable as far as our argument goes, cfr. T. LECCISOTTI, *Le conseguenze dell'invasione longobarda per l'antico monachesimo italiano* in «Atti I Congresso internazionale studii longobardi», Spoleto, 1951, 369-376.

The vicissitudes of the relics of St. Benedict and the questions attached to them have been amply dealt with in the two volumes *Il sepolcro di S. Benedetto,* Montecassino 1951, 1982 (Miscellanea Cassinese, 27, 450.

The most recent edition for use, after that of B. ALBERS, *Consuetudines Monasticae,* III, Montecassino, 1907, can be found in *Corpus Consuetudinum Monasticarum,* I, Siegburg, Schmitt, 1963, pp. 93-175 (*Casinensium Ordines antiquiores*).

The most ancient evidence on the liturgy has been examined by G. MORIN, *Les quatres plus anciens calendriers du Mont-Cassin,* in «Revue Bénédictine», 25 (1908), 486-497. A considerable part of the medieval liturgical textes can be found in E. MARTÈNE, *De antiquis monachorum ritibus,* Lyon, Amission, 1960.

For the case of Ratchis see: C. G. MOHR, *La monacazione di Ratchis e la diaspora friulana,* in «Ce Fastu», 32 (1956). For the mission and the return to France of Carloman: G. TANGL, *Die Sendung des ehemaligen hausmaier Karlomann in das Frankenreich im Jahre 754 und der Konflikt der Brüder,* in «Q.F.I.A.B.», 40 (1960), 1-42.

The thorough study of N. CILENTO, *Le origine della Signoria Capuana nella Longobardia minore,* Rome, Istituto Storico M.E., (1966) (Studi Storici, 69-70) vividly illustrates the environmental conditions in which the Cassinese Lordship found itself, and had to cope with, until the Norman conquest.

To conclude, the recent study of A. O. CITARELLA and H. M. WILLARD, *The Ninth Century Treasure of Monte Cassino,* Montecassino 1983, (Miscellanea Cassinese 50), provides a useful view of an area until now neglected in the life of the Cassinese community in the ninth century.

III.

ON THE ROAD TO EXILE

> *«Like... Rome, like all Italy, Monte Cassino suffered the onslaught of barbarians, coming now through the mountains and now from the sea; devastations, ruins, flights; also returns and restorations.»*

1. AT TEANO.

The survivors of the great disaster took the road to exile just as their fathers did three centuries before. This time, however, the monastery was not at the beginning of its existence, and the fugitives could choose the most suitable refuge among the many cells and possessions in the patrimony of St. Benedict.

These exiles withdrew to their dependency in Teano under the guidance of Angelarius. Besides safety from new incursions, the place offered the possibility of keeping an eye on the devasted house, which was nearby, and this kept alive the hope of returning. They brought with them the bulls, diplomas, and whatever they had been able to save from the marauding horde. Again this time they did not leave behind the most precious remembrances of Father Benedict: the autograph copy of the Rule, the measures for bread and wine, and the sacks found at the monastery gate miraculously full of flour. Once again they did not take with them the remains of their saints, who were safe in their underground tombs and perhaps guarded by some survivor.

The tenth, the «iron» century found the exiles at Teano. This period has been painted, perhaps, in excessively dark tones; still, the fact remains that after working for a long time, the forces of political and economic disestablishment brought forth at that time their most deadly fruits. The renewal of the terrible invasions and devastations brought back ruin, changing entire regions into desert, and the particularism of local lords became more and more damaging due to the absence or weakness of the central authorities.

In fact, with the deposition of Charles the Fat (887) the Carolingian empire ceased to exist. Among the ever-spreading disorders and ever-continuing struggles, the lay lords succeeded in enslaving the Church. The monasteries, especially those that had escaped the fury of the invasions, could not avoid falling under the control of strangers; the monasteries were turned, completely or in part, into private dwellings. They were abandoned by the monks, who were forced to roam the country, except when they were tolerated and allowed to live wretchedly in some corner of their old buildings. It is not surprising that monastic life practically disappeared in some regions.

The papacy itself became the sport of the powerful Roman factions: they fought over the chair of holy Peter, which was passed from one mighty family to the next that was able to seize it in the ever-shifting balance of power. «No human tongue could tell how much Italy had suffered after the death of Charlemagne»: this declaration made by the Italian representatives at the depositon of Charles the Fat expresses tersely what the situation in Italy was in this calamitous age for western Christendom. Monte Cassino in particular continued to suffer from the contrasting ambitions and from the covetousness of the Lombard princes in southern Italy.

With the uncertainty and the various changes necessary because of their precarious situation, the monks of Cassino were all the more exposed to the sufferings that the difficult times brought. After the death of the bishop of Teano, their Abbot Angelarius assumed the succession (889). While the monastery was ruled by Ragemprand (889-899), a fateful fire destroyed their quarters in Teano. It was at this time that the original manuscript of the Rule, apparently written on papyrus, was lost. According to tradition, only the last chapter was salvaged; this too disappeared at the time of the French invasion and sack at the end of the eighteenth century [1]. What was left of the treasure was deposited in the episcopal palace of Teano, and it seems that part of it remained there.

Abbot Angelarius had already tried to partly restore the buildings on Monte Cassino, and after several years of tenacious efforts the church and some other parts of the monastery above were rebuilt in the best way possible under the circumstances. Safety, however, could not be assured, and, therefore, it was not possible at the time to make a complete return to the old home; instead, after about thirty years, the monks made another move, this time to the rich plain of Capua. Surely, the trials suffered, the uncertainties of the times and the lack of a home suitable to their needs seemed to justify the decision.

Actually they were simply giving in to the temptations and intrigues of the princes of Capua. It certainly was not piety that led the masters of Capua to offer a shelter to the displaced monks, but the desire to control that powerful community by keeping the monks away from their monastery and by forcing them to become city dwellers. This would have made it easy for them to lay their greedy hands on the patrimony of St. Benedict.

The singular diligence of Abbot Leo (899-914), who succeeded Regemprand, in the restoration of the Cassinese monastery by making possible a return there forced, in effect, the princes Landulf and Atenulf to execute their plan without any delay. Without a leader or a home after Leo died (August 17, 914) the monks were uncertain as to the choice of a successor. The princes seized the opportunity and forced the election of a relative of theirs, John, archdeacon of the Church of Capua and thus a stranger to the community. For the occasion he became a monk and through him the princes succeeded in their design.

2. At Capua.

After assuming his position the new abbot began to entice the monks with bright prospects of a better life in order to convince them to leave Teano and go to Capua, a major city of the region and the residence of the princes. It does not seem that the abbot had to try too hard to persuade them, because in a very short time the Cassinese community was in Capua. There, with the help of relatives and friends, abbot John built, from the ground up, a large monastery in honor of St. Benedict, in which fifty monks resided. He made every effort to care for their welfare, and the buildings were splendidly appointed, as witnessed by some narratives and charts of the period that have survived. The abbot extended his attention also to the rebuilding of the basilica at Monte Cassino. He was a learned man and a good diplomat, and as such was sent by the princes of Capua as ambassador to Constantinopole to urge, successfully, the help which had been promised against the Arabs.

Yet, in spite of these undeniable merits, the results of John's work were ruinous for the future of the abbey. By moving to Capua, the monastery not only lost its independence but became enfeoffed to the lay princes. Moreover, contacts with the Capuan court and city living caused a rapid break-down in discipline, perhaps already in the last years of John (March 31, 934). So the plan of Landulf and Atenulf had fully succeeded: «While the monks were busy enjoying the new found pleasures, the princes hastened to make themselves masters of the whole patrimony of St. Benedict» [2]. Unexpected allies of the princes in this, the Hungarians with their terrifying and destructive raids, made it more difficult for the monks to return to their solitude.

Under the circumstances outside help was needed, somebody who cared and was willing to extend a powerful hand to restore the fortunes of the Cassinese community. This help, in fact, was not long in coming. A reforming monastic movement had been building in a remote corner of Burgundy. Odo, the abbot who had started the recovery at Cluny, was invited to Rome by Albericus, *princeps et senator omnium Romanorum**, to restore discipline in the monasteries of the city and those others in his domain. Under papal mandate he took under his care also the mo-

---

* «Prince and senator of all the Romans».

nastery of the monks from Cassino.

Soon he placed his disciple Baldwin as a successor of Abbot Adalbert (934-942). The new Abbot, even after being called back to Rome by Marinus II, did not relinquish completely his rule over the abbey where he had served as coadjutor and later as successor to Maielpoto. Baldwin, convinced that no lasting good could be achieved in Capua, asked the aid of pope Agapitus II (946-955) to obtain from prince Landulf freedom for the community, while leaving a few older monks to take care of the house of St. Benedict in Capua. The papal order, however, was not fully carried out at this time.

3. THE GLORIOUS RETURN.

The complete realization of the plan was the work of Aligernus. Elected abbot at Capua in 949, like Baldwin he was a disciple of Odo. Born in Naples, he had chosen the monastic life at St. Paul in Rome during the governance of Baldwin.

The great chronicle of Monte Cassino, popularly known as the *Chronicon,* begins the second book with his election to mark the beginning of a new era. And truly, the «almificus pater», as another great abbot, Hugh of Farfa, called him, must be considered the third founder of the abbey. The importance of his rule, which lasted almost thirty-six years, was truly exceptional. New forces, emerging after the terrible crisis of the tenth century, were shaping the future of the people of Italy. It would not be long before the western empire would be restored, and the new Saxon dynasty, in pursuing its far-ranging policies would bestow many favors on churches and monasteries. Monte Cassino, placed almost at the geographical limit between the territorial ambitions of the western empire, trying to extend its control to southern Italy and the area under Byzantine control, soon became the establishment whose success and security was uppermost in the hearts of the German rulers. It became, in fact, an imperial chamber, enriched with privileges and concessions, and its political power was restored and increased. The work of restoration, which in the political sphere had led to the *restauratio imperii**, soon made great progress also in the social, economic, and religious order.

The choice of Aligernus was, indeed, providential; it led the house of St. Benedict on new and more glorious paths. He began by re-claiming the patrimony usurped by the neighboring lords; he did not back away from any obstacle. It was he who built the castle which dominates the town below and which took the name of Rocca Janula from its position as an access gate; even now this ancient structure is a significant landmark in the Cassinese landscape. It was there that the abbot was caught off guard by Atenulf of Aquino and was chained and exposed to the mocking and tauntings of the local mob. Freed at last by the Prince of Capua, he nobly forgave his aggressor.

The organization of the Patrimony was a splendid example of prudence and Christian wisdom. The plan of Aligernus was ahead of the times and gave new directions to the feudal system of the region. The *placiti libellarii* granted by the abbot to his tenant farmers were advantageous emphyteutic contracts: the land was given in free lease for twenty-nine years, against the payment of one seventh of the crops and one third of the wine. To stimulate trade, which struggled in a purely consumption economy, he encouraged the formation of numerous centers, building churches and helping in the construction of homes and castles.

Aligernus took no less interest in the internal life of the monastery. Before all, he improved the buildings, and both in the observance and in liturgical splendor, monastic life reached one of its happiest moments. St. Nilus, the austere ascetic, welcomed at Monte Cassino with the pomp of a major solemnity, had nothing but praises for the strict regularity of the monks' life. He was a guest in a dependency of the abbey at Valleluce. St. Romuald sent from far Catalonia the early fruits of his apostolate in that region. Olibano Cabrera, count Bisuldinese, and

---

* The restoration of the Empire.

Ceritanese; John Grandenigo, who lived an outstandingly virtuous life and whose memory was glorified by numerous miracles after his death, came here and there were others in their company. One must add that the fame of the holiness of their lives attracted to Monte Cassino monks from other faraway monasteries, even from Germany. They came to consult with the Cassinese about their observance, which was quite different from that of Cluny, undertaking the long journey to gain first-hand knowledge of it.

The recovery was therefore vigorous, and while the early stirrings of a new beginning were becoming apparent among the peoples of Italy, the community of St. Benedict also enjoyed a new spring. As elsewhere, in Monte Cassino we find early evidence of the Italian language in the *giudicati,* known generally as *placiti,* of the era of Aligernus. Even through some unavoidable short-lived changes of direction and some brief storms, the recovery produced in due time the abundant fruits of a rich summer.

In fact, at the death of Aligernus (November 23, 986), Princess Aloara of Capua, the widow of Pandulf Ironhead, as a new Marozia succeeded in having Manso, her husband's cousin and the then vicar of the monastery of Fondi, elected as successor to the great abbot. Some of the monks refused to accept him and set out for different places. Most took the road to Jerusalem. Among them were two future abbots, John III and Theobald, while Liuzio, who stayed for some time in the area where later he founded the monastery of Cava, built on a mountain near to Monte Cassino the monastery of St. Mary dell'Albaneta.

The rule of Manso which started during these disturbances and animosities was not a happy one. It cannot be denied that he succeeded in consolidating and enlarging the Cassinese domain; he not only built castles like Roccasecca but managed even to bring the county as well as the diocese of Aquino under the control of Monte Cassino. It was, perhaps, this extraordinary greatness that made him adopt a princely life style even while undertaking long journeys beyond the Alps. The reaction in the congregation, which was very austere in the observance of the Rule, was very strong. It was this, perhaps, that caused Manso's sad end. His designs, which included seizing Capua itself, convinced Count Pandulf to accept and support the wicked proposals of Alberic, the cruel bishop of the Marsi. This latter, using some corrupt monks, had the Abbot blinded so that he could take possession of Monte Cassino. Manso died of a broken heart (996), but the bishop, struck by the hand of God, failed in his design.

Manso's death was a signal to the neighbors to move against the abbey, and his successor John II (996-997) soon gave up his office. Old and in poor health, he was seized by violent remorse, when, in repressing an uprising of the inhabitants of Pignataro, the abbey forces set fire to the church of the village. He decided, therefore, to withdraw to solitary life, not far from the monastery, on a slope where later was built a church in honour of St. Peter and St. Damian.

John II was succeeded by John III (997-1010), a native of Benevento. A dour and austere man, he was among the monks who, during the rule of Manso, had made a pilgrimage to the Holy Land. For six years he had lived a solitary and austere life of penance on mount Sinai, he then moved to mount Athos from where he returned to Monte Cassino after the fall of Manso.

St. Romuald came to Monte Cassino during his rule (998). The great monk came to the gate of the Abbey, even then guarded the symbolic lions [3]. As a sign of humility he rode an ass obtained in exchange for a beautiful mare which had been given to him by the son of a king of the Slavs. During his stay he fell gravely ill, but he was restored to health by God's help. A little later emperor Otto III also came to the abbey. He was atoning through holy pilgrimages for the cruel excesses which took place in Rome in the repression of the uprising of Crescenzo Nomentano.

With these visits which provide strong evidence of the vigor of the life brought back by Aligernus, the tenth century, which had opened with the mournful exile, came to a close. With the eleventh century the splendid rebirth of the Italian people began, which saw the birth of the communes in the North and the beginning of Norman power in the South, both forced to coexist with the constrasting claims of the two supreme medieval powers, the Papacy and the Empire. The attention and creativity of the organizations designed by Aligernus led to a full flowering of the arts and Monte Cassino reached the summit of its grandeur both morally and materially. There was no break in the life of the community: the sacrifices and the expiations of one generation prepared for the joys and triumph of another, «Euntes ibant et flebant mittentes semina sua, venientes autem venient cum exultatione portantes manipulos suos *». The words of the prophet could apply also in this sense to the legacy of St. Benedict on the holy mountain.

------

* «The first went scattering the seeds in tears, the others came happily carrying the bundles of the harvest».

NOTES

[1] P. MEYVAERT was the last one to study this fragment and its authenticity in «Problems concerning the "Autograph" manuscript of St. Benedict's Rule» in *Revue Bénédictine*, 69 (1959), 3-21. There is an argument contrary to his conclusion in T. LECCISOTTI, *I Regesti dell'Archivio di Montecassino*, II, Rome 1965, XLIV, n. 76.

[2] L. TOSTI, *Storia*, I, 86.

[3] These lions, watching the gate of Monte Cassino until the last destruction have now been placed in a more secure place. The lions were the traditional symbol of the Cassinese domain; they were placed not only at the entrance of the monastery and of the abbot's palaces, but also at the borders of the territorial possessions. As symbols of vigilance and guardianship, they were placed already by the Egyptians as avengers of sins and profanations, at the entrance of temples, they also served as ornaments to the temple of Jerusalem. They appear also on buildings and in the possessions of ancient monasteries.

The two greyhounds, in mosaic of the Desiderian age, which are still on the sepulcher of St. Benedict, served the same purpose of vigilant custodians.

BIBLIOGRAPHY

The literature of this century of Cassinese history is not very large and, perhaps, judgements on it are susceptible, in part at least, to correction, not unlikely to what has happened for the history of the Church of Rome of the same period.

One should note the following: T. Leccisotti, *S. Romualdo e Montecassino,* in «Rivista Camaldolese», I, (1927), 200-207 and by the same author: *Una lacuna della storia di Montecassino al X secolo,* in *Studia Benedictina in memoriam gloriosi transitus S. P. Benedicti,* 1947, 273-281 (Studia Anselmiana, 18-19); also, *Il secolo X e l'influsso della riforma monastica romana a Montecassino,* in «Archivio della Società Romana di Storia Patria», 1982.

These «placita» (judgements) have been edited several times, and with other documents of the language also, in the fourth edition by M. Inguanez, in Miscellanea Cassinese, 24, Montecassino, 1942. A new photographic edition of the placita only was done, on the occasion of the millenary (1960), by A. Mancone, *I documenti cassinesi del X secolo con formule in volgare,* Poligrafico dello Stato. To commemorate the same events other noteworthy studies have been added to those done in the past years on them. For their critical evaluation and for the various editions of the texts, see the lucid and exhaustive examination by F. Sabatini, *Bilancio del millenario della lingua italiana,* in «Cultura Neo-latina» 22 (1962), 1-2. One can also find there the useful and complete bibliography of every thing that has appeared since the edition by Inguanez (1942).

To conclude, let us also remember for the many connections with the history of Monte Cassino, J. Gay, *L'Italie méridionale et l'empire byzantin...,* Paris, 1904.

IV.

THE MOST GLORIOUS DAYS

«In the whole of western Christendom, there was nothing comparable to the basilica of Monte Cassino during the times of Desiderius».
(E. BERTAUX, *op. cit.*, p. 162).

1. THE ASCENT.

This statement by the eminent historian of art in southern Italy, can, without exaggerating, be extended to the whole complex of the Cassinese monastery in the eleventh century. The forces now blossoming in the country were renewing Italian life and contributing to the rising splendor of one of her most expressive centers of culture.

Abbot Atenulf (1011-1022) of the family of the Princes of Capua, who when still a young boy had been brought to Germany as a hostage and had been raised there in a monastery, was a cautious administrator and admirable for his support of the arts. A mild-mannered man, he established friendly relations with the Byzantine empire, and this drew on him the wrath of Emperor Henry II. When Henry II came to Italy, Atenulf tried to escape to Constantinople but perished at sea.

In the presence of the Emperor and Pope Bendict VIII, Teobald (1022-1035) was chosen as new abbot of Monte Cassino. A disciple of Aligernus, he also during the rule of Manso, had made a pilgrimage to the Holy Land. His rule, which marked the beginning of a new era in the history of culture in southern Italy, was, notwithstanding some difficulties, rather felicitous and thus the upward movement continued.

The Bavarian Richerius (1038-1055), firm in his intent to free the imperial abbey from the grasp of the Normans, who were continuing to expand and strengthen their conquests in southern Italy, carried on with German tenacity the work of consolidation. In fact, the *Chronicon* itself recognizes that the basis of the ensuing splendor was strengthened during his abbacy. Richerius also was captured and held prisoner by a Count of Aquino but was set free through the intercession of Guaimar V, Prince of Salerno.

As a successor to Richerius the monks chose Peter, who had been at the monastery since he was a child. Their choice was rejected by Pope Victor II. The Pontiff wanted at Monte Cassino an abbot who would be capable of asserting himself vigorously both in the current difficulties and in the coming political contests but, most important of all, one who could hold the Normans at bay; thus, through his legate the Cardinal Umberto di Selvacandida, supported by the humble and pious Peter, he obtained the nomination of Frederick of Lorraine (1057-1058). Already a cardinal and chancellor of the Roman Church, Frederick had been a legate with the same cardinal Umberto at Constantinople in the context with Cerularius. Later he sought refuge at Monte Cassino and donned the monastic habit, moved not only by a desire for a more perfect life but also to escape the wrath of the emperor, who suspected that he was a supporter of his brother Gotfridus, Duke of Lorraine and Tuscany. The rule of Frederick was brief but noteworthy because of the new directions taken in politics and in the fields of culture and the arts. At the death of Victor II on May 23, 1057, Frederick was elected Pope and took the name of Stephen IX. he was the first Cassinese monk to ascend the throne of Peter, and he decided to retain the governance of the abbey, not only because of the deep affection he had for it but also because by that time Monte Cassino was a strong and precious ally for the embattled Roman Church.

Upon the death of Frederick (March 29, 1056) in Florence, the monks elected Desiderius (1058-1087) as his successor. He was of the family of the Princes of Benevento and had to surmount grave obstacles to embrace the life of his choice. The Popes had already put to use his diplomatic skills on several special missions. He was, in fact, in Bari as a papal legate ready to set sail for Constantinople when a delegation of monks came to inform him of the death of their abbot, Pope Stephen IX, and to invite him to return to Monte Cassino. Pope Nicholas II confirmed and blessed him as new abbot, made him a cardinal of the title of S. Cecilia, and also named him his vicar for the whole of southern Italy. In the annals of the abbey his achievements endure; he made it into a splendid, outstanding center of monastic life, culture and the arts as well as a political force to reckon with.

Monte Cassino was now assuming a position of first rank in the region and had a well defined character of its own.

2. THE SUMMIT.

The gravest crisis in medieval history was approaching: the beginning of the great struggle between the Empire and the Church. At the same time, throughout southern Italy the tempo of the Norman conquest was accelerating. At the beginning, Monte Cassino was mistrustful and hostile, as were all Italians, and the Roman Church above all. Slowly, however, a change of course took place and in the end, it was Monte Cassino that helped make possible the reconciliation between the Church and the newcomers. The storm was approaching; the Church, preparing to oppose the Empire in a tremendous struggle, needed trusted supporters. The new state that was rapidly forming on the southern border of the pontifical domain could provide the needed help. It was therefore Monte Cassino, trusted ally of the Popes, whose abbots now became stable members of the Roman Curia, to act as mediators in this alliance that was to produce such notable results.

Geography clearly favored Monte Cassino in this role of power broker. The Cassinese domain, the natural gateway between the papal state and southern Italy, was by now also an important element in the political stability of Italy. The «Land of St. Benedict» stretched from the Tyrrhenian to the Adriatic Sea. In the greater part of the *Terra di Lavoro*, in Samnium and the Abruzzi, and in far away territories that the abbey owned, from

Apulia to Illyrium and even Sardinia, the Abbot of Monte Cassino had public and religious authority. In the vast domain entrusted to him, he was the only bishop and the only ruler. He did not recognize any superior authority other than the Pope. The neighboring Princes and the foreign rulers came to him in the humble dress of pilgrims or benefactors. Less than a century after Aligernus had led his flock back to the mountain of St. Benedict, a Benedictine state had risen in the middle of Italy, another ecclesiastical domain, better defended against intrusions from lay lords and less open to dissensions than the papal domain. At times the two domains were ruled by the same man. A century of extraordinary growth of Benedictine power brought two of its abbots to the throne of Peter: Frederick of Lorraine (Stephen IX, 1057-1058) and Desiderius (Victor III, 1086-1087). They both retained the governance of the abbey; Victor, in fact, returned to the mountain which he had left in search of the clean air and the safety that Rome could not assure even to the leader of the Church. Thus for a whole year the Pope resided at Monte Cassino, making it the center of Christendom [1].

Fifty years later the abbey produced a third Pope, Gelasius II. As knights of Christ, the monks through their works and their words went about spreading the Roman thesis of ecclesiastical reform. Drawn from Monte Cassino's monastic family came a steady stream of administrators and legates who represented the Pope in the most distant regions. Baronio called it «a seminary of holy pastors» [2] and the phrase was not an exaggeration. To the three Bishops of the ninth century and the four of the tenth one must add in the eleventh, two Popes, thirteen Cardinals, and fourteen Archbishops and Bishops; in the twelfth century the abbey gave the Church one Pope, fifteen Cardinals and twenty-six Archbishops and Bishops. This enumeration was done by Gattola, and although doubts remain about some names, one may be certain that the list is not complete. Therefore the principal monastery of Christianity had earned the trust of the whole Church and was a strong supporter of the cause of reform.

As solid stronghold, the abbey from time to time gave

hospitality to almost all the Popes of that troubled period. Leo IX, Stephen IX, Nicholas II, Alexander II, Gregory VII, Victor III, Urban II, Paschal II, Gelasius II, and Callixtus II, among all the Roman pontiffs who in the course of the centuries made their way to the sacred mountain of St. Benedict, were the ones who left the most vivid memory of their visits, because they were linked with the memory of the days of sorrow. With them came a crowd of followers and collaborators. Many members of the sacred college often took part in the solemnities of the liturgical year, finding at Monte Cassino the right atmosphere both for the exercise of political power and the pursuit of sacred studies. The sternly austere Peter Damian profusely praised the Cassinese community for its favorable environment which also contributed to the splendid flowering of the arts and culture, all useful weapons in the defense of the Church.

This is what the abbey had become through a century of constant labours. As it was in the wishes of its abbot Desiderius, Monte Cassino became the worthy heir of a very old and proud tradition. They abbey at that time was the most beautiful in western Christendom, surrounding that wonderful basilica to which there was «nothing comparable in the West». More will be said later concerning the learning and the skills of the monks living in the shadows of those glorious buildings. It is no wonder then that Monte Cassino became one of the centers most qualified to support and defend the Church.

The most significant moment, which was clearly the reflection of the vital role of the abbey in the continuing struggle, was the consecration of the splendid basilica of Desiderius (October 1, 1071). Pope Alexander II, continuing the policy of his predecessors, had made even closer the ties between the Roman Church and the great Cassinese abbey, whose abbot was one of the most influential members of the Curia. The Pope himself sent the invitation notices for the exceptional event. Present were five Cardinals, ten Archbishops, forty-three Bishops and a large crowd of Abbots and monks. Among secular princes, all the most powerful lords of southern Italy where there. In a rare display of cooperation they set aside their jealousies and contrasting aspirations in honor of St. Benedict. The crowds of people were very large and the providential liberality of the monks furnished gratis all the necessary food for the eight days during which worshippers kept coming. Our eyes have been able to enjoy the extraordinary scene recreated by the magic brush of Luca Giordano on the great end wall of the Cassinese basilica.

The solemn dedication was so great an event that the *Chronicon* attributes to it not only the faster rate of growth of the monastery (in two years the number of monks living there grew considerably) but also of Monte Cassino as an attraction for travelers. Powerful and humble people. for various reasons, crowded more than ever around the Abbot of the great Campanian abbey, forming a solid line of men ready, in the name of St. Benedict, to defend the embattled Church. This gave the reformed party renewed fervor and hope for the future.

Among those present at the consecration was Cardinal Hildebrand. In a few years the abbey would again offer him hospitality when as a worried fugitive from the violence in Rome toward the end of his troubled pontificate, he was seeking a safe asylum.

Gregory VII died in 1085 outside the house of St. Benedict in Salerno, in the arms of the Cassinese Alphanus, an exiled martyr, and was succeeded by Desiderius of Monte Cassino. Desiderius carried on faithfully the program of Gregory, but his serene and sensible mind did not have the iron rigidity of his glorious predecessor. Convinced that in the bitter dispute, both the ecclesiastical as well as the temporal powers, were threatened with serious dangers, he tried vainly to smooth over Gregory's uncompromising stand. After refusing the papacy for a year, he finally accepted in 1086, retaining, however, like Stephen IX, the governance of the Abbey.

After the synod held at Benevento, Desiderius returned home to die on September 16, 1087. He was buried first in the chapter, like all preceeding Abbots. His remains were later moved to where they are today in the rich chapel dedicated to him, which Luca

Giordano decorated with scenes from Desiderius's life and glorious achievements.

The abbot's chair then passed to Oderisius (1087-1105), a cardinal deacon from the family of the counts of the Marsi. Oderisius was not an unworthy successor to Desiderius; he carried on the artistic program and shared Desiderius' zeal for the Crusaders, to whom he offered liberal hospitality at the abbey and whose efforts he supported with letters to the Byzantine Emperor, Alexius. Oderisius's piety for the dead was extraordinary. He established the rule, still observed at Monte Cassino, that after the death of each monk, his rations are assigned for thirty days to a pauper, and four psalms are sung for the repose of the dead. Another four psalms are sung for the dead every day in chapter and on each Friday a Mass, with absolution, is celebrated at the cemetery.

3. THE FIRST SHADOWS.

The eleventh century, which saw the most splendid period in the history of the abbey, came to an end during the abbacy of Oderisius. The dreadful struggle between church and empire was not over yet, and its repercussions in the life of the monastery were felt continuously.

Otto, of the family of the counts of Fondi (1105-1107), was succeeded by Bruno (1107-1111), already bishop of Segni and outstanding for his knowledge and the holiness of his life; later on he was canonized by Lucius III. Ardently devoted to the memory and the examples of Gregory VII, he did not act very respectfully towards Pope Pascal II, who in his prison at Tribuco yielded to the demands of emperor Henry V in an effort to avoid worse evils. The Abbot was therefore forced to resign from the governance of the abbey and to resume the administration of the diocese of Segni where he died in 1123.

His successor Girardus, also of the family of the counts of the Marsi (1111-1123), had been a soldier for a long time. In the middle of Rocca Janula he built a tall, strong tower and, in that same redoubt, he held in custody for some time the antipope Burdino (Gregory VIII). During his abbacy another Cassinese ascended the pontifical throne with the name of Gelasius II (1118-1119). He was Giovanni Caniulo from Gaeta, to whom was credited the restoration of the rhythmic *Cursus* in the papal chancery. His pontificate, brief but exceedingly painful, ended with his tragic flight from Rome and his exile at Cluny.

It is possible that Gelasius' extraordinary sufferings led to a more rapid conclusion of the peace that was signed at Worms (1122). Unfortunately, however, it was a compromise rather than a real peace, and so the struggle resumed again shortly thereafter under various pretexts.

Monte Cassino was forced to maneuver carefully among the different factions, amidst the struggles and the schisms. In 1130, for instance, it supported the party of Anacletus. The position of the abbey was made all the more difficult because of her location within the Norman domain; in one episode she was forced to pay out of her treasury the expenses of the war between king Roger II and Pope Innocent II. The pope, in fact, was captured by his adversaries in an ambush right below the abbey in San Germano (1146). Like Leo IX at Civitate, Innocent II also was treated with all possible reverence and soon set free.

The regular way of life at the abbey was not, however, shaken or weakened by the course of events. The Abbots continued to occupy preeminent positions both at the Curia and the royal courts; often they were raised to the cardinalate. Their elections, however, often became the subject of disputes because of the interference of higher authorities. Popes and Emperors frequently took part in the elections. When Guidobaldus was elected in 1137, for instance, Emperor Lothair III, the Empress and St. Bernard were present, while Pope Innocent II was close by in San Germano. It was on that occasion that the great abbot of Clairvaux addressed the monks in chapter and insisted, together with the Emperor, on visiting barefooted all the churches of the monastery. The Empress Richiza also had come up the mountain to Monte Cassino on foot as an act of reverence to St. Benedict.

With the opening of the Norman succession, which placed the southern kingdom in German hands, the difficulties became more acute. There were many grave and painful moments. Only death had prevented Guarino, the chancellor of King Roger, from driving out almost all the monks from the monastery and using it as a fortress against the Germans (1136).

It was left, however, to another chancellor, Asclettinus, the archdeacon of Catania and minister of William I, to change the house of Benedict into an army barracks twenty years later. After expelling all the monks, except twelve who favoured pope Hadrian IV, Asclettinus placed there a contingent of troops. This situation did not last long because the Pope and the King soon came to an accord, and the Abbot, Rainald of Collemezzo (1137-1166) died at peace with the royal party

Abbot Roffredo dell'Isola (1188-1210), a Cardinal of the name of saints Peter and Marcellino, displayed a considerable political activity. Although a follower of the party of Emperor Henry, he was nevertheless sent hostage in Germany for some time by the suspicious sovereign. Upon the premature death of Henry, the abbot was charged by Pope Innocent III to watch over the security of the kingdom of southern Italy to prevent German usurpation. Memorable was the siege that the Germans lay to Monte Cassino after seizing the localities of S. Pietro in fine, S. Vittore, Cervaro, and San Germano. Besides the abbot and two other cardinals, about a thousand people had sought refuge in the abbey (1199-1200). After two months, the commander Marqualdo was forced to withdraw the siege of the monastery, but he vented his wrath on the people of San Germano and surroundings. Until our own days an image of the Crucifix, much venerated in the collegiate church of Cassino, had preserved the memory of the outrages suffered at the hands of those brutal soldiers. To prevent new dangers the abbot strengthened the fortifications of San Germano and the Rocca, expelled all Germans from the country of Sora, and, allied to Gualtieri Count of Brienne, kept at their heels as far as Sicily. During his last years,

Roffredo gave hospitality to Innocent III who, after holding a parliament in San Germano, spent a few days at the abbey (1208). The Pope also asked him to supervise the reform of the community of St. Paul in Rome. Roffred died not long after.

His warlike spirit and political awareness remained alive in some of his successors, including Adenulfus (1121-1215) and Stephen of the family of the counts of the Marsi (1215-1227). It was, indeed, a necessity imposed by the times. In northern Italy free popular armies organized by the communes carried on with the support of the church the struggle against the totalitarian German empire. The southern regions, unified in the Norman kingdom, were fighting to escape being caught in the German vise. Had the imperials succeeded in enforcing their claims both in the north and in the south it would have been easy to suppress the freedom of the Roman church, the only power still capable of resisting their quest for absolute dominion. Monte Cassino, therefore, as a great fief at the very gates of both contestants, had to fight not only for its particular rights, but as always, for the greater cause of the Church.

NOTES

[1] E. BERTAUX, *op. cit.*, 157.

[2] «One can surely state, however, without the least doubt or error that in the whole Christian world there was never a monastery from which came out so many personages so eminent for holiness and learning and so many were promoted to the governance of the Apostolic See, that one can affirm in truth that for a time Monte Cassino was a seminary of bishops...»: *Annal. Eccles.*, 716.

BIBLIOGRAPHY

E. BERTAUX, *L'art dans l'Italie méridionale,* Paris 1906, (new anastatic edition 1968) gives us a lucid synthesis, although his point of view is basically artistic.

For the history of this epoch especially, one cannot leave aside the general events, with which it is tightly connected, particularly from the facts of the Norman occupation and those of the struggle for the investitures. For the first, in spite of its shortcomings, F. CHALANDON, *Histoire de la domination Normande en Italie et en Sicilie,* Paris 1907 (reprint. New York, B. Franklin, 1960) is indispensable. For the other, A. FLICHE, *La réforme grégorienne,* 3 vols. Louvain, 1924-1937, although not everybody shared his views.

The reconstruction work of Richer, in particular, has been thoroughly studied by W. WHUR, *Die Wiedergeburt Montecassino unter seinen Reformabt Richer von Niederaltaich,* in «Studi Gregoriani», III, Rome, 1948, 369-450. To our knowledge of the Cassinese environment of the period contributes a great deal also, W. HOLTZMANN, *Laurentius von Amalfi. Ein Lehrer Hildebrands,* in *Studi Gregoriani,* I, 1947, 207-236.

In the same volume, 319-327, the exaggerated conclusions of Fliche about the action of Desiderius as Pope have been refuted by T. LECCISOTTI, *L'incontro di Desiderio di Montecassino col re Enrico IV ad Albano.* On the same topic see also, E. AMANN, *Victor III,* «Dictionnaire de Théologie Catholique», Paris 1948, 2866-2872.

For the rule of Desiderius at Monte Cassino see, G. B. BORINO, *Per la storia della riforma della Chiesa nel secolo XI,* in «Archivio Società Romana Storia Patria», 38 (1915), 457-513.

For the twelfth century, cfr. E. CASPAR, *Petrus Diaconus und die Monte Cassineser Fälschungen,* Berlin 1909 and the more recent study by H. HOFFMANN, *Petrus Diaconus die Herren von Tusculum und der Sturz Oderisius' II von Montecassino,* in «Deutsches Archiv für Erforschungen des Mittelalters», 27 (1971), 1-109.

Part of the customs of the twelfth and thirteenth century have been preserved in the Constitutions or statutes newly edited by T. LECCISOTTI and F. AVAGLIANO, in *Corpus Consuetudinum Monasticarum,* VI, Siegburg, Schmitt 1975, 201-258.

Access avenue

Entrance cloister

The death of St. Benedict (A. Selva)

St. Benedict

BENEDICTUS
QUI VENIT IN NOMINE
DOMINI

St. Scolastica

The choir

◀ St. Benedict's sepulchre

Monument to Piero dei Medici

Chapel of the Virgin Mary Assumption ▶

St. Peter liberated from prison.
(S. Pistolesi 1979)

The Baptism of Jesus.
(B. Long 1979)

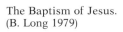
The Crypt

▲ Polish military
cemetery

German military
cemetery

English military
cemetery

V.

TOWARDS NEW TIMES

«Speluncam latronum de templo Domini facientes».
(Reg. Bern. I ab.)*

1. THE SWABIAN OPPRESSION.

As already mentioned, the disputed Swabian succession at the death of William II (1189) was the cause of many grievous evils for southern Italy. The troubles increased when the new young emperor, Frederick II, a former pupil of Pope Innocent III resumed the struggle between the Church and the Empire.

With the consolidation of Norman power, the Cassinese abbey had lost a great deal of her political importance, and in the harsh confrontations, especially in the later years, the peace of her cloister was beset by the tragic necessities of sieges and the horrors of war. Yet she remained a power of the first rank and her position on the borders of the rivals caused her to feel the effects of the wrath of both opposing parties. Many times the land of St. Benedict was subjected to fire and sword; more than once those who survived the slaughter, with the vision of horrible cruelties still in their eyes, wandered in search of safer shelters. The horrors kept increasing with the mounting hostilities and the alternating fortunes of war.

In 1229 the monastery, which was held by the Emperor's men, was besieged by the Cardinal legate Pelagius, leader of the papal forces. After a bitter fight in the surrounding mountains, he was able to capture the monastery and occupy it with a force of over a hundred armed men. The damages to the abbey were compounded; the vicars of the Emperor, then on a crusade in the

---

* «They changed the temple of the Lord into a den of thieves».

East, began to drive out the Cassines monks from the various dependencies, stripping them of all their goods and treating them so harshly that many of the monks had to change their clerical clothing in order to escape. Compounding the troubles, Cardinal Pelagius laid his hands on the treasure of the monastery.

During the same year, the Cardinal legate became frightened by the return of the Emperor and sought shelter in the abbey. He began to strengthen the place with his men; thus the unlucky monastery was subjected to another siege. This time it was the imperial army that moved to capture it. The troops abandoned themselves to every possible excess in the surrounding area. The Saracens were especially notorious being responsible for the destruction of the church of the nearby abbey of St. Matthew. In all this confusion, the imperial fisc exacted its share, appropriating the demesne and the possessions of the monastery.

During the summer of the following year, on July 23, 1230, Frederick II signed a peace treaty with the Pope in the main church of San Germano, where once before he had held court before leaving as a crusader for the Holy Land. Afterward, the Emperor was prevailed upon to restore his favor to Monte Cassino; at first only partially, but finally, through the intercession of the Duke of Austria to full favor. This provided a period of relative peace.

This accord between the Pope and the Emperor was not sincere, and did not last long. In the year 1239, the Cassinese monastery, burdened heavily with debts, was once again subject to persecutions and tribulations because the Emperor, anticipating the resumption of hostilities, wanted to neutralize the power of the monastery. Moreover, the community, after the death of Landolfo Sinibaldo (1227-1236), was for several years without an Abbot because it was not easy to find a candidate that would be acceptable to both the Pope and the Emperor. Not until 1239 was it possible to obtain the dual assent to the choice of Stefano di Corbaria, who was installed with great rejoicing.

Soon, however, the joy turned into mourning because the following month the excommunications launched by the Pope against the Emperor marked the beginning of a new and more violent struggle. In the month of April the Cassinese monastery, by order of the Emperor, was made ready for war and some of the monks were expelled. The following June an edict of Frederick II banished from the kingdom all religious born elsewhere, and in the same month other monks were forced out of Monte Cassino, but were allowed to settle in Valleluce. Finally in July all but eight monks had to abandon the monastery and withdraw to Valleluce or return to their own families.

Now there was total desolation on the sacred mountain. The site made famous by the veneration of Popes, Emperors and entire generations of people was reduced to a den of thieves for twenty-six years. The Abbot, deprived of his civil jurisdiction, was forced to become a follower of Caesar or to remain in San Germano, where since the time of Theobald (1022-1035) there had been an abbatial house on the spot where once had stood the ancient monastery of the Saviour. At one time we even find the ailing Abbot in the shelter of the dependent monastery of St. Liberatore on the Maiella.

Conditions at Monte Cassino improved only with the arrival of the Angevins. On March 29, 1263, Pope Urban IV had already nominated a new abbot in place of Teodino, one of Mandred's supporters. In reality the new abbot was able to take his office only after the battle of Benevento (Feb. 26, 1266) and after the death of Manfred. He was Bernardo Aiglerio, born in Lyon and formerly abbot of Lerins; he was a good friend of Charles of Anjou, who supported him firmly in his difficult task, which also included important missions on behalf of the Pope and the King. Bernard's accomplishments were so great that he deserves to be numbered among the abbey's great Abbots. He restored monastic discipline and the authority of the abbey in the domain of St. Benedict. His commentary on the *Rule* and the volumes of *Regesti* furnish us with ample evidence of his activity while his *Speculum monachorum* testifies to his enlightened piety. This latter work, though not quite original, became very popular in monasteries where for a long time together with the *Rule* and the

Dialogi of Gregory the Great formed an ascetic manual for the use of the monks.

The rule of Bernardo, which had received a heavy blow when the Angevin king deprived him of his criminal jurisdiction, ended with his death on the 4th of April, 1282. Once again the community had begun to flourish in the new atmosphere of peace and tranquility. In this same century the number of monks sometimes rose to one hundred eighty and from the community three were appointed Cardinals and ten others Archbishops and Bishops.

The attempt of Celestin V formed only a passing cloud over the abbey. Surrounded by his fanatic monks, he wanted to unite Monte Cassino, the capital of monasticism, and the congregation that he had founded. He honored the monastery with a visit and bid the monks to change their lifestyle and the habit. The majority of the monks chose to go elsewhere, abandoning the monastery, which Celestin V had placed in charge of one of his followers, Angelario (1294). Calm was restored with Boniface VIII. Later, Angelario was entrusted with the custody of Celestin after this Pope had resigned his office, but he allowed Celestin to escape. This so enraged Boniface VIII that he therefore deposed Angelario in 1295.

The new century turned out to be one of the most tragic in the history of the abbey. The weakening of the two great universal powers, Papacy and Empire, and the rise of nationalistic and particularistic forces led to continuous wars, which threatened to destroy the Cassinese monastery. And yet in spite of the wars and a terrible earthquake, life resumed with renewed vigor when anxiety and fear disappeared towards the end of the fourteenth century.

Misfortunes resumed, although indirectly, with the Pope's exile at Avignon (1305-1377). Out of reverence to St. Benedict, who had lived and was buried there, and for the convenience of the local population, Pope John XXII decided that the Cassinese abbey, which among its pastors numbered so many cardinals and two popes, should henceforth (May 2, 1322) become an episcopate, depending directly from the Roman Church. To safeguard the character and the very life of the monastery, the Pope also decreed that the bishop should always be elected by the monks. This clause, however, was not observed and this led to a new decline because the majority of the bishops, elected in Avignon, often were not even monks and so remained indifferent to the needs of the abbey with which they were not acquainted, ruling it from afar through appointed vicars.

The needs of the abbey kept mounting. First the Hungarians, who marched into Campania to avenge the death of their king Andrea, attacked and sacked Monte Cassino as well. The vassals, especially Jacopo da Pignataro, took advantage of the disorders, while the fraudulent behavior of the episcopal vicar Guglielmo Calderi allowed his followers from Calabria, called up to defend the abbey, to become impudent plunderers of Monte Cassino property. More damaging by far were the deeds perpetrated by Jacopo: he made himself master of all the land and dependent villages; moreover, he drove away almost all the monks, so that for over a year «that church so resplendent for religious fervor and attendance» was left without any religious worship. When Jacopo finally departed, only the walls of the abbey were left standing.

Even those walls, however, were destined to fall. On the morning of Sept. 9, 1349, a terrifying earthquake reduced the monastery, which was still the most beautiful in all Christendom, into a mass of ruins. All the monks survived but were forced to abandon the large halls and the long porches built by Desiderius, which had either collapsed or threatened to, and to take shelter in wooden barracks. During the same century other quakes kept causing still more damage to the structures.

Angelo della Posta (1357-1362), the only Cassinese among the Bishop-abbots, worked hard to rebuild the church and at least one dormitory and a refectory for the monks as quickly as possible. It was left, however, for Pope Urban V (1363-1370), the former Abbot of St. Victor of Marseilles, to complete the work. He abolished the episcopal see for many reasons of practical utility and, above all, to prevent the election of strangers. Thus the

Pope reserved for himself for several years not only the title but also, in the true sense of the word, the office of Abbot of Monte Cassino. He directed all Benedictine institutions to contribute a fixed amount to the rebuilding of the abbey, and in order to restore life to the community he invited monks from other monasteries. As one can learn from the letters that have survived from contemporary monks, the Pope followed progress at the abbey step by step. The work of reconstruction advanced so rapidly that already under abbot Pietro de Tartaris (1374-1395), who succeeded Andrea da Faenza (1369-1373), the first of the new Abbots, planning began for the decorations of the new buildings.

The Western Schism, however, brought new struggles, which were particularly violent in the kingdom of Naples because they were entangled with the contest for the dynastic succession. Not only the abbot de Tartaris, who played an important role in the election of Urban VI and who was entrusted with very important posts in the kingdom, but also his successors, Enrico (1396-1413) and Pirro (1414-1442) Tomacelli, found themselves implicated in various ways. The two Tomacellis, in fact, ended up as political prisoners, the first of King Ladislaus in the stronghold of Spoleto and the second of Pope Eugene IV in castle S. Angelo. In addition, King Ladislaus drove all the monks out of the abbey, allowing only twelve to remain under the rule of the Cistercian abbot Andrea da Capua. The monks were permitted to return only after the death of the King in 1415. Not long after, the abbey suffered a new disaster. Francesco Blando di Piedimonte S. Germano managed to seize the abbey and plundered it, torturing and killing many monks.

After the death of Abbot Pirro, Pope Eugene IV entrusted the fortunes of the abbey to Cardinal Lodovico Trevisan, better known under the name of Scarampa (Sept. 4, 1443), to begin reorganization of the domain of St. Benedict. He tried to transfer the monks of the congregation of S. Giustina of Padua to Monte Cassino, but was unsuccessful. The following year Eugene IV granted the monastery of S. Gregorio al Celio as residence for part of the community. Also at that time, in 1440, in spite of the lack of manpower and many financial burdens, five monks left for Monserrato, invited there by the new king of Naples, Alfonso of Aragon.

It was not until 1446 that the Pope finally gave his assent to the nomination of the monk Andrea Carafa, who had already been elected Abbot with the approval of King Alfonso. The rule of Abbot Carafa, which lasted until 1454, was quite lamentable and painful because his extreme attachment to his parents led him to a vexing avariciousness which was very painful for the community. When he died (Feb. 1, 1454), Pope Nicholas V, on May 18, 1454, appointed as abbot Cardinal Trevisan, who had been Patriarch of Aquilea, either because he wanted to provide a strong leader to the monastery, then threatened by the nephews of Carafa, or because he wished to accede to the request of the King of Naples who wanted to reward a loyal follower.

2. THE COMMENDATARIES.

With him the series of commendataries began. The commenda, that is the placing the administration of a monastery in the hands of a trusted person, had come by now into universal use. This practice at the start had been beneficial, but soon greed changed it into one of the main causes of ruin for many of them. The trustees, in fact, even when most favorably disposed towards the welfare of the monasteries, were in general by temperament and upbringing not qualified for the office; moreover, their long or habitual absence was further obstacle to any good intentions. In addition, most of the times the monastery represented for them only a part of their fat patrimony or the means by which to restore losses, in which case the monastic community became a useless burden on the balance sheet. Thus, the monks were abandoned to the care of a Prior, mostly unable to exercise any authority, with revenues limited to what the commendatary was willing to give him. Soon both discipline and buildings began to deteriorate.

Monte Cassino also was a victim of this system. Upon the

death of Abbot Trevisan (1465), Pope Paul II, resisting every pressure, kept the abbey under his control, for political as well as moral reasons. The efforts of Ferrante I of Aragon obtained from Pope Sixtus IV what he had been unable to get from Paul II, the concession of Monte Cassino for his son Giovanni, then only eighteen years old. In spite of his youth his management gave rise to good hopes for the future. Giovanni must be given credit for the reopening of the school for oblates in the monastery of S. Maria dell'Albaneta (1481), while attempts continued to introduce the observance of S. Giustina at Monte Cassino. Giovanni also ordered an identification of the sacred remains buried under the main altar (Nov. 18, 1484), in addition a new, beautifully carved choir was put in place.

After Giovanni's death — he had been a cardinal since 1478 — all the monks with the exception of four were expelled by order of the King because of the war between Ferrante of Aragon and Pope Innocent VIII. Peace was concluded in 1486, and in the treaty due consideration was given to the interests of the abbey.

The regime of commendataries went on and so Monte Cassino was given to the son of Lorenzo the Magnificent, Giovanni dei Medici (1486-1505), the future Pope Leo X. Unfortunately, because of this election Monte Cassino found itself involved in yet another war. The French invasion of the kingdom of Naples reopened a period of violent struggles which continued with the Spanish counteroffensive. Although far removed and almost unknown to the abbey, Giovanni dei Medici ordered Monte Cassino to partecipate in these hostilities.

During their cavalcade through Italy, the French were joined by various Italian lords who wanted to obtain favors from them, including the Medici, who had been banished from Florence. In 1501 Giovanni dei Medici, abbot of Monte Cassino, pleaded with the French King Louis XII in Naples the case of his brother Pietro. The king easily found the way to satisfy Pietro's desires, appointing him governor of the Cassinese domain. Thus, on his account, the abbey found herself firmly in the French camp and became the theater of more bloody encounters. In fact, not only was the territory of the abbey badly devastated in a war that was decided on her very border, but the monastery itself saw its cloisters stained with blood in numerous acts of violence.

While Consalvo di Cordova, commander in chief of the Spanish forces, was fighting the French along the Garigliano River, Monte Cassino was transformed into a powerful fortress held by a strong French contingent. It does not appear that the community, quite small in number as a result of the rule of the commendataries, had been banished from the abbey; nevertheless the soldiery did not refrain from profaning the sacred place.

Consalvo, the Spanish general, had offered terms of surrender to the French defenders, which they had accepted only in the event that the expected relief forces should not arrive; meanwhile, an armistice was concluded. When Consalvo who had left for the assault on Gaeta, found out that the French had broken the agreement and were raiding the surrounding valley, he decided to assault Monte Cassino. After repeated efforts, the Spanish troops broke into the cloisters, pursuing the enemy and cutting down everyone they caught.

Along the banks of the Garigliano the war lasted a while longer because the troops, stuck in the mud of the wintry season, were unable to score a decisive blow. Finally, on the 27th of December, Consalvo was able to force his way across the River Suio, surprising the French camp. Pietro dei Medici met his death in the precipitous flight when the barge with four artillery pieces in which he was trying to get to the sea capsized in the river. His corpse was found and brought to Monte Cassino, where later a magnificent monument, by Sangallo, still standing today, was dedicated to him.

For southern Italy the battle of the Garigliano river (1503) marked a decisive date in her history; it set the condition and the boundaries which remained unaltered until the modern era. For the venerable house of St. Benedict, however, the damages inflicted by a war that had been fought even in her cloisters and came to an end at her very gate might have proved irreparable if Providence had not again come to her aid in a new way more in tune with the times marking a decisive turning point in her thousand year history.

BIBLIOGRAPHY

For the last Swabian period the sources, in part, are the RYCCARDI DE SANCTO GERMANO NOTARII, *Chronica,* last edition by C. A. GARUFI in *Rer. Ital. Script.,* VII, part II, Bologna, Zanichelli, 1937-1938.

The same period has been sketched by T. LECCISOTTI, *S. Tommaso d'Aquino e Montecassino,* Montecassino 1965 (Miscellanea Cassinese, 32). The rule of abbot Bernard, has been illustrated by A. CAPLET in the edition of the *Regesti Bernardi I abbatis casinensis fragmenta,* Rome, 1980, and narrated by A. SABA, *Bernardo I Ayglerio,* Montecassino, 1931, (Miscellanea Cassinese, 6). Cfr. also T. LECCISOTTI, *A proposito dell'abate di Montecassino Bernardo I,* in «Bollettino Diocesano di Montecassino», 27 (1972), 415-428.

For the same century the fundamental study is M. INGUANEZ, *Cronologia degli abati cassinesi del secolo XIII,* in *Casinensia,* Montecassino 1929, 409-456.

For the period of the bishops one must note the contribution of A. MERCATI, *Un vescovo mancato di Montecassino,* in *Casinensia,* 247-286, and, *Statuta Casinensia (saec. XIII-XIV)* in the already mentioned *Corpus Consuetudinum monasticarum,* VI, Siegburg, Schmitt 1975, 201-258.

For the restoration of Urban V: T. LECCISOTTI, *Documenti Vaticani per la storia di Montecassino. Pontificato di Urban V,* Montecassino 1952 (Miscellanea Cassinese, 28).

A. ALBAREDA, *Monios de Montecassino a Montserrat,* in *Casinensia,* 209-216, deals with the expedition of the Cassinese at Montserrat.

The tormented events of the government of Pirro Tomacelli have been studiede by T. LECCISOTTI, *Aspetti della crisi dell'età moderna a Montecassino,* in «Archivio Storico Terra di Lavoro» 2 (1960), 133-157; 3 (1964), 173-211.

The period of the commendataries by N. PICOZZI, *Gli abati commendatari di Montecassino (1454-1504),* Rome, Tip. Agostiniana, 1946.

For the period of Giovanni de' Medici in particular, there is an interesting work by G. B. PICOTTI, *La giovinezza di Leone X,* Milan, Hoepli, 1927; the war events of the beginning of the sixteenth century, which find some parallel with the events of '44, are described by P. PIERI, *La battaglia del Garigliano del 1503,* Rome, Proja, 1938; by the same also, *La guerra Franco-Spagnola nel mezzogiorno (1502-1503),* in «Archivio Stor. Prov. Napol.» 72 (1952), 21-69.

An attempt to abolish the commenda by the introduction of the Olivetan monks at Monte Cassino has been revealed by V. CATTANA, *Per la storia della commenda a Montecassino. Un progetto del re Alfonso II d'Aragona,* in «Benedictina», 19 (1972), 437-444.

VI.

THE MODERN AGE

1. THE VIGOROUS RECOVERY OF THE SIXTEENTH CENTURY.

The process, which in Europe through long medieval toil had brought about the formation of large, modern national states, in Italy gave more limited results. The pride and the strength of provincial forces, together with the survival, as in Germany, of the great universal ideas, led to the formation of regional states. These, as they grew stronger and more centralized, hardly tolerated limits to their absolute power. In this new political climate the existence of isolated monasteries, especially those that owned vast feudal estates, encountered great difficulties; they ran the risk of being absorbed by the great lords who fought to become their commendataries.

To fight against the evils of the time in Italy, since the beginnings of the fifteenth century, a federation among some abbeys had been formed. St. Benedict certainly had established his monastery as a complete family and as an independent unit within the local ecclesiastical life. Groupings of various forms which had taken place in the course of the centuries had been determined either by bonds of dependency or by other people's will or by the necessity to face dangerous situations. Thus the *congregations* had come about. The name assumed now a much larger meaning than the one found in the *Rule*, where it indicated only the monks and the community. The congregation of S. Giustina originated in Italy in the fifteenth century. It was a reform movement striving to raise the ancient abbey of Padua from the abyss of desolation into which the commenda system had precipitated her: in the end many monasteries joined and the organization extended throughout the peninsula.

The form that its organization took shows clearly the necessities it tried to meet. Formed to prevent the evils of the commenda system, it aimed at destroying its very roots. Thus, under the influence of ideas already current it aimed, through the monastic order at establishing a central authority so strongly organized that it would prevent the return of the evil system. The congregation, it must be pointed out, was the response of the monastic communities to new times and circumstances rather than, as is still wrongly repeated, an imitation of the political organization of the Venetian state. The abbacy was made into a temporary office, and its election was reserved to the general chapter, which was the supreme authority of the congregation; thus it was placed beyond the control of extraneous forces. The new organization spread rapidly and soon imposed itself to the admiration of contemporaries for its cohesive strength and for the holiness of life and strong character of its monks. It also found kind and strong support from the popes, especially Eugenius IV, who can be called a cofounder of the congregation.

It was, indeed, Pope Eugenius who, as we have already mentioned, first conceived the idea of entrusting Monte Cassino, torn between wordly ambitions and contrasts, to this national congregation which was better able to cope during the difficult times. The attempt, though renewed at the time of cardinal d'Aragona under Sixtus IV, had no success.

The credit for the realization of this project must go to Consalvo di Cordova, «the greatest soldier of the Renaissance» [1], who knew by personal experience the kind of difficulties that fortifications could create for adversaries. At any rate, it was in the interest of Spain that Monte Cassino, a very large barony at the very gates of the kingdom of Naples, be neutralized in this way. The Catholic rulers were determined now to destroy the power and reduce to submission the turbulent barons of the kingdom, any fief that remained strong and autonomous would be a problem. This explains the personal and constant interest of the king who repeatedly addressed popes, cardinals, and the commendataries. What was requested was not a division of the income between the commendatary and the monks, as in previous occasions, but the total liberation of the Cassinese domain.

Consalvo had therefore decided to call in the congregation of

S. Giustina, which was about to celebrate its first hundred years of existence and which now controlled many important monasteries in Italy. How had he learned about it? According to one tradition, St. Benedict had appeared to him in a dream before the battle of Cerignola, promising him the victory and entrusting to him the welfare of his monastery. On the day of his triumphal entry into Naples, Consalvo recognized that the habit of the abbot of St. Severino was the same one St. Benedict had on during the apparition; it was the habit of the monks of St. Giustina.

The invitation this time came from the Spaniards. All the necessary initiatives were set in motion and followed by the King personally. The resignation of the commendatary, the cardinal dei Medici, was obtained by payment of a large compensation, and Pope Julius II granted the decree of annexation. With the bull «*Super cathedram*» (Nov. 15, 1504), published with several other pertinent documents, the Pope decreed also that henceforth the congregation, due to the name and the dignity of the monastery that headed all others, should bear the name of Monte Cassino. The annexation was for the congregation a happening of exceptional importance. The monks who joined it wanted the moment commemorated with suitable paintings, which were placed by the second gate of the cloister. It took place on Sunday, Jan. 12, 1505.

A few days before, about one hundred monks from the closest monasteries had gathered in San Germano. They were housed in the palace of the Abbot, and on January 11, the election of the new Abbot, who would remain in charge until the next chapter, was held. The Abbot then presiding, Eusebio Fontana da Modena, at that time Abbot of Perugia, was elected. The new Abbot, together with Abbot Ignazio Squarcialupi, a Florentine friend of the former commendatary, who was the general counsel of the congregation, had been charged with conducting the negotiations on behalf of the congregation. The following day the monks ascended the sacred mountain in solemn precession. Early in the morning, in the presence of the people and the notables, among whom there was the governor general of cardinal dei Medici who was the vicar of the abbey and a loyal friend of Consalvo, the Spanish viceroy, Alarcone, president of the congregation, sang a pontifical Mass in the church of San Germano and concluded with the homily «*Venite ascendamus ad montem Domini*» *. The procession was then formed, headed by the citizens of San Germano carrying lamps, and others dressed in white linen clothes. They were followed by all the clerics of the abbey wearing surplices; among them eighty priests preceded by twelve silver crosses: the last two of them carried the very precious robe that Consalvo wore at his triumphal entrance into Naples and a very large piece of gold silk cloth, both gifts that the conqueror was donating in honor of St. Benedict. The rich cape that was made out of that robe was kept in the sacristy until the end of the eighteenth century, when it was destroyed in the French sack of the abbey. Bringing up the rear came all the monks, the first carrying the pontifical bulls and, in the middle, twelve monks from the choir school, singing psalms. At each of the five oratories stationed along the way, the procession stopped to sing the proper antiphons and prayers. After the last one, that of S. Agatha, the president intoned the *Te Deum,* which was sung until the procession reached the second gate of the monastery. There Eusebius handed the bulls to a notary and ordered that they be read; then he opened and closed the main gate to indicate that he had taken possession of the house. Singing the *Benedictus,* the procession then reached the church. The Abbot closed and opened the door, ascended the main altar and, with tears in his eyes, touched the four corners. He descended next in the choir, at that time in front of the presbytery, and sat in his seat. He then moved over to the sacristy, here also opening and closing the door. Finally, he proceeded to the chapter, where the only bull addressed to the monks was read, after which they pledged obedience to Eusebius. In large part they were the ones that the congregation had assigned to Monte Cassino. There were twenty-nine of them and four clerics, mostly from northern Italy and Florence. Of the old

---

* «Come let us ascend the mountain of the Lord».

monks, some agreed to stay on with the newcomers; others elected to withdraw to dependent houses of the abbey.

When the ceremonies came to an end, all the participants were invited to dinner; in the afternoon almost all took their leave with the exception of Alarcone and a few others who were invited to remain. On the following day a solemn funeral Mass was celabrated for Queen Isabel of Spain, who had died on November 25, shortly after Monte Cassino had been liberated. In the afternoon Squarcialupi gave a sermon on the theme: «introibimus in tabernaculum eius, adorabimus in loco ubi steterunt pedes eius» *.

As it began its new life, the monastery was reaching the thousandth year of its existence. It was now losing its autonomy to become part, albeit a very important one, of a larger organism. The time limit placed on the office of Abbot eliminated the individualism that marked previous abbatial rule; hence uniformity was the pattern of all succeeding administrations. The abbey, of course, lost most of its political importance after the union, but she retained a large patrimony in addition to its moral influence [2]. In the new political climate, a life full of involvement and vitality, even though troubled by passions and contrasts, was no longer possible as in the Middle Ages. Instead, a long period of calm and peaceful prosperity began at Monte Cassino. The monks could now dedicate themselves fearlessly and with renewed zeal to their own religious lives and to peaceful pursuits. Recovery followed quickly and the sixteenth century can reasonably be compared to the eleventh, standing out with it as one of the most noble periods in the life of Monte Cassino.

The work of reconstruction soon began to erase the marks left by the war. Most of the buildings, both because of direct acts of war and of fires, were in ruins and the monks lived in wooden huts. The work of restoration of the buildings was a prelude to the magnificent constructions which would grace the summit of

---

* «We shall enter his tabernacle ; we shall lie prostrate where his feet touched the ground».

the mountain in that century. Much care was also given to the reestablishment of rent payments and the recovery of the patrimony, as the beneficiaries died out or relinquished their holdings. Thus, large resources began to flow again into the abbey's treasury and this allowed the funding of many charitable enterprises and works of embellishment lending Monte Cassino great distinction.

The Cassinese congregation has enriched Italy with many monumental monasteries, thus one would hope that it would be of great interest to have an artistic and, especially, an architectonic history of these works, but after so much grievous destruction of archives and documents one wonders if this is still possible. At Monte Cassino, in particular, the congregation had raised a hymn of incomparable glory to the father of western monasticism, leaving until our own days a magnificent monument of sixteenth century monastic architecture.

Almost all the Abbots contributed to this work. The one who distinguished himself most in the first quarter of the century was Ignazio Squarcialupi. The abbey owed much to his hard work and recognized that its artistic renewal began during his tenure. He used his influence with Pope Leo X to obtain several favors, among them the abrogation of the payments the abbey had to make to him for giving up his position as commendatary. At the death of the Pope, the people of San Germano, taking advantage of the fact that Squarcialupi was away in Rome, revolted on December 2, 1521; among other acts of violence, they broke down the gates of the abbey, killed some of the monks and sacked the place for three days.

There was also the danger of a return of the commenda and the possibility that the armed rabble, which sacked Rome in 1527, might next turn on Monte Cassino after robbing nearby towns and villages. These proved to be temporary fears. Misfortunes befell the population, especially at San Germano, with the plague of 1527, where the sufferings were mitigated by the great charity of Abbot Crisostomo de Alessandro; in 1593 famine and bands of robbers again brought great sufferings to the people.

In the words of Minozzi, who found his opening quotation in one of the thirty splendidly illuminated choir books ordered by Squarcialupi, Monte Cassino

«As Christ's small ship sailing on the lake conquered the waves of the times and gave new wings to hope. Life was bursting out all over, like flowers in spring. The Cassinese soul was truly rising again with Christ, sitting with him at the banquet of life, gathered hopefully around the great tree of the Church in contemplation of the supreme mysteries and glorious beauty, embracing the spirit of renewal» [3].

The one, however, who distinguished himself the most in the renewal of Monte Cassino in the second half of the century was the Abbot Angelo de Faggis, named Sangrino from his village, Castel di Sangro. To the holiness of his life and great learning he added an exceptional building activity which makes him appear as a second Desiderius. He also fought valiantly to preserve the rights of the monastery. One must remember also Abbot Girolamo Scloccheto who on March 13, 1545, while some works were in course in the church, conducted a new recognizance of the remains of St. Benedict and St. Scholastica and, on the following day showed the sacred relics to the magistrates and the leading citizens of San Germano. Abbot d. Girolamo Brugia (1590-1595) built a new paper mill at S. Elia and improved the old factory that produced pins and needles in San Germano.

The renown of the place and the high repute of the monks' lives drew always, but especially during Holy Years, thousands of pilgrims and prominent people. Ignatius Loyola withdrew there for forty days to train Pietro Ortiz in the Spiritual Exercises; it was there that Diego de Hoces died; Filippo Neri was there during his youth; Torquato Tasso sought peace and tranquility there. The brushes of the brothers Da Ponte gathered all these souls together around St. Benedict in the beautiful painting of the Cassinese refectory.

«... which together shone more
luminously of reflected light» [4].

2. THE MAGNIFICENCE OF THE SEVENTEENTH CENTURY.

In the following century life at the abbey followed the same pattern of the preceding one. The Abbots, who according to the ordinances of the congregation, served for only short terms, could not leave a mark of their personality; still they were all watchful keepers of discipline and of the rights of the monastery. All were equally diligent to see to the completion and the embellishment of the buildings which became more majestic and monumental. Amongst them excelled d. Simplicio Caffarelli; d. Domenico Quesada, who undertook the total rebuilding of the church; d. Angelo della Noce, who in 1659 supervised the last recognition of the remains of St. Benedict and St. Scholastica; and d. Andrea Deodati, who placed the relics in a nobler and more dignified vault.

Concerning monastic observance at the abbey, Cardinal Aguirre and the fathers Bollandisti and Mabillon are faithful witnesses. The first wrote enthusiastically, «the personal edification that I experienced in observing the exceptional fervor with which those holy monks serve God in that sacred solitude, the continuous attendance at the choir day and night, and the scrupulousness with which they observe their ordinances...» And the famous authors of the *Acta Sanctorum* wrote: «... as Leo of Ostia writes about St. Odo abbot of Cluny... we also can say: what we had heard said, we have also seen in the city of the Lord of Hosts and the city of our God and on His sacred mountain. It is not our task to describe the buildings of the monastery or the church, not even the exquisite charity with which we have been received and the glow of holiness that we have seen in the faces of those pious monks...» [5].

Witnesses that the spiritual vitality remained as vigorous in this century were those English monks who prepared themselves at Monte Cassino for their missions in the homeland, the restoration of the Benedictine houses destroyed during the schism, and the foundation of the Polish monasteries. D. Roset, prior of the monastery of SS. Vitus and Idulfus in Lorraine, came to Monte

Cassino to learn the customs and rituals to bring back to his country, where the monks of the Cassinese congregation were establishing a new one in Lorraine, from which later came forth the congregations of St. Maur in France and St. Placide in Belgium. In 1608, Pope Paul V chose two monks of Monte Cassino, d. Felice Passer and d. Benedetto Sangrino, to inspect the congregation of Melada in Dalmatia; they were chosen by the monks as presidents of their congregation. Besides giving the Church eight archbishops and bishops, Monte Cassino gave to heaven many saintly souls, among them d. Zaccaria Petronio, endowed in life and in death with the gift of miracles, who had already been named in the process of beatification.

The influx of those who came to venerate St. Benedict remained very great in spite of the fact that access was very difficult and travel was unsafe. During the Holy Years, the numbers increased greatly: in 1600 there were daily at Monte Cassino more than one hundred pilgrims, and the monks, according to the *Rule*, washed their feet and served them meals; in 1625 the total number reached eighty thousand: in 1650 they numbered forty-seven thousand, reaching a peak of nine hundred on some days. There was, of course, no lack of illustrious visitors, who came accompanied by glittering escorts, at times as many as three hundred, among them, sixty knights and numerous cardinals who came for prayers and meditation. Pope Clement VII had planned to come but was forced to cancel the visit, fearing the disorder and disturbance the monastery would have to suffer because of the number of attendants who were ready to follow him.

The administration, both spiritual and temporal, of the dependent territory required special care. Pope Urban VIII confirmed to the Abbot «all episcopal prerogative rights»; synods were held frequently. It was also necessary to defend the rights of the monastery, not only those affecting the patrimony through the acquisition and the redemption of debts, but above all the jurisdictional rights about which litigation was characteristic of that age.

In 1669, after various attempts, the rights of criminal

jurisdiction were reacquired by a payment of thirty-four thousand ducats; the abbey had lost those rights during the reign of Charles of Anjou, and the restitution that Pope Pius II had tried to make had not been successful. During the insurrection of 1647, the Abbot d. Andrea Arcioni (1645-1647) had to furnish troops and money to the royal party, to which he had given his support. He was also the ambassador of the congregation at the courts of several princes, among whom one must remember in particular the Duke of Savoy Amadeus, and in 1649 he represented the Duke of Parma, Ranuccio II, at the Vatican during the papacy of Innocent X.

Abbot d. Isidoro Agresti (1614-1617) was praised for the peace and tranquility he maintained at the abbey during his rule, especially at S. Germano, where he installed a ruling committee of fifty deputies in place of the tumultous popular council.

Work meanwhile continued on refining and completing the buildings of the preceding century. The splendid and imposing scale of the design required great efforts, large expenditures, and time. The mountain provided only the stones; everything else, from sand to lime, beams and lumber, had to be transported with great difficulties from the outside, and the craftsmen and artists would not come to work on the isolated mountain without the assurance of better pay than they could obtain in the city. All these expenses were not covered by the regular income of the abbey, but by the generosity of benefactors. The distinguished historian of the abbey, d. Erasmo Gattula, intended to preserve their memory in a work that he never had the opportunity to write.

The greatest care was devoted to the church, which in this century was completely renovated. This, in the wonderful richness of its marbles, the splendor of its gold, and the magnificence of its colors, proved to be the best work of the Neapolitan school of the time, its hymn to the glory of St. Benedict.

3. THE SPLENDID AND PEACEFUL WORK OF THE EIGHTEENTH CEN-
   TURY.

As the new century opened, this grandiose building program
gave the house of St. Benedict an appearance of imposing
magnificence, and the range of its jurisdiction became larger. In
fact, at the close of the preceding century, in 1698, through an
agreement worked out with commendatary Innico Caracciolo,
Bishop of Aversa, Pope Innocent VII decreed the annexation of
the abbey of S. Vincenzo al Volturno to Monte Cassino. The final
approval of the commendatary was given only at the end of 1700.
The Cassinese had also worked out an agreement with the Bishop
of Isernia, who had some claim on the territory, by turning over
to him jurisdiction of the village of Pesche, which until then
belonged to them. In 1701 Pope Clement XI granted daily plenary
indulgence to all visitors of the basilica.

These auspicious beginnings were soon disturbed by the
repercussions of the war for the Spanish succession (1700-1714),
which placed the whole of Europe in turmoil. As a result of it, the
kingdom of Naples passed from the domination of Spain to that
of Austria. Monte Cassino, as usual, due to her position seemed
headed for new troubles. Spanish troops had taken quarters in
San Germano and had erected some small fortifications on the
mountain in the vicinity of the monastery. The presence of these
troops certainly brought no benefits either to the abbey or the
populace. The worst was avoided, however, because of the
respect and deference of their leaders, who even asked that the
Abbot to be present at their military councils. After the precipitous
retreat of the Spaniards, the German forces under their supreme
commander, Count Daun, arrived. The general staff took
residence in the abbatial palace of San Germano until their departure for Naples (July 1). In addition these military chiefs also invited the abbot to be present at their deliberations and, when they
were visiting Monte Cassino, according to ancient custom left
behind at the gate of the monastery their swords and whatever
other weapons they were carrying. Their stay, although brief, still

caused many anxieties and annoyances, mainly because they wanted the monks to make for the troops a quantity of bread four times greater than they could produce, and it was only with the greatest difficulty that it was possible to limit the quantity to the lesser number of seventy-thousand rations.

Later the political situation changed again; this time the kingdom of Naples fell to the Bourbons of Spain. The new king, Charles III (1734), demanded the tithe but recognized the rights of the abbey. Another cause of great danger and fear was the terrible storm of Feb. 20, 1712, in which the monastery was repeatedly hit by lightening.

The calm, however, was not seriously disrupted until the end of the century, and this allowed the work to proceed with great alacrity, especially on the church, which was finally completed after eighty-seven years. Coincidentally, on the chair of Peter sat Pope Benedict XIII. The austere Dominican, zealous in the worship of God and ecclesiastical liturgy, for a long time had had a very special love for the abbey, where he felt quite at ease. He had already visited Monte Cassino in 1676 when he was on his way to take possession of his see in Manfredonia. He had returned in May, 1721, after the conclave that had elected Innocent XIII; his stay remained memorable because of the great devotion he showed.

When he arrived at the first gate of the monastery, he dismounted and, on his knees, kissed the ground remaining some minutes in prayer; he repeated the same procedure at the small shrine of St. Benedict then proceeded to the second gate reciting the *Magnificat* with his companions. He did not want the monks to accompany him and, when he reached the church — it was nighttime — he had all the candles, which had been lit on occasion of his arrival, extinguished and by the light of the perennial lights around the sepulchre of St. Benedict, memorized the saint's hymn *Inter aeternas* with the accompanying prayers and recited Matins and Lauds with his secretary, Nicola Coscia. Afterwards without taking supper, he went to the novitiate to sleep in one of the cells, first asking on his knees for the benediction from novice master d. Anastasio Perrone. He participated punctually in day and night choirs, and in the refectory limited himself to drinking only water. Before leaving, he went to the lodgings of the Abbot to ask for the benediction of the prelate. After he was elected Pope, he wanted to bless the Abbot of Monte Cassino, d. Sebastiano Gadaleta, personally in the church of St. Calixtus in Rome on June 10, 1725. It is not surprising, then, that he later accepted the invitation of the same Abbot Gadaleta to come again to Monte Cassino, on his way back from Benevento to Rome in order to consecrate the new basilica.

According to Abbot Tosti, «there was feverish activity at the abbey in preparation for the arrival the Pontiff and his retinue. At the time the viceroy of Naples was Michel Federico d'Althann, Bishop of Vaccia and cardinal of the Church. He, with all his court and a company of Cuirassiers, met the Pope at the border of the kingdom and escorted him to Monte Cassino. On May 16, the Pope left Capua on his way to Teano; Althann preceded him and arrived on the evening of that same day at San Germano. The following day he ascended the mountain accompanied by Abbot Gadaleta and the procurator general Tansi; at the gate of the monastery he was met by the monsignors Tedeschi, Archbishop of Apamea, Mariconda, Bishop of Trivento, Pazzancri, Bishop of Imeria, some Cassinese abbots and monks, who offered their respects and let him inside with many signs of honor. Gadaleta and Tansi returned to San Germano, where they joined the Abbot of St. Paul in Rome and monsignor Accoramboni, auditor of His Holiness, and travelled a few miles outside the city to meet the Pope. The reception at San Germano, was modest rather than splendid, by express will of that most humble Pope. At the gate of the city, the Pope mounted a white horse with the saddle covered with a cloth of purple velour with gold pendants. He was dressed most modestly in white tunic, a black mantle, and a red hat. He set off for the monastery immediately. Two cavalrymen preceded the whole cortege. Following immediately behind was the cross bearer, Monsignor Piersanti, holding the cross, wearing his biretta under an umbrella that he himself held. He carried, suspended

from his neck, the sacred Eucharist placed in a silver pyx, enclosed in a velour purse richly adorned with gold thread. He was
flanked on one side by a Dominican friar and on the other by a
prelate, each carrying a lighted silver lamp in honor of the Blessed
Sacrament. Next came the Pope with his court and the Abbots.
When he reached the first gate of the abbey, the Holy Father dismounted and, carrying a blazing torch, bareheaded followed the
Holy Eucharist on foot as far as the three cloisters. Here Piersanti
opened the purse and took out the consecrated Host, which he
handed to a monk, who, followed by all the bishops, abbots, and
the Pontiff, carried it to the altar in the chamber of St. Benedict.
After a brief prayer, Pope Benedict withdrew to a small cella furnished only with four chairs, a small sleeping mat, and a writing
table. Those who know how humbly this Pope lived his pontificate will not be surprised at the modesty of the quarters that he
himself chose, refusing to stay in others better furnished and
more richly decorated. He joined the monks in singing the psalms
in choir and at meals in the refectory. He did not want anyone at
his meals except the monks, bidding the prelates to withdraw
because the food was not fit for their rank but was poor repast
prepared for a monk (alluding to himself) and for the other
monks.

On May 18, the Pope went in the church of St. Martin, which
at that time must have been larger that the present one, with Cardinal d'Althann, the Archbishops of Apamea and Corfu, and the
Bishop of Trivento. There he put on the sacred robes and with all
prescribed church ceremonies enclosed the relics of the saints in
five small chests which had to be placed beneath the walls of the
altars that were to be consecrated; then they were all locked in a
larger chest marked with the pontifical seal. Quite early the next
morning, on the day of the consecration, the Pontiff returned to
begin the solemn ceremonial rites with the three prelates mentioned above and the viceroy, who were deputized to consecrate four
of the altars, while the Pope himself performed the ceremony at
the main altar. These and the Pope dressed in the sacramental
robes while the monks recited the penitential psalms. When

everything was ready, four Abbots, d. Leandro di Porzia of St. Paul's, d. Massimo Albrizio of the Santissima Trinità of Cava, d. Serafino Tansi, procurator general, and d. Placido Sala of St. Scholastica of Subiaco dressed in red capes and white bonnets, placed the chest containing the relics on their shoulders and came to the door of the basilica preceded by a long procession which included the Pope, singing the Litany of the Saints. Here was a dais with a chair in which the Pope sat; at his feet sat the four Abbots, bearers of the relics, acting as his assistants. On another dais to the right, the four consecrators were seated. As soon as everybody had taken his place, the Pontiff launched a most profound discourse on the rite of dedication for churches, in particular that for Monte Cassino, which was about to begin. At the end of his sermon, he entered the church and consecrated it with all the pomp of the Roman rite» [6]. At the very lengthy ceremony, which lasted eight hours and was captured by the brush of Paolo De Matteis, were present besides the Cardinal-viceroy, thirteen Archbishop and Bishops, seven Abbots, many prelates and members of the nobility, and a very large number of commoners. The Pope remained at Monte Cassino until the May 21, offering examples of singular piety and paternal benevolence towards the monks. He seemed to have regained his youthful happiness with this return to monastic life away from the heavy burden of his office. Because of his interest in the security and preservation of the ancient charters, he especially enjoyed spending time alone in the archives in pleasant conversation with the archivist, d. Erasmo Gattola, condescending sometimes to holding the ladder for him while he climbed to get documents from the highest drawers. After his return to Rome, he sent the Abbot (Aug. 27) the brief «*Qui prosperum fecit nobis iter*», which contained high praises for the Cassinese community and the concession of ample privileges. In recognition for such great generosity the name of Benedict XIII has been remembered by the monks in daily prayers in his honor for the dead, and up to the present his statue stands among those of other benefactors.

Among the Abbots worthy of special mention in this century

besides Gadaleta we find the names of d. Gregorio Galisio and d.
Archangelo Brancaccio. In the large community, where to the
number of monks, which varied between sixty and ninety, one
must add the many novices, oblates, and servants, there was also
a Norwegian, d. Agostino Olao Worm from Cristiania, a converted Lutheran, in addition to several Poles. The number of
pilgrims and famous personages that came to visit remained very
high throughout the century; all were received with customary
charity and ritual ceremonies.

This century brought also increased hostility to ecclesiastical
immunities, which had to be defended sometimes even by excommunication. Because of these litigations, the very large administrative expenses, and a management not always wise, the
large domain provided very small financial gains. What constituted the major characteristic of this century, however, was the
flowering of scholarly research, especially in the field of history.
Through this scholarship Monte Cassino kept pace with the
evolution of Italian culture, which in this field reached great
heights. The abbey thus became a beacon for scholars from all of
Europe.

NOTES

[1] P. PIERI, La guerra, op. cit., 21.

[2] PICOTTI, op. cit., 105 reports that in the: «warehouses of the monastery in the
month of November of a year that had not been one of the best for the South of Italy (and
we must add that it was during the epoch of the commendataries) there were available for
export 5676 bushels of wheat, which we do not know whether they were part of the tithe
that went to the Abbot's revenue».

[3] G. MINOZZI, op. cit., 52.

[4] DANTE, Paradise, XXII, 23-24.

[5] Acta SS. Martii, II, 297. Mabillon's evidence will be reported in chapt. 2 of part II.
His companion, d. M. Germain, on his part wrote (cfr. E. DE BROGLIE, Mabillon et la
société de l'abbaye de Saint-Germain des Près, Paris, Plon 1888, vol. II, 16): «... l'observance est très belle dans cette illustre monastère, l'astinence continuelle, le silence et la

ponctualité exacts; l'office divin y est très bien fait. Les religieux, qui sont noble, ont bonne grâce et la meilleure physionomie que j'ai encore vue dans une communauté entière».

[6] L. Tosti, *Storia*, III, 266-269. The small church of St. Martin, mentioned above, does not exist any more. It was on the north side, close to the present small cloister of St. Ann.

BIBLIOGRAPHY

As sources for the history of the sixteenth century, we must remember the two *Cronache* in manuscript kept in the archive of Monte Cassino, by P. Petrucci and O. Medici.

Always noteworthy the contribution of G. Minozzi, *Montecassino nella storia del Rinascimento,* Rome, Ferrari, 1925, although, as the author himself warns it should have been revised. The revision has been done by M. Inguanez, in «Riv. Stor. Bened.», 12, 1925, 173-184.

For the union of Monte Cassino to the congregation of S. Giustina, see: T. Leccisotti, *La congregazione «de Unitate» a Montecassino,* in «Casinensia», 561-584, and *Documenti per l'annessione di Montecassino alla congregazione di S. Giustina,* in «Benedictina» 17 (1970), 58-91. For the conditions of the buildings at that time, T. Leccisotti, *Montecassino agli inizi del Cinquecento,* in «Benedictina», 2 (1948), 75-94.

For the fervor of its spiritual life see, T. Leccisotti, *Tracce di correnti mistiche cinquecentesche nel codice Cassinese 584,* in «Archivio Italiano per la Storia della Pietà», 4 (1965), Rome, Edizione Storia e Letteratura, 3-120.

For the next two centuries, besides the manuscript diaries see, T. Leccisotti, *I monasteri fondati da S. Benedetto e il loro stato alla metà del secolo XVII,* in «Benedictina», 27 (1980), 63-82; *Carlo di Borbone a Montecassino,* in «Arch. Stor. Prov. Napol.», III ser. 1 (1961), 289-326, and *La giurisdizione criminale cassinese nel '700: l'ultima intestazione nello Stato di S. Germano,* in «Atti dell'Accademia Pontaniana», n. 7, XI, 133-157.

The narrative of the coming of Benedict XIII in 1727 has been edited by T. Leccisotti, *La consacrazione della Basilica Cassinese nel 1727,* in «Benedictina», 14 (1967), 320-330.

VII.

THE SUPPRESSIONS AND THE RECOVERY

«Succisa virescit» *

1. THE FRENCH SACK AND THE FIRST SUPPRESSION.

The eighteenth century would not end in peace. The age of gold, predicted by the rosy illusions of the Illuminism, turned instead to bloody repressions and atrocious warfare. The whirlwind that from France spread to all of Europe reached southern Italy in 1796.

It was then, in fact, that war preparations began. The main body of the Neapolitan army, under the command of general Mack, took position along the banks of the River Liri. The king, the Queen, and the court, with all military chiefs and the army treasures, and with a guard of two hundred grenadiers made their quarters at Monte Cassino, remaining there for a long time. The movements of troops in the region continued for three years. The abbey, as one of the main baronies of the kingdom, was asked to contribute to the heavy expenses, and a greater part of the treasure was consumed by the demands of the war.

All those preparations were in vain; the royal army did not put up much of a resistance, and the French poured into the kingdom right through the valley of the Liri. Without meeting any resistance they reached San Germano on December 30, 1798. Immediately, cruelties and depredations began. The abbatial palace became the headquarter of the various generals that took their turn in command. On the very day of his arrival, General Matthieu came up to the abbey to search in the library for the

---

* «The cut-off shoot grows verdant again».

topographical maps of the kingdom of Naples. When he could not find them he broke into threats and insults.

The new year, 1799, began with the arrival of General Championnet with two-thousand soldiers. To meet his demands, in part at least, all the silver objects that were left in the treasure of the abbey, including two large statues of St. Benedict and St. Scholastica, had to be handed over. The people who lived on the other side of the Liri saw in the tree of freedom not the symbol of a liberal government but «the sign of a new foreign tyranny» [1]; bristling with outrage, they offered to shelter the Abbot and the monks, promising to defend them to the last man. The generous offer was not accepted, however; instead, great efforts were made to calm the indignation of those faithful, for fear of worse evils.

The French domination did not last long, and the withdrawal of the troops of the Republic from the region promoted violent reactions which caused many sufferings to the populace and to the Abbot in particular.

In their retreat from the kingdom away from the victorious advance of the royal forces, the French moved toward San Germano, arriving there May 10 of the same year. The town had been abandoned by the inhabitants, who had taken refuge in the mountains. At the abbey shortly after Mass, the rattle of heavy guns firing on San Germano was heard. The monks, taking with them the most precious relics, took shelter in Terelle, where they were received hospitably, especially by the Jannarelli and Grossi families. In the monastery, the venerable d. Giovanni Battista Federici, the young d. Enrico Gattola, and novices encouraged by exhortations of Federici stayed on. Fifteen-hundred soldiers of the column led by General Olivier invaded the abbey. The first eighty, with drawn swords, searched and robbed the monks who had come forward to greet them.

The pillage began right away. All the doors were broken down, and the store room, the cellars, and the bakery were emptied; what could not be carried — furniture, bedding, linens and other objects — were left strewn in the garden. Even the library and the archives were invaded. At the entrance of this precious treasure of Cassinese history, Gattola tried with urgent prayers to stay the rampaging horde but was hit on the neck with a sword and dragged away. The devastation in the church was even worse. Lines of soldiers, wearing sacred robes and driving donkeys, milled through the marble aisles singing obscene songs and upturning and scattering the relics on the floor and even pouring out consecrated hosts from the stolen precious vases. Vestments were cut into pieces and burned on great fires to retrieve the gold and silver woven into the cloth. In this manner the mantle of the great commander Consalvo of Cordova was destroyed. Eyewitnesses later recounted that the mantle was burned in the corner of the cloister of the Benefactors closest to the old hostel, where later the college was built. All these fires and the myriads of candles gave the monastery the appearance of a burning furnace, while San Germano also was engulfed in flames.

At dawn of the following day, the marauding bands withdrew from the abbey, of which only the walls remained standing. On the poorly guarded place, other people poured «they were not French and pounced like vultures on a carrion» [2], completing the devastation. They operated so thoroughly that it is estimated that half of the spoils ended up in the hands of the peasants. The desolation was so complete that some of the monks doubted that they would still be able to live in the monastery.

Political stability was not restored with the departure of the French. The unsettled political and military situation caused many more sufferings. A letter of the newly elected Pope Pius VII (1801) brought, therefore, a measure of comfort. A former Cassinese monk of the abbey of Cesena, he answered the Abbot's letter of congratulations and homage with this message: «Our heart is saddened that this house of prayers has suffered so many calamities through the recent vicissitudes; it is our desire that the monastery be restored to its old splendor and discipline as it stood for such a long course of centuries for the edification and glory of the Church. In this we promise our help through our resources and the use of our apostolic authority, in such a way that it will never be necessary again to implore our favor in behalf of your community» [3].

Papal support was, indeed, badly needed. On his way to Naples, after the new expulsion of the Bourbon king, Joseph Bonaparte passed through San Germano on February 14, 1805. He was extremely courteous with the monks, who were quite suprised, since memory of the French devastation was still so fresh in their minds. As he was departing, he went so far as to promise, «If you need anything, write to me directly and I will be at your service». What came next instead was not only the abolition of the feudal domain of the abbey but also the suppression of all religious orders. Thus Monte Cassino, after thirteen centuries, came to an end not through barbarian violence or act of war but by the decision of new legislators (February 13, 1807)» [4].

The royal decree, however, declared that the new dispositions would take into consideration «because of the great respect that we have, those celebrated places that during the barbarian age preserved the sacred fire of religion and saved for the ages the learning of past generations of men and those sanctuaries deserving so much respect» [5]. Therefore, the buildings of the abbey of Monte Cassino, together with those of Cava and Montevergine, were preserved under the guise of an «*establishment*». The monks, about fifty at Monte Cassino, without their religious garb, were deputized for the preservation of the artistic and cultural patrimony, with the Abbot acting as *director*. At the beginning the monks were judged as politically unreliable, and they were therefore guarded by soldiers as if they were prisoners. A certain calm returned during the reign of Joachim Murat, who was always kind towards the Cassinese.

2. THE ITALIAN SUPPRESSION.

After the fall of the Napoleonic star, the abbey recovered its juridical personality. It was due above all to the firm desire of Pope Pius VII, who had the clause included in the concordat he signed with the king of Naples. It was, however, not possible to recover the ancient feudal privileges nor the old possessions which were by now almost all lost. The abbey was granted an annual revenue of 19,000 ducats, which in reality never came to more than 14,000 net, and a few of the old possessions, among them, Fiumarola.

The new conditions at Monte Cassino were, obviously, a far cry from the splendid state of old; still, they allowed life to continue on new bases and with different horizons. The discouragement of the old monks was now replaced by their hope of survival, which was soon reinforced by the re-opening of the old school for oblates with eight students.

The political convulsions of 1820 brought back new troubles. Once again military detachments were seen in the abbey, but the isolated voices that demanded other suppressions found no echo, probably because of the speedy reestablishment of order.

The abbey thus was able to resume activity, and with the restoration of the old discipline attention soon turned to repair the buildings. «Strong in the observance of the old Benedictine traditions», the monks kept their house «always opened to welcome the most outstanding and learned men in Europe, who came to find peace in the exercise of the monastic obligations of the hospice and held their minds and hearts firmly in meditation on Jesus Christ, according to the prescription of their legislator, without paying any attention to opinions and credences, eager to help any aspiration of Holy Mother Church and their community» [6].

In 1834 the vicariate of Atina was annexed to the spiritual jurisdiction of Monte Cassino, i.e., what was left of the «Land of St. Benedict». At the same time, Monte Cassino relinquished its jurisdiction over the land of Cetraro in Calabria in favor of the Bishop of St. Mark and Bisignano. The possession of Cetraro had been donated to the abbey by Sikelgaita, the beloved second wife of Robert Guiscard.

To make more available the many fruits of the learned activities at the abbey, in 1842 a printing press was installed. There was also a project for the establishment of a great periodical,

L'Ateneo Italiano, with which most of the outstanding scholars
of the time had promised their collaboration. The design was not
realized mostly because of the prohibition of the cowardly Bourbon police.

When voices began announcing the birth of a new day for
Italy, they found an immediate echo in Monte Cassino. From
here the Risorgimento received votes of success, advice, encouragement, and offers of help to restore the historical unity of
Italy, an idea that had never died in the hearts and consciences of
all her people [7]. The Cassinese, as it is well known, did not
withdraw and were not hostile; in fact, they favored the movement that wanted Italy united under the leadership of the Papacy.
This position cost them pains and persecutions. In 1849 the printing house, which had recently published, among others, two
works by Tosti, *Storia della Lega Lombarda* and *Il Salterio del
soldato,* which were judged to be worth a military victory, was
shut down, accused by the government of being a source of
subversive propaganda. Some monks had to go into hiding;
others were placed under police surveillance, and everyone in the
abbey was full of apprehension under the threat of more severe
measures.

Then the movement for the unification of Italy, the
Risorgimento, took a course decidedly hostile to the Church: one
of the most odious measures adopted was the new suppression of
religious corporations, approved by Parliament in 1866. «When
the news spread through Europe, a large number of scholars
rallied around the abbey, fearing that the policies of the Italian
fisc might permanently damage the cause of civilization and
historical studies. There was great commotion in the academies of
France, England, and Germany, and innumerable pleas were
heard to preserve that seat of scholarship, to which for so many
centuries travelled the learned men of Europe. The Chancellor of
the new German empire manifested this wish to the Italian
minister; the French academy expressed similar entreaties, and in
England not only scholars, like those of the Archeological Society, but all those who had read in the history of European civiliza-

tion the name of Monte Cassino, pressed their leaders and Parliament with the force of public opinion to open private negotiations with the Italian authorities on behalf of the abbey. And it was a joy, indeed, to see how this small piece of Italian soil fired the enthusiasm of so many learned people for its preservation. Among them we gratefully want to remember the names of Gladstone, Clarendon, Stanley, Forbes, Russel, Pertz, Saint Marc Girardin, and Dantier» [8].

Neither this universal concern, however, nor the memory of the great services of St. Benedict to Italy and to civilization nor the patriotism and the sufferings by some of the monks and the efforts of some illustrious members of the Italian parliament, one of the most kind and authoritative of whom was Gabrio Casati, succeeded in overcoming the sectarian ill will. The iniquitous ordinance, after some hesitation, was enforced against Monte Cassino in 1868.

Once again deprived of its juridical status and of whatever possessions that remained, the works of art and of cultural interest were catalogued and the abbey became property of the state. It was declared, however, a national monument and the monks became the custodians, while still serving in the cathedral since the Abbot was also bishop of the area.

This arrangement, later adopted for other famous establishments, originally was worked out to preserve all the buildings of the Cassinese community with all the treasures that they contained in their traditional unity. Thus there was some compensation «to the severity of the law, and this resulted in the preservation of Monte Cassino» [9].

In spite of this it did seem at the time that the days of the abbey were coming to an end. Instead, in the changed political and social climate, this marked the beginning of a new and noble life.

3. THE RECOVERY.

«The Suppression decree has given back to the country, that is the fisc, all the lands of our abbey. The spirit, however, cannot be confiscated». Thus wrote Luigi Tosti, the great historian of Monte Cassino [10].

His words truly hit the mark, because the life of the abbey was not in the buildings and the possessions, but in the spirit that animated the community, in the vigor of the tradition that stretched through the long centuries. Everything else formed only the changeable exterior appearance, which through the years kept conforming to various exigencies, both social and political. This time also adaptation to the changed circumstances came quickly; it became possible then, after the initial dismay and uncertainty, to start once again.

«Succisa virescit» became the motto of the new recovery. The old tree, indeed, grew verdant with new shoots in the old branches. Discipline, organization, and studies in the arts again brought honor to the house of St. Benedict and made it illustrious.

Stricter discipline once again led to a closer observance of the Rule. After the suppression, the old organization, conforming to time of exigencies now gone by, was set aside in favor of a new constitutional concept closer to the original one; the Abbots once again served for life with greater autonomy, and the *Conventus Casinensis* resumed its ancient structure. The unrelenting zeal of the Abbots — d. Carlo de Vera (1863-1871), d. Nicola d'Ogremont (1872-1896), d. Giuseppe Quandel (1896-1897), d. Bonifacio Krug (1897-1909), and d. Gregorio Diamare (1909-1945) — lifted the community up in numbers and quality. From the almost furtive welcome of the first novice, d. Gaetano Bernardi, soon after the suppression, with only dim hopes for the future, up to our own days when the community, although still short of the old number, had moved steadily towards it, it was all hard work and sacrifices that only God knows. From d. Carlo de Vera, who in spite of the harsh conditions imposed managed to avoid any changes in the quality of life at the abbey, to d. Gregorio Diamare, who in the promising group of young people (it was he who opened the monastery once again to the oblates in 1912) saw a return to better times, from the multifarious activities of the Abbots to the humble daily dedication of those called to perform the modest and obscure tasks, it was all a sacrifice joyously offered for the greater glory of God.

Scholarly work was again pursued in the aristocratic college, in the diocesan seminaries and, above all, in the archives, whose learned publications were printed on a chromolythographic press. While the old buildings were restored and renovated, Monte Cassino hosted new artistic manifestations.

The course of this new flowering can be placed between two significant dates, 1880 and 1929. 1880 commemorated, according to tradition, the birth of St. Benedict. That fourteenth centenary was celebrated throughout the world with extraordinary solemnities but many manifestations had their natural setting in Monte Cassino. Large throngs of people gathered there during the course of religious observances held in the month of April, while in May the ceremonies assumed a tone prevalently monastic.

That year, due to its closeness to Easter, the feast of St. Benedict was transferred to Tuesday, April 6. A solemn Triduum took place from the fourth to the sixth presided over by Cardinal Domenico Bartolini. The main sermons were given by mons. Alfonso Capecelatro and by the Benedictine Bishop Placido Schiaffino, who were later both made cardinals. On Monday a solemn mass according to the Greek rite was also celebrated by the monks of Grottaferrata to commemorate the reverence that their founder St. Nilus had for the tomb of St. Benedict. On the same day the pontifical Mass was offered by the saintly Bishop of Catania, later a cardinal, the Benedictine Giuseppe Benedetto Dusmet, who on that occasion laid on the tomb of the Father the gold medal that he had been awarded in recognition of his heroic charity. Then on the feast day, in place of the slightly indisposed Cardinal Bartolino, the sacred rites were presided over by His Highness the Prince and Benedictine Archbishop of Salzburg over an extraordinary crowd from the top of the great staircase of the central court.

The celebrations during the month of May were held around the time of Pentecost, which was for Monte Cassino, from the most remote times, the date of the most typical pilgrimages. For the first time since the days of Louis the Pious (IX century) representatives from all Benedictine monasteries gathered together, with those coming from the new regions of the world sitting next to those from the old European communities. It was also the first time since the Vatican Council that so many prelates, decorated with papal insigna, about fifty, were seen together. To symbolize the strengthened bonds among the many branches of St. Benedict's followers, the venerable remains of the edifices where the holy Patriarch had placed the foundations of his institution were consecrated as a church.

The May festivities were also held in a three-day cycle from Pentecost, May 16, to Tuesday, May 18. On that day, the pontifical legate, Giovanni Battista Pitra, at the time Cardinal-bishop of Frascati and a Benedictine monk, consecrated the «Torretta», which had been renovated with contributions from all the Benedictine monasteries.

From that time onwards the expansion of all Benedictine communities, which revolutions had greatly hindered, went forward again and the meeting at Monte Cassino laid the foundation for the fraternal congregation formed in 1893. To commemorate that centenary a special medal of St. Benedict, endowed with many indulgences, was coined.

In 1929 another papal legate, Cardinal Pietro Gasparri, came up the sacred mountain. These were no longer the years of the depression, and the date, which traditionally marked the XIV centenary of the foundation of the abbey, saw there a renewed life and vigor. The Church also was at a historical threshold of her existence, the day after the great happening which had marked the end of her conflict with Italy. In addition the peace so much desired and favored by the Cassinese was to be sealed in their house, just when the whole world commemorated her beginnings and the countless fruits she had contributed to the progress of mankind.

The solemn ceremonies which were attended by huge crowds lasted from March 21 to November 13 and reached their highest point during the stay of the Cardinal legate, who arrived on April 26, promptly at 11:35 A.M. by special train, after a triumphal journey, and was welcomed by Abbot Diamare, the Minister Giuseppe Belluzzo, who represented the Italian government, and by many other high ranking officials. While a company of grenadiers, drawn up along the railroad station, which had been completely done over for the occasion rendered military honors to the echo of martial tunes, a twenty-one gun salute greeted the papal emissary from the mountaintop. The dignitaries, in a four-horse carriage which had belonged to the royal house of Naples, with postillion and grooms, made their way towards the palace of the Abbot by the boulevard along which, besides the honor guard, were lined the mayors of the 92 towns of the province.

Here all the officials and numerous delegations were introduced to the legate, who blessed the exulting crowd from the great balcony.

At 5:00 P.M., heralded by a cannon shot, the cortège began moving towards the mountain. Near the small church of St. Agatha it was met by the Bishops and the Abbots present, together with the whole community. From there in procession they accompanied the Cardinal legate, who vested in a purple mantle and protected by a rich canopy proceeded to the church. The choir, under the direction of Licinio Refice, took part in the religious ceremony, after which the cortège proceeded to the chapter hall. After the papal brief, accrediting the cardinal for the important mission, was read, abbot Diamare approached the throne and offered expressions of homage and welcome, which were graciously accepted by his eminence.

On all following days, many crowded pilgrimages alternated through the ample lobbies and cloisters of the abbey to receive the blessing of the legate. Among the celebrations that made memorable that period, one must remember the openings of the exposition of Monte Cassino, that of arts and crafts at Cassino and the official reception at City Hall.

Sunday, April 28, was reserved to the great liturgical commemoration, presided over by the legate while the homily was given by Abbot Schuster (later Pope Pius XII); a choir formed of cantors from the Roman chapels joined that of the monks to sing the Mass composed for the occasion and directed by maestro Refice. At the end of the great banquet in the vast refectory, for the first time, representatives of the Holy See and the Italian government exchanged the ritual toasts.

Unforeseen developments forced Cardinal Gasparri to cut short his visit at Monte Cassino. The celebrations, however, continued. Worth remembering are the festivities in July presided over by Cardinal Alessio Ascalesi with the participation of all the Bishops of Campania; those in October, with the II Eucharistic Congress presided over by Cardinal Camillo Laurenti; and the closing ceremonies in November, with the participation of representatives from all religious orders, who came on a pilgrimage with the presence of the prefect of religious order, Cardinal Alessio Lépicier and the arrival of His Royal Highness the Hereditary Prince of Italy, in addition to pilgrimages coming from almost every region of the peninsula.

At the close of the centenary year, Pope Pius XI, who had ushered in the celebrations with his brief «*Non sine numinis instinctu*», commented upon them with paternal affection in the consistory of December 16. He had already, with the apostolic letter «*Sancti Benedicti*» of October 17, granted a plenary indulgence *toties quoties* to all visitors of Benedictine churches on the feast day of St. Benedict [11].

Newspapers in many countries showed a lively interest in the centenary, and numerous were the publications, narrative as well as scientific, which helped to preserve its memory. Among the latter one must point out especially the two volumes of the collection *Casinensia,* in which outstanding scholars joined the monks in gathering new and interesting contributions for the history of Monte Cassino. There was, in addition, an issue of commemorative stamps.

The meeting of the Royal Italian Historical Institute (May 28-29, 1930) and that of the historians of medicine (Sept. 18, 1930) were both held at Cassino in connection with the anniversary celebrations. The results of the first were gathered into a volume, while the physicians, remembering the special merits of the abbey in the field of the healing arts, presented to the monastery a magnificent bronze plaque designed by A. Mistruzzi.

Almost as a preparation for the solemn celebrations of 1929, the bicentennial anniversary of the church consecrated by Pope Benedict XIII in 1727 had been commemorated two years before. The celebrations held in May and October, the latter presided over by Cardinal Laurenti, attracted many pilgrimages.

Besides the first meeting in 1880, all Benedictine abbots and prelates had gathered at Monte Cassino in 1913. Then as in 1929 Cardinal Gasparri, a beloved old friend was chosen as president of that venerable assembly. The focus of the celebrations was the reopening to public worship of the restored crypt with the consecration of its three altars. The solemnities lasted a little over a month (May 4 to June 8), and large crowds attended, to whom the Holy Father Pius X, with his brief «*Archicoenobium Casinense*», had granted a special jubilee. The altars were consecrated on May 6, the main one by Cardinal Gasparri, the side ones by the Benedictine Archbishops Serafini and Bonazzi. The main liturgical ceremonies were held on May 8: the Cardinal celebrated the mass and participated in the procession, assisted by about one hundred prelates wearing mitres and pastorals who were placed in special stands with other participants, including the college of St. Anselm in Rome, the clergy and diocesan confraternities, the seminaries of Monte Cassino, and the abbeys of Cava and Aquino.

Pontifical functions were celebrated every week by various prelates; noteworthy was the one on June 1st conducted according to their rite by the Greek monks of Grottaferrata and the closing ceremonies officiated by Cardinal Diomede Falconio.

One of the most characteristic manifestations was, without

doubt, the *Ludus* which, reviving a noble medieval tradition, staged some episodes in the life of St. Benedict at Monte Cassino.

The concourse of visitors and pilgrims to the sacred mountain remained steady, not just on exceptional occasions. Among these visitors were many rulers and members of the reigning families of Europe, sometimes welcomed with solemn ceremonial; many Princes of the Church, among them Cardinal Achille Ratti, who remained there a whole month before taking possession of the diocese of Milan; also many political leaders; and, most numerous of all, scholars from all over the world, who joined the crowds of people drawn by the fame of the place or by their feelings of devotion. One must also remember the conferences on social studies, those of the Catholic youth, the courses in spiritual exercises, the yearly reunion of the bishops of Campania, and the large attendance by personages from aristocratic and political circles at the sacred functions, especially those of Holy Week. After March 8, 1887, a new roadway made access to the abbey easier. Work had begun in April 1865, financed by the ministry of Public Works, headed by Silvio Spaventa. The road was greatly improved and hard topped in 1929. In 1930 a boldly designed cable car was added; in 1931 a new aqueduct which brought to the abbey a larger volume of purer water was constructed.

The activities of the monks, besides the uninterrupted choir services, studies, duties of hospitality, and the training of the young, were centered on the care of the 71 churches of the area that were still dependencies of Monte Cassino. The Abbot Diamare, whose abbacy marked a decisive stage in the last recovery, also made a profound impression in this field, renewing and improving conditions as required by the changing times. Thus, resuming a tradition that had been interrupted at the beginning of the nineteenth century, he established again a small community of monks at Cassino in the Abbot's palace, which still kept its old name of «*Curtis Major*». This made possible a closer and more readily available ministry for the spiritual needs of the people.

In the same palace was located, as in the old days, the

episcopal curia with its various offices as well as various Catholic associations particularly active at the time. It was, in fact, with their help that the Abbot was able to carry out the great work of social assistance and welfare which drew universal admiration and was rewarded with a gold medal and various honors from the Italian government.

Always ready to meet the needs of his flock, Diamare proved to be as brave as his predecessors, especially Abbot d'Orgemont, in ministering to the victims of cholera in 1911 and those of the earthquake of 1915. To him goes also the credit for the organization of the Catholic associations, especially those for the young; for years he devoted his most assiduous care to them and provided a suitable residence for them, aided by the generous munificence of Pope Benedict XV. Equally well appointed were the new living quarters prepared at Cassino for the Sisters of the Stigmata. He encouraged the pastors to establish kindergartens, to promote religious institutions, and to welcome nuns into their parishes. When the ancient abbey of S. Vincenzo al Volturno was given back to Monte Cassino through the generosity of Duke Enrico Catemario di Quadri, new roads opened for the spiritual well-being of the area. Many churches were restored; others were built anew or transformed into parishes. More accurate catechetical teaching and the awakening of Eucharistic fervor were the foundation of this movement of renewal. These were the goals pursued in three diocesan congresses in 1924 (May 22-25), 1929 (Sep. 18-22), and 1932 (June 8-12). Yearly, Eucharistic days were set aside in the various parishes to preserve the fruits of the congress, and a Diocesan synod was also in advanced stages of preparation.

On March 12, 1928, Abbot Diamare, by gracious will of Pius XI, was consecrated titular Bishop of Constantia in Arabia by Cardinal Ascalesi, assisted by two Benedictine archbishops, mons. Anselmo Pecci of Acerenza and Matera and mons. Gregorio Grasso of Salerno. On that occasion, together with the monastic community, all the faithful gathered around their beloved father as they did on the anniversaries of his monastic, priestly, and abbatial jubilees (1913, 1916, 1934, 1938 and, especially, 1941).

On the eve of the fourth destruction, Monte Cassino, in the last recovery of its millenary life, remained faithful to the better traditions of its long activity. In and around the abbey, in the basilica, glittering with gold and mosaics, in the solemn, marbled cloisters, around the matchless artistic treasures, a fervid activity went on without pause. The workshops, the schools, the *scriptorium*, and the hospital were continuously active, while along the mountain and down in the plain the monks laboured assiduously in Christ's domain like industrious bees around their center. Like soldiers of Christ, the immortal King under whose banner they served, they were armed with the glorious and indestructible fire of love and obedience.

NOTES

[1] L. Tosti, *Storia,* IV, 21.

[2] *Ibid.,* IV, 33.

[3] *Ibid.,* IV, 38.

[4] *Ibid.,* IV, 40.

[5] *Ibid.,* IV, 41.

[6] *Ibid.,* IV, 45.

[7] C. Calisse, in *Convegno storico di Montecassino,* Roma 1932, XXXVI, («Bul. Ist. st. Ital.», 47).

[8] L. Tosti, *La biblioteca dei codici mss. di Montecassino,* in *Scritti vari,* Roma, Pasqualucci, 1896, II, 291-292.

[9] *Ibid.,* 292.

[10] *Ibid.*

[11] Pius XI mentioned the centenary also in a letter to Card. Gasparri of April 15 and in the encyclical *Quinquagesimo Anno* of Dec. 23 and in the secret consistory of July 15, for the election of Card. Schuster, always in terms of deep veneration.

BIBLIOGRAPHY

About the beginnings of this period see the two excellent studies by E. Jallonghi, *Borbonici e Francesi a Montecassino* (1796-1799), in «Arch. Stor. Prov. Nap.», 34 (1909) and *Montecassino nel primo cinquantenario del secolo XIX* (1806-1856), in «Riv. Stor. Bened.» 7 (1912), 195-222 and 416-431; both make use of the archival journals and contemporary relations, materials which now, unfortunately, are in part lost. The *Storia* of Tosti, IV, 71-112, contains the summary of the relation of d. G. B. Federici on the French devastation. Some of the maltreatments suffered by the monks are reported by T. Leccisotti, in *Episodi di storia Cassinese,* in «Benedictina», 22 (1975), 182-187, while L. Fabiani in the III volume of *Terra di S. Benedetto, op. cit.,* speaks about the division of the patrimony. The study of T. Leccisotti, *Luigi Tosti agli inizi della sua attività intellettuale,* in «Benedictina», I (1947), 259-317, deals also with the period from 1819 to 1848.

Concerning the Abbots of the XIX century, T. Leccisotti has reported in *Bollettino Diocesano,* 1972-1980.

On the events at Monte Cassino at the time of the suppression much light is shed by the correspondence of L. Tosti, especially, that part published by F. Quintavalle, *La conciliazione tra l'Italia e il Papato nelle lettere del P. Luigi Tosti e del sen. Gabrio Casati,* Milan, 1907, and by T. Leccisotti, *Uno dei tentativi di Conciliazione del 1861,* in «Arch. Stor. Prov. Nap.», 1963, 419-456. See also T. Leccisotti, *A proposito di un autografo Manzoniano,* in «Archivio Storico Pugliese», 14 (1961), 108-112.

About the typography some news have been given by A. Mirra, *Inizi e fasti della tipografia di Montecassino,* in «Rassegna Romana», 5 (1933), 11-21.

The environment of the new times, with its multiform and varied activities, is in part portrayed in the work of C. L. Torelli, *Montecassino nella storia e nell'arte,* Reggio Emilia, Guidetti, 1916, in which one can find also biographical notices and bibliographical indications about some of the more illustrious monks. For the rule of the abbots De Vera and Krug one can see their short *Commemorazioni* written, as for other Cassinese of that time (Tosti, Bernardi, Postiglioni), by Card. Capecelatro, in *Opere* etc., ed. Desclée, but published several other times. A complete study, however, is still lacking, especially for the period of the rule of Abbot d'Orgemont, which was, in fact, the longest and the most constructive. The greater part of the documentary material of the last few centuries was lost in the rubble. For the years going from 1893 to 1940, a good deal of information may be found in the *Annales Ordinis S. Benedicti,* Rome, 1910-1940.

Printed relations are available about the two periods of festivities of 1880; the first of them includes also the three sermons of the triduum. About those of 1913, there is an ample report by P. Cauchi in «Riv. Stor. Bened.», 8 (1913), 256-282. Also the talks, given by I. Schuster and C. Mercurio for the occasion, were published in a special pamphlet.

A detailed chronicle of the first period of the festivities of 1929 is found in *Civiltà Cattolica,* 2 (1929), 358-367. The same periodical, to commemorate properly the occasion, devoted large space for noteworthy articles on Benedictine matters.

We must note with regret, the thoughtlessness, inaccuracies and factiousness with which the Cassinese festivities of 1929 are reported in the notes written by C. Cerruti to some passages of the *Memorie del Cardinale Gasparri,* edit. by G. Spadolini in *Il Cardinale Gasparri e la Questione Romana,* Florence, Le Monnier, 1973. One had wanted to see a strong political emphasis to what was, in fact, a spontaneous manifestation of joy by the Cassinese for an happening so much wished for, even in their own house. There is no doubt that the government of Italy took advantage of that first solemn manifestation to express its gratitude to one of the chief architects of the «Conciliazione».

The copious material on the organization and the various manifestations of that centenary has, unfortunately, been lost in the destruction. The *Atti* of the II Eucharistic Congress, however, were printed at Montecassino in 1929.

VIII.

THE UTTER DESOLATION

«*Vix autem obtinere potui,
ut mihi ex hoc loco animae cederentur*» *.
GREGORY THE GREAT, *Dialogi*, II, 17.

1. THE PREMONITORY SIGNS.

It was a gloomy night in October, 1943: Saturday, 16. All around the wide valley of the Liri river deep shadows and terror lurked. Big guns thundered not too far away and above one could hear the droning of war planes, the dreadful heralds of death and desolation. The ancient abbey, completely isolated from the outside world, without water or electricity, had sheltered now for a little over a month thousands of people who, uneasy and terrified, had come seeking cover and protection in the house of St. Benedict.

In the trembling light of a few candles, the whole monastic community gathered deep down in the top of the mountain around that tomb which is the heart of the community and her source of life. From the hearts, more than from the lips, of the seventy odd people dedicated to the service of God, came once again the words of the hymn which for centuries daily renewed the memory of two Saints: «Pronae mentis visceribus, caelum detis incolere quos vultis terram spernere» **. When the echo of the last amen subsided against the golden vault of the chapel, after the «perseverantem in tua voluntate famulatum» ***, the fearful silence was broken by the voice of the Abbot. The follow-

---

* «I obtained with difficulty that in this place lives would be saved». St. Benedict's words in foreseeing the destruction of Monte Cassino.

** With humility, we ask that you grant life in heaven to those that by your will despised the world».

*** «... persevering in service according to your will».

ing day, he said the family of St. Benedict would once again be driven along the roads of exile and that «*excelsa domus*» (lofty mansion) might once again become a battle field and the prey of death. He himself was old and could only hope that someday his tired bones could find their way back to rest with his fathers, but what future was in store for the community and above all, for its growing youth? Against the threatening waves, however, one had to stand firm under the hand of God who tests those he loves, ready always to accept his will without reserve: «God's will be done». Shouting this assent even with tears filling their eyes, this last reunion broke up. The following day the painful evacuation began.

For sometime now, the winds of war had been coming closer to the centuries old walls of Monte Cassino. Nothing, however, seemed to justify any prediction of impending doom. Officials of the Italian government, in fact, shortly before Italy signed the armistice with the allies (Sept. 1943), had transferred there, as a safer place, works of art from the museums of Naples which until then had been stored in the abbey of Cava.

During the preceding month of May, a notable influx of German soldiers in the region, many of them in Cassino, had caused the first alarms. The first air attack in the area took place during the night between July 19 and 20. The objective was the airport of Aquino. Other raids of various intensity followed. It was only on Sept. 10 that the town of Cassino was the target. There were extensive damages there and in the Abbot's palace, as well as about sixty casualties. On the same day the gross imprudence of a German flier, who repeatedly attempted to show off by flying his craft in the space through the metal cables, put out of work the cable car that joined Cassino to the monastery. It was the beginning of the war-time state of emergency for the region and, especially, for the abbey.

The Abbot, in fact, who remained in Cassino for some time giving all possible aid to the stricken people, was forced to provide shelter in the temporarily empty college to the Sisters of Charity, the Sisters of the Stimmata with the young orphans, and also to the Benedictine Sisters, whose houses had been destroyed or badly damaged.

In addition, the monastery had to be opened to the many refugees from Cassino and the surrounding area, whose number grew to over a thousand, while the mountain also was full of people. The water supply dwindled and then stopped completely, and the wells, quite low because of a prolonged drought, were inadequate to the need. Electricity and all public services — mail, telephone, telegraph, railway — also ceased. General conditions of hygiene and safety were thus seriously impaired. The daily air strikes on various targets in the region added to the uncertainty and panic, especially when one of them again hit Cassino. One night a small bomb landed about three hundred yards from the monastery, and at the beginning of October anti-aircraft batteries came into action and their fire sometimes crisscrossed right above the abbey. On the evening and through the night of October 10 a heavy bombardment of unknown origin hit Cassino and also the mountain. The buildings of the abbey were clearly and accurately avoided; only a few incendiary flares fell on the monastery with, fortunately, only minor damages, while only a short distance away however, large fragmentation bombs fell.

In the meanwhile, many attempts to place military installations or observation posts on Monte Cassino were repeatedly foiled, while suspicions were allayed and threats dismissed. Everything, therefore, seemed to strengthen hopes that, in spite of other unavoidable sad days, the storm would pass without grave and irreparable consequences.

2. Evacuation.

While anxiety for the future dominated and life continued in an atmosphere of sufferings and emergencies, on the morning of October 14, Captain Maximilian J. Becker, a medical officer, and Lt. Colonel Julius Schlegel, both coming from Teano but traveling separately arrived at the abbey. The Abbot, who received them, reported that they claimed to be sent by General Conrad, commander of the Göring division, with the agreement of the Italian minister of education. They held several confidential meetings with the Abbot [1], who afterwards gathered the community and disclosed that he had been invited to evacuate from the abbey all the works of art and items of cultural value, given the imminent advance of allied forces, and to draw the necessary plans. On October 16, however, the two officers returned and ordered without euphemisms, the total evacuation of the abbey, which within a few days would be right on the line of defense that had been chosen.

As the captain informed one of the monks in French, «Your monastery will follow the same fate of S. Chiara in Naples and the churches of Rome (meaning St. Lawrence). It is painful because your monastery is so beautiful and so important. *Mais c'est la guerre*. The order is to stop them here. They will never have Rome».

All sorts of difficulties were raised but to no effect; the declaration of the Abbot that he could not consent to hand over all those treasures of art and history received no consideration. The German military authorities assumed all responsibilities; besides, they asserted, all objects carried away would be placed in a safe place and later handed over to the Italian authorities. No better result was obtained by pointing at the very difficult task of packing all those objects. The Abbot, in fact, was still unconvinced that the belligerents would dare to attack the monastery, but the opinion of the military differed. This, as the events unfolded, unfortunately proved to be closer to reality. Thus, on that same day, German soldiers brought up to the abbey a large quantity of packing materials. The lack of the necessary workers was remedied by assembling them from among the refugees.

At the start, the German officers had planned to take away first of all the archives and the old library (which legally had belonged to the Italian government from the time of the Suppression) and with them, also the items on deposit from the museums of Naples. Everything that was considered state property was taken over by the Germans, leaving no possibility that the monks, who were left in the dark as to its destination, could oversee the transport and care for the future custody of those precious items. Only later it was possible to learn that all items had been stored in a villa near Spoleto. The Germans promised that, within the limitations imposed by war operations, at a later date they would also allow the community to leave with as much of their own property as they could take with them. This disposition was soon changed.

Thus on October 17, a Sunday, a single truck left carrying archival materials; the following Tuesday, two left for Rome with some of the private property of the monastery and four monks as escort. It was only then possible to bring the news of what was happening at Monte Cassino to the outside world.

From that day until November 3, such sad caravans arrived in Rome almost daily, transporting monks, sisters, orphans, and everything else that it was possible to move in such an emergency. The evacuation undoubtedly lasted longer than had been anticipated because of the resistance that the Germans were able to mount near Capua. Almost all the evacuation operations were entirely filmed by German cameramen, who, for effect, made sure not to miss the sorrow and tears that showed on the faces of all those who watched the approaching ruin of a monument so outstanding for its sacred memories and who grieved over the dispersion of beloved people and most precious relics.

The deep bitterness of the situation was alleviated somewhat by the tactfulness of Lt. Colonel Schlegel, who used as much delicacy as possible in carrying out his difficult and thankless task. Some of the monks and then also the Abbot were allowed to remain at the abbey as custodians. Their number, at first limited to three or four during the evacuation, was increased by a few and, one day, Schlegel was happy to announce that the abbey itself would not be used as one of the bastions in the defensive line [2].

Almost all the refuges from Monte Cassino were affectionately welcomed by the most Reverend Abbot Primate of St.

Jerome and St. Paul, who, (more than anybody else) followed with loving concern and firm cooperation the fortunes of the Cassinese community. Meanwhile, this forced exodus which was the prelude to the mass deportation of the whole population of the area, evoked deep emotion everywhere [3]. In fact, after the desperate alarm was sounded by the first monks who reached Rome, both German embassies in Rome, the German Archeological Institute, the Superintendence of archives and that of the Ancient Art of Latium, the General Direction of Antiquities and the Arts and that of the Academies and Libraries worked very hard to avoid the dispersion and loss of the treasures that had been removed. In addition, His Highness the Hereditary Prince of Italy took the fortunes of Monte Cassino very much at heart, as he had already seen that eventual war damages were a possibility.

The action of the Holy See was the most efficacious and prompt of all. Right from the beginning the Holy Father took a personal interest in the fate of the abbey. This deep concern of his was shared most sincerely by his aides. This writer will never forget the tears that filled the eyes of the late cardinal Maglione when informed of the imminent danger. It was due to their efforts that the archives and the library were handed over on December 8 to the Italian authorities in Castel Sant'Angelo, from where they were transferred to the custody of the Vatican Library. No possibility was overlooked to ensure the safety of the monastery, and any military use of it was firmly prevented so that legitimate hopes for the future could be entertained.

In a way this situation seemed a repetition of what happened in the sixth century shortly after the death of St. Benedict. The community of Monte Cassino, forced into exile by the fortunes of war, arrived in Rome to find shelter in the sanctuaries of the city and protection of their most precious relics by the Apostolic See.

Meanwhile, in the deserted abbey, there remained together with the Abbot five fathers between the ages of thirty and forty; five brothers, all quite young, except one that was over eighty years old; the priest who was director of the office of diocesan administration, an oblate and a few domestics to help with the upkeep of the house. The Abbot also obtained permission to let a few families of farm workers occupy some nearby buildings and annexes. Thus, over all, there were about 150 people in Monte Cassino.

This number kept growing substantially, for many refugees, sometime encouraged by the Germans themselves, ran to find shelter in this place that they supposed safe. In fact, at the beginning of December, the German High Command informed the Abbot that, in order to protect such a famous monument from any war damage, a three hundred yard wide zone had been marked around the abbey, in which any military installation was strictly forbidden [4]. Only at the main gate of the monastery, upon request of the Abbot. three guards were posted.

Outside of this area, everything was progressively destroyed. At Cassino the Germans blew up all the houses in the outskirts and at the beginning of December also the railroad station.

At the beginning of January [5], the inhabitants of many surrounding towns, including Cassino, were driven out and it was also announced that the neutral zone around the monastery was abolished. All the civilians, who had found shelter at the abbey, including the farm workers and the domestics who had a permit to stay, were forced to leave, with the exception of three families whose members were almost all gravely ill.

The monks also were ordered to leave, but they declared that after all the promises they would not leave except by force. They knew, of course, of the grave danger they were exposing themselves to, for the Germans refused to assume any responsibility for their safety. They once again received, however, assurance that the buildings of the abbey and the surrounding neutral zone would not be utilized for military purposes. And yet, even if withdrawal from the mountain by the German forces was out of the question, it would seem that the concession of a few more yards would not have compromised the efficiency of that strong defensive line which was anchored to the chain of the rugged mountains of Abruzzi. At any rate, even in this defensive system, the house of St. Benedict remained until February 17 defenseless, almost a peaceful, sublime statement of spiritual value in the war madness that surrounded it.

After the allies' landing at Anzio [6], the guard posted in front of the gate of the monastery was withdrawn. This was the only entrance into the abbey and had stayed closed to everybody for a long time. There was a feeling that the Germans were about to leave the area. In the abbey, by now completely isolated from the outside world, there remained the monks mentioned above, the secular priest, a domestic, and the three families of farmers.

On January 11 [7], some stray artillery shells fell on the monastery. From that day, grenades of the opposing artilleries fell on the buildings in growing numbers, doing considerable damage also to the great fresco of Luca Giordano above the door of the church.

On February 5 [8], a very violent bombardment against the mountain drove a group of about forty women, who had taken shelter in S. Giuseppe and the surrounding area, up to the gate of the abbey. Insane with fear, they screamed, imploring asylum and even threatening to burn down the door. Feelings of Christian charity persuaded the Abbot to order the gate opened, but with the women rushed in a great crowd of civilians, who once again invaded the monastery.

They settled themselves as well as they could along the great entrance stairway, in the carpentry shop located under the monumental library, in the porter's lodge, in the postal office, and in the hall of the curia. Many others were in the warren beneath the monks' shelter, which had a separate entrance from the garden.

The place proved of no help for the safety of many of them. The artillery shells that kept falling not only caused damages to the buildings but killed many of them. The very day they came in, at about 2:00 P.M., a man died while he was drawing water from the well in the central cloister; two women died from the violence of the explosion under the porticoes and a boy also died in the central cloister. This continued in the following days. By February 8 it was estimated that more than one hundred shells had fallen on the abbey without any hostile reaction at all from it.

A German grenade on February 5 had already gravely damaged the bronze doors of the abbey, which went back to the eleventh century.

The monks, faced by the growing danger, had adapted the cellar under the college as a shelter. Here they also celebrated the divine office without omitting, however, the necessary occupations and the indispensable surveillance. They also were kept busy providing spiritual assistance and maintaining order among the refugees, a task far from easy and fraught with danger. They had to take care of the cleaning, the kitchen, and the animals that had been saved from the requisitions. Diseases that raged in those close surroundings tormented by so many privations and dangers, added to the miseries.

A young priest, who had not spared himself even in making boxes for burial of those poor unfortunates, became himself a victim of a disease that could not be identified. On sexagesima Sunday, February 13, while the dreadful storm raged on, he died almost unexpectedly, leaving the survivors in deep sorrow.

Born in Vercelli on March 11, 1911, d. Eusebio Grosetti was eighteen years old when he came to Monte Cassino. A soul, «natulariter» Christian, and art lover (his name will be found again in these pages), he soon found himself in perfect harmony with all that wonderful complex of artistic beauty and incomparable memories that made up the Cassinese world. Now that a destructive fury was about to strike that beauty that had attracted and fascinated his mortal eyes, an act of divine mercy and love opened to him the beauty of eternity, granting his mortal remains to rest in the sacred area, where, around St. Benedict and his Virgin sister, so many Saints wait for the resurrection.

His burial, on the following day, was carried out under very difficult conditions; shells were now falling in increasing number and the abbey was by now seriously damaged. Everywhere there was desolation and death. What was the future going to bring? It had been a few days now since allied troops had moved up the mountain and taken position almost under its strong walls; some units had also seized the higher surrounding hills. Would the storm blow over now or did the Lord ask for more trials?

3. THE CATASTROPHE.

The body of don Eusebio, dressed in monastic garb, laid in the second corridor of the basement. For twenty-four hours the brothers kept the wake with love and prayers before committing it to the final place of rest.

About two o'clock in the afternoon of February 14, two young men burst into that quiet and sorrowful gathering. They brought some fliers that had been scattered over the monastery and gathered at great risk by the refugees housed in the warren.

The leaflets gave a peremptory warning:

«*Amici italiani,*

ATTENTION!

We have, until now, tried to avoid in any way the bombardment of the monastery of Monte Cassino. The Germans have taken advantage of this. Now, however, the fighting has drawn close to the sacred enclosure. The time has come when, reluctantly we are forced to aim our weapons at the monastery itself.

We give this warning so that you may have the opportunity to save yourselves. Our warning is urgent. Leave the monastery. Depart immediately. Respect this warning. It is given for your own safety.

THE FIFTH ARMY»

Meanwhile, other people had crowded into the shelter, and they all waited anxiously for the decision of the Abbot. He advised, finally, that they seek out a German officer in order to inform the Command. This was no easy task. One had to leave the abbey and venture out into the open terrain raked by artillery and small guns fire in order to reach the closest German position between S. Onofrio and S. Comeo. Soon three young men ran out, but when they reached the threshing yard on the way to Albaneta, a violent fire of rifles and machine guns forced them to fall back. Even a second attempt under a white flag failed.

Great agitation and fear seized the crowd of refugees: what

would the monks do? Some proposed a mass exodus under white flag; some dissuaded them, speaking of mass killings in similar circumstances; there were those who wanted to stay there, others that predicted a swift death under the ruins; there was also somebody who suspected a trick of the monks with the help of the Germans to force the refugees out of the abbey. The monks, instead, urged that people decide for themselves what was best for them.

Meanwhile, through these convulsed hours, the body of d. Eusebio was placed in a box improvised from bed planks. Some volunteers, accompanied by a monk, carried it on the run along the inside stairs of the abbey down into the chapel of St. Ann, placing it in the middle of the presbytery.

In the evening, two young men renewed the risky attempt to reach the German line and, more lucky than the others, succeeded in approaching the crew of a German tank along the road below San Giuseppe. For some days now, but only during the night, two tanks had moved along the road firing on the allies' position, but they never went beyond the garden enclosure or moved into the flat area of S. Agata [9].

The young men showed the leaflet to the soldiers and told them that the Abbot wished to speak with a German officer as soon as possible. Unfortunately, it was not possible to get in touch with one until five o'clock of the following morning. They would permit the secretary of the Abbot, who spoke German, to come accompanied by one man only. A larger group would have been immediately fired on.

In the shelter, the monks, in case of an emergency, gathered the barest necessities in hand bags and some small suitcases. After supper, a young refugee in the warren began to shout in German trying to draw the attention of the soldiers to the urgency of solving the serious impasse. There was, however, no answer. They had to resign themselves to wait until the next morning; at five they would try again to reach the officer.

Thus that terrible day, Tuesday Feb. 15, arrived [10]. The liturgical calendar commemorated the SS. Faustinus and Giovita from Brescia. Their worship and the famous relic of St. Faustinus came to Monte Cassino with abbot Petronax, at the dawn of the first restoration.

At five in the morning, while the secretary of the Abbot was preparing to go out, the long awaited officer, Lieutenant Deiber, arrived at the abbey accompanied by one soldier. He was led to the Abbot, shown the allied leaflet and apprised of the desire of the monks, who had been previously allowed by the German command to wait at the abbey the arrival of the allied forces, to make contact with the lines of the Fifth Army without delay. At the same time the civilian refugees would be evacuated through the German lines.

The answer was very encouraging. The fliers, evidently, were a means of propaganda and intimidation. No one could be allowed to reach the enemy lines. As for the refugees, if they left the monastery now, they would expose themselves, as past experience showed, to losses of thirty percent. In any case, the monks had to assume the responsibility of any eventual exodus. The officer declared further that during the night he had informed his Commandant, Schmidt, about the serious situation at the abbey, and the Commandant had ordered the opening of the mule trail that goes down to the via Casilina (S. Rachisio-Colloquio) from midnight to five the following morning to allow passage to those trapped on the mountain. The departure had to be made in complete silence in order not to attract the attention of the enemy; furthermore, anyone trying to go to Cassino would be fired on. When he was told that the day after might be too late, he replied that it was not in his power to change the disposition and that he would not want to assume the responsibility of changing the hour chosen as the best, which, on that day, had already gone by [11].

Before leaving the monastery, which was off limits to the military, the officer expressed the wish to be led for a brief visit to the church. The visit was made in complete darkness that even the fleeting light of his pocket lamp was unable to pierce.

It was broad daylight now. At 8:30, the monks recited Prime, Tierce, and then celebrated the Mass of the Octave of St.

Scholastica in that part of the shelter which had been turned into
a small chapel. Above the altar they had placed the beautiful
Madonna painted by de Matteis, which previously hung above the
tomb of St. Benedict. Soon afterward in the small room of the
Abbot, they recited the Sext and the Nones. Finally, singing the
Marian antiphon, they invoked on their knees Our Lady's help.
At 9:45, while they were singing the «pro nobis Christum exora»
they heard a sudden terrible explosion.

Then other explosions followed without pause. Dismayed
and frightened, the monks grouped together in a corner. The Abbot imparted the absolution to the kneeling religious. Death appeared imminent. The thick walls were trembling perilously;
through a narrow window smoke and dust poured in, and one
could see the bursts of flame of the bombs hammering the side of
the college. Panting, crying, and covered with dust, a figure rushed into the small group praying in the corner. It was the oblate;
unable to speak, he indicated with gestures that the church had
collapsed. That wonderful work, the heart of the fourteen hundred and fifty years old abbey, was the first to be hit. The ordeal
lasted one hour and a half, but the small community was still
alive, and so were the brothers who had taken shelter in the
bakery.

The Abbot went out of the shelter to assess the damages. In
the central cloister he sadly realized that only the lower floor of
the abbey was still standing; even though the facade of the church
was still standing, where once was the vault, now with horror, he
could see the sky.

The three families of farmers insisted on staying in the
monks' shelter, in spite of the fact that the place was unsafe. A
number of refugees, mad with fear, had left their shelters and
were in the open under the artillery shelling, which hit several of
them. Many others died trying to flee the abbey. Finally, many
who were swept away in the collapse of the cloister of the Prior
were still alive among the ruins. A few, generously trying to give
them help, were caught in the open by still another wave of
bombers and perished.

This second round began just when the Abbot, after returning to his small room, was arranging with his secretary for the
disposition of the Holy Sacrament, which the sacrist had gone to
take out of the chapel of the Pietà in the Torretta. Once again a
series of tremendous explosions were followed by worse quaking
of the walls. A more violent explosion completely blocked the access to the small rooms; another one made the obstructions even
thicker; the area was sealed off, but the strong walls held.

From the adjoining rooms one could hear now the desperate
screams of the women and children of the three families. One
could also make out the voice of the sacrist who had returned
unhurt with the Holy Sacrament, bringing the divine comfort of
the communion under the form of the viaticum for the others and
himself, and thus all the sacred hosts were consumed.

Fortunately, the thick wall between the Abbot's room and
the adjacent premises had, just below the vault, a small arch closed with a thin metallic net. Thus it was possible to speak with the
sacrist. He said that they were all safe and that the entrance to the
shelter, although obstructed in part, was still usable. Nothing was
known about the rest, not even of the monks who had taken
shelter in the farther recesses of the basement. Breaking open the
small net, the Abbot was helped to pass to the other side, and the
secretary followed him. Then, through the semiblocked entrance
they all went out.

What a sight! The center of the first cloister was a deep
hollow around whose edges were piled up the ruins of the surrounding buildings and the massive stumps of the pillars. The
central cloister with the loggia of Paradise no longer existed.
Even the well cover had sunk down and at the bottom one could
see some water, strangely red colored. Only in the entrance
cloister part of the portico was still standing. Of the cloisters
up on the summit, like the cloister of the Benefactors, nothing
was left. After the Lombards, the Saracens, and the earthquake,
the fourth destruction of Monte Cassino had now been accomplished.

Among the ruins, the survivors stood dazed and dismayed in

the face of such unbelievable disaster, while bombs kept exploding all around them.

Meanwhile the monks trapped in the more remote area of the basement had succeeded with great difficulty in forcing a passage out for themselves following a small opening that let in a little light. The Abbot left all the people free to provide for their own safety. During a brief pause in the artillery barrage, some of the religious together with most of the refugees were able to escape along the road to Rome. Six monks, the domestic, and the three families of farmers remained with the Abbot. Unable to cross the ruins to go in the warren, they decided to take refuge in the lower chapels of the Torretta. At the door of the Torretta, which was still free, they heard heart-rending screams and found a woman who had lost both her feet; they helped bring her inside. The large stairway and the lower chapels had been taken over by hundreds of people. The monks stopped in the chapel of the Pietà while one of the brothers and a refugee went to fetch the provisions left in the shelter. They made it just in time; shortly afterwards a landslide blocked the entrance completely.

In the Torretta there was great agitation, cries, moaning, and voices begging for help. Nearby, in the rooms of the Curia, a fire broke out. Darkness came and made the situation even more painful. The Abbot was seated on a chair on the left side of the altar; lying on the floor around him were the monks and the lay brothers. Among the latter there was one with a very high fever moaning on a mattress. Everyone had a little bread and cheese, but there was no water.

About 8:00 P.M., the German officer that had come in the morning returned and gave the Abbot the following communication:

«The German Fuhrer, A. Hitler, acceding to the wishes of the Pope (auf wunsch des Papst), will ask the Americans for a truce, so that the Abbot with the monks and all civilians can be evacuated from Monte Cassino. The Abbot, with the monks, the wounded, and the children will be taken by trucks via Cassino, but they must reach the transports on foot, because the road leading up to the abbey has been destroyed by the bombing; the others, on foot, will have to make their own way out of the fire zone. It is the wish of the Pope that the Abbot and the monks be taken to the Vatican. It will take a day or two to get the answer. During the night, Field-marshal Kesselring will ask for the cease fire. We hope that the Americans will grant it; otherwise they will have to bear the blame».

The officer then asked the Abbot if he could issue a written statement declaring that both before and during the destruction there were no German troops in Monte Cassino. Because this was the truth, the Abbot, by moral duty, could not refuse. The declaration was written out and the Abbot signed it on the altar of the Pietà.

The cease-fire never took place. There are, in fact, doubts that the request was ever made or was ever meant to be made. The same day, it must be noted, Marshall Kesselring declared that the ruins of the abbey would form henceforth part of the German defensive system, and after all the monks left on the 17th, German troops moved in. Thus the war was able to invade that oasis of peace. The fatherly solicitude of the Pope, speaking for the whole civilized world, had been able to keep it out of the line of fire until then. Now the struggle became even more fierce and the task of the assailants much more difficult [12]. In fact, as soon as the Germans were free to occupy the height, the allies were forced to evacuate the surrounding hills which were already in their hands.

The promised cease-fire, although many had little faith in it, did bring some sparks of hope during the long and sleepless night; hope is always the last to leave.

All the alternatives to the truce were frightening. How could the sick and the wounded be carried out of the danger area? How could the octogenarian Abbot reach Roccasecca? Remaining there among the ruins with the sick, the children, and the old with no food or water, meant sure death.

Suddenly in the somber darkness a frightful noise jolted those that were dozing and those too frightened to sleep. They all found themselves in a thick cloud of dust. Soon they discovered that part of the lower vaults of the Torretta had collapsed; fortunately, nobody was hurt.

At dawn on the 16th, almost all the refugees still in the abbey left; only the three families of farmers, some old people, some children abandoned by their parents, a few of them gravely wounded, remained. In all, only four or five sound men were left. A lay brother by chance found that a small well near the kitchen was intact, so finally they could have some water. It was impossible, however, to celebrate even one Mass, because everything needed was missing. There was only a breviary for the divine service. The Abbot and the other two priests remaining recited it standing in the vestibule of the Torretta.

Soon, however, they had to abandon even that shelter, not so much because of the wind and the cold but because of the violence of the artillery barrage. They were forced to move onto the landing of the great stairway. Towering over them was the large fresco of Moses praying on the mountain between Aaron and Hur who held up his arms, while on the plain below the battle between the Jews and the Amalekites raged on.

The continuous artillery fire did not allow the monks to assess the damages to the house. In fact, for fear of being swept away by a collapsing vault which was dangerously covered with very heavy mounds of debris, they even avoided staying in the chapel. The small group of survivors gathered around the little altar of St. Benedict next to the gate of the old citadel; thus if the bombing continued they would die embracing the altar in the place that held so many famed and sweet memories of the healing virtues of the Patriarch.

Almost directly across, in the «hall of the sleepers» an old man was dying; the sacrist gave him absolution, but could not administer the viaticum or the extreme unction. Beyond the great entrance stairs, three children lay on a straw mattress; their mother was killed in the bombing and their father had cruelly forsaken them. The two little brothers cried desperately, and their little sister, completely exhausted, moaned piteously. The Abbot himself took care of them, gave them a little food to hold up their strength. Whatever food and wine left was shared with the other survivors. In the afternoon new fears arose. Planes flew above, but they only fired their machine guns and dropped a few stick bombs.

The survivors waited anxiously for the return of the officer with the news of the truce to provide, especially, for the sick and the wounded. The few healthy men were asked to prepare a passage through the main gate, which was completely blocked by ruins. After some hours of hard work, they succeeded in moving the very heavy door and opened a narrow passage. They waited however, in vain, with darkness, despair and sadness mounted. The German officer did not return. By now no human help was forthcoming, and they spent a sleepless night in dejection and prayers.

Even in such great uncertainty, the Abbot and the monks decided without regard to their own safety, not to abandon the sick and the wounded. An old woman died in the cell of St. Benedict, assisted to the end by her daughter who, unlike her son, refused to leave her.

Dawn was about to come, and the first light showed that by the progressive crumbling of the cracked walls, a great deal of debris had accumulated, threatening more and more the precarious safety of the lower levels. Above all, the conclusion was reached that in these conditions no assistance could be given to the suffering people. There was only one way of escape left, to hope to take advantage of the relative calm of the early morning hours to carry the sick and wounded and, in God's name, to venture across the fire zone to reach the area behind the lines. Within a few minutes they were ready; any delay now could be fatal. To transport a sick woman and the one who lost her feet, they used ladders.

In the great entrance hall, the Abbot gave absolution to everybody; then, carrying a large wooden crucifix he advanced with great difficulty through the tight passage dug in the thick debris. It was now 7:30 A.M. One by one all followed after him

Montecassino as it was

Cassino's valley as it was

Southern side as it was

North-west side as it was

Southern side as it was

As it was

The entrance as it was

The entrance cloister as it was

The middle cloister as it was

The middle cloister as it was

As it was

As it was

As it was - The Observatory

Cloister of the benefactors as it was

As it was

As it was

They wanted to take the three wounded children with them, but the girl had only moments left, and one of the boys was near death; when they tried to pick him up his cry of pain made it clear that this would only increase the sufferings of his last moments. The other boy was in better condition, though his legs were paralyzed. One of the lay brother carried him on his shoulders.

To carry out this act of charity they had to leave behind the few things left to them, even some money and the precious pectoral crosses stored in the Abbot's small case. The line, formed of about forty people, wound slowly and with difficulty among the ruins; the Abbot could not walk by himself and had to be supported. It took a good half hour to cover the short distance to the little church of St. Agatha, with all reciting the rosary as they moved along. At this point, they turned on to the mule trail and from there took the road, now called Anzino, which was still in good condition. Before the intersection with the road for S. Rachisio, they passed a machine gun position and, soon after, three soldiers sheltered by a crevice. At the sight of the unusual group preceded by the cross, they were surprised and, perhaps, also moved. The party asked the soldiers to allow them to pass, said that they had evacuated the monastery with the approval of the German command and were trying to get behind the lines. The three soldiers did not answer, but one of them covered a nearby weapon with some branches.

The group moved on. The road here was all torn up; high above, flying very slowly, they saw a reconnaissance plane. The group of fugitives, because of the full light and bright colors of the traditional costumes worn by the women, was clearly visible against the somber landscape. A short distance from S. Rachisio, a grenade exploded on the side of the road, no more than ten yards from the group. They kept going all the same, under the protection of the cross and praying.

From the rear cries of warning were heard; the stretcher-bearers found it impossible to carry the mutilated woman on the road torn and ripped by bomb craters. They were begged from afar to persevere in their efforts, and the cries were no longer heard as they resumed their trek. When they arrived on the plain at a late hour, they discovered with horror that the poor woman had been abandoned to her destiny by the exhausted porters. There were more explosions, prayers and invocations for help.

From the lower foot-hills of the mountain, somebody spotted Carlomanno Pelagalli, an octogenerian lay brother, who had preceded the group, on his way towards the Casilina highway. At that time they lost track of him. Later on, it was learned that he had died on March 3 among the ruins of his abbey. God knows what hidden voice brought him back to die there where he had lived for over fifty years [13].

After passing through a torn up pine grove, they reached the dry bed of a mountain stream; beyond they found a redoubt and, near the small chapel of the Colloquy, a cottage bearing the sign of the International Red Cross. The time was about 10:00 in the morning.

At the entrance there was a broken piece of statuary, inside a first aid station. In the basement there were beds for the more seriously wounded; the others had to stay on the main floor.

They explained their plight to some German soldiers coming from the direction of Albaneta, and kept asking to be allowed to contact a military command. This was impossible because all telephone lines were down and the closest command was at Villa S. Lucia, over two and a half miles away. The Germans, instead, urged them to move on right away because the artillery fire was mounting in intensity. They suggested following a path not yet spotted by the Allies along the base of the mountain, avoiding with care the roadbed of the Casilina, which was under fire from both sides, proceeding in small detached groups, and falling quickly to the ground when they heard the hissing sound of a falling grenade. A trooper at the door was just pointing out to the Abbot's secretary the small path, when they were both slightly wounded by an explosion.

The fugitives started in small groups, the sacrist led the first one; the Abbot would be the last to follow, to make sure no one else was left behind. The old man was very tired by the precipitous descent from the mountain and showed symptoms of physical collapse; the soldiers noticed this and offered him some coffee. Just at that very moment, a soldier entered the cottage and announced that the German command was anxiously looking everywhere for the Abbot. When he was told that the Abbot was there, he informed him that the Regimental Command had received a radiogram with strict orders, following the personal request of the Holy Father, to see to it that the Abbot of Monte Cassino got safely out of the combat zone. Someone hinted at the possiblity that an ambulance might arrive in the afternoon to take out the wounded and that the Abbot should take advantage of the opportunity. It was evident that the old man was near exhaustion and would not go very far on his own, so they convinced him to stay. The soldier that had come by his own initiative to search for the Abbot returned under the heavy shelling to the command to announce that he had been found.

The Abbot, his secretary with the paralyzed child, the only one left behind, withdrew into the shelter and recited the office. Soldiers came and went to snatch a little rest. Three women from Cassino, who could not go on any longer, found their way there.

An allied plane circled above the cottage, near which there was the wreck of an ambulance hit by artillery fire. An ash blond boy was trying to repair it with no good results; another with a bandaged neck said that he had been wounded on the mountain; still another, between one explosion and the next, asked seriously to no one in particular, what the devil Tommy wanted in Europe, with all the good things that he had back home. And so the hours glided by.

In the afternoon aerial activity increased greatly. Tremendous explosion could be heard; perhaps they were bombing Monte Cassino again. About 4:30 P.M., the ambulance finally arrived. A sergeant notified the Abbot that he had been charged with his rescue and handed over a letter from the command. The note explained that in the morning a long search had been conducted in the abbey and its vicinities to find him and now, after

expressing his gratification that he was safe, the writer invited him
to follow the bearer of the letter, because from the supreme command had arrived an order to take him out of the danger zone.
The sergeant was very kind, urged them to make haste, offered
them oranges, helped to place the paralyzed child on a stretcher,
let the women aboard, and finally helped the Abbot and the
secretary to get in. He started the engine and began to apologize
for the rough ride. They had to go as fast as possible on account
of the strong artillery fire on the via Casilina.

The ambulance lurched forward. It was a bumpy and rapid
run. From a small opening in the drapes one could see a squadron
of planes raining bombs on the abbey, causing violent explosions
which raised columns of dense smoke. For the fugitives it was the
last view of their beloved home. The survivors (in small groups)
finally reached Rome [14].

This time also, as in the first destruction, St. Benedict had
obtained that the lives of his children be spared. On the day of the
Octave of St. Scholastica, February 17, he saw them cross
unscathed the circle of steel and fire that surrounded their home.

The destruction, however, did not end then. The Germans,
logically, now felt free to move into the ruins, and they turned
them into a defensive bastion. In the two cloisters adjacent to the
central one, they placed two heavy mortars while the inner cor-
ridors were used as troop quarters and ammunition depots. In addition, a complex communication network was installed.

The traces of the military occupation were later found in the
filth, the graffiti, and the sketches left behind. At the northwest
corner of the shelter, that had been occupied by the monks, a
skillful cartoonist had drawn Churchill standing in the desolate
plain of Cassino, smoking his huge cigar and pulling behind him
guns and airplanes, while a gigantic German paratrooper standing
on the ruins of Monte Cassino confronts him, saying: «Denk'ste»
(Think it over!).

On a German observation post, there was another sketch
showing the eastern side of Cassino and a woman dressed as a
soldier, eying with curiosity the rangefinder while two soldiers

watch her intently. Of all the inscriptions, only one shows a gentle soul: above the drawing of a river there were the words, «On the lovely banks of the Rhine».

To secure interior communications and to search for treasures, the Germans broke into walls and floors. In the room located under the chapel of the Holy Monks of the Torretta, they found two bodies, that of the German monk d. Gabriele Wüger, a painter, and that of cardinal Bartolini. The first has disappeared since; the other, without the pectoral cross and the ring, was later found in a tub in the garden. Other profanations were committed, like the sacrilegious parody played at Arpino using ecclesiastical vestments stolen from Monte Cassino. Several Germans killed in the fighting were buried in the ruins of the abbey, all, however, as it can be seen from the dates on the tombs, after March 15.

The bombings and artillery fire continued to pour without pause, culminating in the intense saturation bombing which reduced Cassino to ashes and destroyed what was left of the abbey, the eastern part, that until then had remained in fair condition [17].

It was only on May 18, after three months of German occupation, when the allies finally broke into the plain, that the brave Polish soldiers succeeded in taking the monastery, advancing along the only possible direction, the hills on the northern side that surround and dominate the position. It was on those heights, in the sector of Caira, Pozzalvito, Albaneta, Calvario (593 m.), that the fierce fighting took place. Then, as always, the abbey was not involved in the battle [18]. At 10:30 in the morning of May 18, anniversary of the dedication of the Torretta, the Polish flag was raised on the ruins of the abbey. On the following day, a military chaplain celebrated Mass next to the great decapitated statue of St. Benedict, on the spot where the central cloister once was.

NOTES

[1] A plan to withdraw the Axis forces to the Gothic line, i.e., along the Tuscan Appenines, was not accepted in order to keep enemy aerial bases as far as possible from the German war production centers. Thus the defensive line was established on the other mountain chain that divides Italy from one sea to the other. The massif of the Cairo mountain, which formed its western end, included Monte Cassino.

The Lt. Colonel JULIUS SCHLEGEL, an artillery man and a flier, in his articles, *Mein Wagnis, op. cit.,* followed by Böhmler, takes credit for the whole operation of evacuation and salvage of the archives and the library.

The medical officer is given a secondary role: Böhmler mentions him briefly (p. 248, 293) and Schlegel only in the last of his articles, n. 50, speaking of his collaborators: Lt. Paolo Raab and Lt. Manegold, who was already dead.

On the other hand, according to Capt. Becker the initiative was his. It was he who proposed the operation to the Quartermaster and the Adjutant of the division Göring, then stationed at villa Lerro, not far from Teano. The proposal was discussed and the captain was directed to the transport pool of the division. The date was Oct. 13, 1943.

The idea of evacuating the archives and library of Monte Cassino occurred to him when he was placed in charge of establishing a military hospital in the convent of S. Antonio in Teano. In the three rooms set aside there were books from libraries in Naples which had to be moved. To save the precious books, he had the idea to ship them to Spoleto, where the food and munitions depots for the Göring division were located. He decided that the same thing could be done for the collections of Monte Cassino.

The captain came to Monte Cassino accompanied by the Franciscan fathers, Giovanni Giuseppe Carcaterra and Baldassarre Califano, to whom he explained his plan. He was preceded, however, by Schlegel, who was in charge of transports for the division, and took over the operation.

At the beginning, the archives and the library, i.e. the part evacuated by the Germans, were placed in the villa di Colle Ferretto, owned by the March. Marignoli. In Dec. 1947, they were transferred from the Vatican library to the abbey of St. Jerome, also in Rome.

There are a number of inaccuracies in the account of Schlegel, as, for instance, the order of departure of the trucks, the transport of the relics, and not of the «body» of St. Benedict, which took place in the first trip, and this author was the consignee, together with the treasure of St. January, Shelley's ashes etc.

[2] This was an initiative of Marshal Kesselring. Thus the monastery was in the fortified zone but was not included in the defensive line, the «Gustav line». It was incorporated only after the destruction. The Marshal himself has confirmed this in his *Memorie di Guerra,* cit., 214: «I can affirm in clear terms, that the abbey was not included in the combat area, in fact, guards were posted to prohibit the entrance».

The irruption of the SS was, in fact, a simple police inspection to prevent the sack of the abbey, a rumor falsely spread by the Allies, see Böhmler, p. 238, 282. Schlegel gave to the police commander the necessary explanations and all ended there. There were attempts to make a war criminal out of Schlegel, but in his defense came Marshal Alexander. In the war he lost his leg and his health and a communist took away his home.

[3] The few students of the college, present at the time of the evacuation of the abbey, found, together with their Rector, generous hospitality at the college of S. Giuseppe. The entire community of Benedictine sisters were welcomed with love and stayed for many months with the Sisters of St. Paul.

[4] A lot has been said about this neutral zone. In reality it was a measure taken by the German themselves without any bilateral, official accord with the Allies. It was, however, well known to both sides that the abbey was not used for military purposes, though there were, obviously, suspicions on both sides, see on this Gen. von Senger und Etterlin, *La distruzione, op. cit.,* pp. 14-15.

According to Böhmler, 336, 398, the neutral zone was entered only by Gen. von Senger, for the Christmas celebrations in the Crypt, Dr. Puppel with two medical corpsmen, on Feb. 10 and 14, to take care of the wounded upon request by the monks and Lt. Deiber, again asked by the monks, to discuss the evacuation. All military positions were outside the «neutral zone» of about 300 yards. On the south-east side there were two tanks at 300 yards distance, four rocket-launchers at 400, and an observation post at the 435 m. altitude. Nevertheless, even now there is talk about redoubts and pill-boxes right next to the monastery.

[5] The so-called battles of Cassino constitute, in fact, one battle which lasted from Nov. 1943 until May 1944, when the Allies pierced the «Gustav Line».

Gen. von Senger und Etterlin (*La distruzione,* 11-13) states unequivocally: «... I wish to make it clear that after the monastery came to be part of the war zone, Fieldmarshal Kesselring not only forbade access to the monastery to all troops, but placed also guards at the entrance to make sure that his orders would be obeyed». These words of the man who was in command of the German forces in the Monte Cassino sector, confirm what this author has stated in a previous edition of this work.

To preserve the memory, the following is a list of the monks who remained to watch over the abbey. Besides the Abbot, there were: d. Oderisio Graziosi, d. Martino Matranola, d. Agostino Saccomanno, d. Nicola Clemente, d. Eusebio Grossetti, all monks and priests; Bro. Carlomanno Pelagalli, Bro Giacomo Ciaraldi, Bro. Pietro Nardone, Bro. Romano Colella, Bro. Zaccaria di Raimo, plus, mons. d. Francesco Falconio and the Oblate Giuseppe Cianci.

[6] The second phase of the battle, the one that interests us most, because it led to the destruction of the monastery is tied up to this landing. The Allies tried to take the Germans from the rear and capture Rome quickly as Churchill wanted.

[7] This happened during the operations for the capture of Mt. Torchio, which was taken that day.

[8] In the confused episodes of this phase, a patrol of the 135th Infantry, commanded by Col. Ward, managed to come close to the walls of the abbey. The monks saw it from the shelter, they even made ready a white flag, thinking they would soon need it. From a cave, below the wall that sorrounded the monastery, the Americans managed to capture 14 German soldiers.

[9] Also in the last days, according to some eye-withnesses, a machine gun kept moving behind the short wall of the carriage-road, below the college, the ammunition, probably hidden in a cave.

[10] The Americans (Fifty Army), exhausted, asked and got help from the English (Eighth Army), whose line joined theirs at Castel S. Vincenzo. The II New Zealander Corps, under the command of Gen. Freyberg, formed of a New Zealander division, II Parkinson and the Indian, IV Tucker, was sent.

How the decision was reached to destroy Monte Cassino it is by now well known. After the first declarations of Gen. Juin, there were those of Gen. Clark, commander of the Fifth Army. What follows is the narrative of Mordal, *op. cit.,* 118 ff., who made use of both sources:

«D'après les plans établis à l'Etat-Major du Corps néo-zélandais, les Hindous devaient attaquer dans la nuit du 13 au 14 février, enlever le mont Cassin, redescendre dans la vallée, couper la Via Casilina, et attaquer Cassino par l'ouest, tandis que les Néo-Zélandais l'attaqueraient de l'est. Les conditions atmosphériques retardèrent l'operation de trois jours. Mais surtout, le général Freyberg [† 1964] venait de poser une question d'une exceptionnelle gravité, celle du bombardement préalable de l'abbaye.

... Le 12 févriere, Freyberg a téléphoné au quartier général de la Vᵉ Armée. C'est le général Gruenther, chef d'Etat-Major, qui prend l'appareil en l'absence de Clark retenu à Anzio. "Je demande le bombardement du couvent", déclare le chef du Corps néozélandais. Gruenther est bien ennuyé. Le couvent ne figure pas sur la liste des objectifs à bombarder, liste qui ne peut être modifée à cette action... Freyberg insiste. Le commandant de la division chargée de l'attaque [Tucker, 4ᵃ indiana; la 2ᵃ Néo-Zélandese, com. Parkinson] a déclaré qu'il considérait cet objectif comme essentiel; il est pleinement d'accord avec lui.

Gruenther appelle le général Marding, chef d'Etat Major de Alexander, consulte Keyes et Ryder qui ne considèrent pas ce bombardement comme indispensable et finit par joindre Clark par T.S.F. pour le trouver, bien entendu, tout aussi ennuyé qu'il l'est lui-même, en raison des difficultés diplomatiques que cet incident risque de soulever entre les Britanniques et les Néo-Zélandais... La discussion dura toute le journée. Alexander inclinait a donner satisfaction à Freyberg, confiant dans le jugement du général néozélandais. Dés son retour d'Anzio, Clark le rappelle au téléphone.

"Si les Allemands ne sont pas dans le monastère en ce moment, déclare-t-il, ils seront certainement dans ses décombres dès la fin du bombardement. Si j'avais affaire à un chef américain, je lui aurais certainement refusé la permission; mai en raison des circostances, j'hésite à susciter une polemique grave. Si vous me dites de le faire, nous le ferons, mais alors, pas à moitié... Nous mettrons tout dessus"...»

Already before (p. 120), the author had said we do not with how much truth:

«Ce n'est d'ailleurs pas Clark qui prit la décision. L'affaire alla beaucoup plus loin. Ellè fut soumise à Alexander d'abord, puis à Maitland Wilson qui tint à effectuer lui-même une reconnaissance au-dessus du monastère et enfin aux chefs d'Etat-Major britanniques à Londres, et par eux, sans aucun doute, aux chefs des gouvernements alliés».

In reality, that of Feb. 12 was not the first request advanced by Gen. Freyberg. Those who monitored closely the Allies radio communications were able to note that on Feb. 10 already, they painted an alarming position about the future of Monte Cassino, almost as if preparing for the worst. In fact, the Benedictines of the convent of Noci (Bari), where a convalescent home had been set up for British soldiers, tell that (see, «Scala», 1964, p. 37): «... just on the 10th of February 1944, Feast of St. Scholastica, we were informed, with hardly hidden satisfaction, of the order of the Allied Command to bomb and destroy Monte Cassino, justifying the order with the presence, in the said monastery, of German troops... During the same day of the 15th, we were told, first that the bombardment was on course and that Monte Cassino was now a mass of ruins».

On the 14th, Freybourg went again to Clark, who tried to dissuade him, especially because there were no proofs of a German occupation of the abbey, see Böhmler p. 331-392. On the other hand, Gen. Maitland-Wilson «après avoir survolé le counvent en Piper-Cub en compagnie du général Devers, à moins de soixante-quinze mètres d'altitude, déclara formellement avoir observé des antennes de T.S.F. et des mouvements de soldats allemands à l'intérieur et à l'extérieur des bâtiments. Ce que nous savons aujourd'hui nous permet de penser qu'ils se trompaient, lui et Devers. Mais nous pouvons aussi penser que cette erreur comblait les voeux des Allemands..., car ils avaient tout intérêt à voir les Alliés s'enfermer dans l'idée qu'ils ne respectaient pas le caractère sacré de ce saint lieu et se décider à effectuer ce bombardement dont Goebbels saurait se faire una arme redoutable pour sa propagande».

The same Wilson, in a telegram to the British chiefs of Staff, declared «qu'il avait la preuve irréfutable» que l'abbaye faisait partie de la principale ligne de défense allemande, que les observateurs s'en servaient pour la conduite du tir de l'artillerie, que les «snipers» s'y embusquaient pour tirer, et que canons, «pill-boxes» et dépôts de munitions étaient répartis sous son ombre...

C'est dans ces conditions que le lieutenent-géneral Ira C. Eaker, commandant les forces aérieennes alliées en Méditerranée, reçut du général Wilson l'ordre de préparer ses bombardiers.

Et comme l'avait annoncé Clark, on n'y alla pas de main morte. Retardé de trois jours par le mauvais temps, le bombardement du Mont Cassin commença donc le 15 février 1944 date que les habitants de Cassino ne paraissent pas decidés à oublier». We, also, would be tempted to ask why should they forget it!

According to the report (see, *La distruzione,* p. 13, note) of Gen. Maitland Wilson of May 10, 1944: «142 flying fortresses dropped 287 tons of demolition bombs of 500 pounds and 66 and a half tons of incendiary bombs of 100 pounds, they were followed by 47 B-25 and 40 B-26 which launched 100 tons of high explosive bombs. Mordal, justly, comments (*op. cit.,* pp. 122-123): «sur un objectif qui ne dévelopait pas deux kilomètres carrés... une belle concentration comme on le voit, mais assez imparfaitement exécutée d'ailleurs, car le général Clark vit tomber sur son poste de commandement seize bombes de fort calibre qui, Dieu merci, ne tuèrent personne, mais par contre terrorisèrent sa chienne et ses chiots!...» (p. 122-123).

«Si seulement, au prix de ce geste fatal, les Alliés avaient pu forcer la victoire... Même pas! Pour des raisons de sécurité évidentes, juste avant le déclanchement des bombardements, on avait fait évacuer la position de l'Albaneta conquise le 6 février, car elle ne se trouvait qu'à quinze cents mètre du monastère, trop exposée aux coups de l'aviation. Occasion inespérée pour les Allemands qui, dès le bombardement terminé, coururent réoccuper cette position dont la comquête avait coûté tant de sang aux fantassins américains et qu'ils n'avaient pu la reprendre huit jours plus tôt, malgré de féroces contreattaques. Cette fois ils étaient bien décidés à ne plus la lâcher de sitôt. On lança sans succès une compagnie du I.er Royal Sussex dans la nuit du 15 au 16 février. Malgré l'appuie de l'aviation et l'envoi de deux compagnies de renfort, ces efforts ne furent pas plus heureux le lendemain. Enfin, au cours de la nuit du 16 au 17, le bataillon du Sussex avait à remettre le pied sur la crête [593 m.], lorsqu'il en fut rejeté avec des pertes sanglantes, laissant sur le terrain douze officiers et cent trente hommes. Les fusiliers de Rjputana, puis le bataillon des Gurkhas attaquérent alors, très bravement, mais sans résultat.

Tandis que la Division indienne s'épuissait ainsi sur le sommets, les Néo-Zélandais n'étaient pas plus heureux dans la plaine... se firent rejeter de la gare de Cassino qu'il avient atteinte dans un premier élan; par contre, ils purent conserver le contrôle des deux ponts qu'il avaient jetés sur le Rapido» (p. 125).

[11] On this passage, Böhmler, (p. 319, 378) comments: «The statement of d. Tommaso Leccisotti that the local German officer had ordered the evacuation on the night of Feb. 16 is as little exact as the one that anyone caught going to Cassino would be shot. What is true is the fact Major Schmidt gave complete freedom to the Abbot, suggesting only that he should take the road towards Piedimonte, where artillery fire was less pro-

bable. Schmidt, who expected an enemy attack at any minute, could do no more».

Actually, our text does not say anything about firing squads, but only of a threat of «opening fire».

As for the hours during which to leave the monastery, they may have been suggested as advice but understood as a command. That is how they were reported by one who took part in the meeting. The road to Piedimonte is, in fact, the one to S. Rachisio-Colloqio.

[12] That the bombing was a serious mistake in the whole botched up compaign, which a reporter (cfr. *Tempo,* Rome, June 13, 1950) defined «as a monument of such ineptitude to shock even the sheep in the mountains of Abruzzi», it soon became evident from the consequences, and there was criticism even in America. Desert tactics, where Greyberg had had some success, did not work in mountain territory. Besides what has been said, after the destruction, the Germans got that freedom of movement that as long as the buildings remained intact, they did not enjoy or was extremely limited. One can say that it was, indeed, in their interest to trick the allies into that action, because under the cover of the ruins they were able to place much better observation points than the ones that Gen. Wilson thought he had seen! No human lives were saved, on the contrary! Undoubtedly, this was the reason that led Gen. Clark to advise against the operation. It was, certainly, a huge tactical error and the opinions of the experts councur, see, *La distruzione,* and MOR-DAL, *op. cit.*

Böhmler notes the rebuttals given by Kesselring to Allied claims (p. 337, 399). The German commander confirmed that the bombing had done no harm to his troops and materiel and, moreover, had given them the opportunity to move into the ruins. The author keeps on listing numerous mistakes made by the Allies. After the first one, rejecting the choice of the Appian road, which could be supported also from the sea, they erred in thinking that the Germans, besides the Cairo massiff, needed also the abbey as an observation point for their artillery. But if the Germans had made the abbey their «eye», it is clear that they would have lost it when the bombing began. If the Allies had had any hints of the many surprises that Kesselring had prepared for them around Cassino, they, surely, would have chosen the Appia for their advance.

And the same author at p. 341, commenting on the declaration of Gen. Wilson on the presence of German troops in the monastery, says that there are many doubts about what exactly he saw. It is possible that a crowd of German soldiers would mill around and inside the monastery with a spy plane flying very low above? If there had been German soldiers, they would take cover immediately.

One must also ask if it was worthwhile to destroy the abbey, even if German soldiers were there. A frontal attack of such a position was a grave error, in fact, both Clark and Juin had tried to outflank it. The German paratroopers, as a matter of fact, were holding on the foothills facing the Casilina, had that position been bombed, there would be no need to touch the abbey, it would have been quite easy to reach the heights north-west of the monastery, from there they could have stormed down, and, without firing a shot, seized the monastery..., Böhmler, p. 342, 404. In the second battle of Cassino, when German artillery fire was directed from observation points in the ruins of the abbey, they (the Allies) blinded them with smoke curtains all day long. They did not break through because their men were exhausted while the German received reinforcements. If the Allied Command was convinced that the abbey had become «the most powerful artillery fortress that ever existed» it would have been easy to anticipate the smoke curtain thus making it impossible for the observers to direct the fire. In this way they would have prevented the destroyed abbey from becoming a fortress in German hands, because this was, indeed, the only military result of the destruction. This was how the German paratroopers were able to occupy the ruins and take strong positions in them, utilizing cover and underground passage, made even stronger by the many feet of debris covering them. Now, indeed, the abbey became the strong point in the German defensive line and Freyberg was hit over the head by the boomerang that he launched against Monte Cassino, which from then on cost the Allies a great deal of blood and materiel (Böhmler, p. 343, 405). No matter how one looks at it, the senseless destruction of Monte Cassino cannot be justified from any point of view, it was a terrible military and political mistake. This is the opinion of Böhmler, who was the commanding officer of the German paratroopers.

We must add, here, that everything has been tried to justify the nefarious act, every means, from flattery to lies, from deceitful proposals of aid to threats, have been employed to snuff out the truth. After the claims of the presence of the Germans, the telephone network etc., all inexistent, the psychological condition of the fighting men has been used. The episode of Reims, where there were observers, does not help that claim. Besides, the action of Gen. Clark, who was certainly informed about the psychological state of his men, and the publications by him and Gen. Juin reveal how things really went refute these miserable pretexts, they condemn the intense compaign of lies, undertaken to justify the decision in the eyes of a world opinion unaware or deceived.

We can conclude by quoting the judgement of the American military critic Hoffman Nickerson, reported by Mordal, p. 138 (cfr., *infra,* n. 17): «le seul résultat de la plupart des bombardements est de détruire les choses pour la sauvegarde desquelles on est supposé se battre», as, in the case of Monte Cassino, strictly connected to moral values, we might add.

Gaetano De Sanctis, speaking about the destruction of Monte Cassino in a meeting of the Pontifical Archeological Academy, had this to say on these tragic results of the war: «It is not our task to isolate and determine the individual responsibilities of this mass of ruins, but this must be said, that to have allowed this to happen will remain for ever the shame of our age and our civilization».

The II volume of the official history of the Royal Air Force while offering extenuating circumstances for individuals, recognizes the gravity and deplores the sad event.

[13] The German paratroopers found him there when they occupied the ruins. He was walking about with a candle through the rubble trying to recognize the familiar places which did not exist any longer. The men of the 4th company, especially Dr. Köhn, took care of him until he died, about the beginning of March. Cfr. Böhmler, *op. cit.,* pp. 325-326, 385-386 and n. 7.

[14] Gen. von Senger und Etterlin has narrated the vicissitudes of the journey and the arrival in Rome of the eighty years old Abbot. In spite of some small inaccuracies, the story is on the whole true. All those who spoke with the venerable old man in those days remember how outraged he was by the fact that while saying that they were taking him to the Vatican and then to the residence of the German ambassdor at the Vatican, they dragged him instead, discouraged, enfeebled and starving, to the radio station and kept interrogating him, while he was unaware of the circumstances, the place and the reasons for that. When he finally realized what they were doing, he rebelled violently and refused to continue, even later, when further pressure was applied. The narration by the general has revealed that this «shameful propaganda», as the Abbot defined it, had been arranged and orchestrated by the Nazi political authorities.

[15] On Feb. 22, Böhmler deployed among the ruins of the monastery the 4th company of his 1st battalion of the 3rd Paratroopers Regiment commanded by Col. Heilmann.

There were altogether seventy men with three heavy machine guns and two mortars. According to Mordal, p. 147: «La position se révéla excellente», car les armes pouvaient battre tous les secteurs de l'horizon». Also large quantities of food and ammunitions were
stored there.

[16] In the ealier editions of this volume, it was stated that the two statues of St.
Benedict and St Scholastica, made out of cedars from Lebanon, which were above the
main altar of the Crypt, had been carted away to present them, according to some rumors,
as gifts to Göring. This was not true and it was proved in the clearing operations, when
fragments of these statues were found in the rubble. The rumor originated from the fact
that some things were carried away in Germany and later some have been returned, as, for
instance, the figure of the angel, also made of the same wood, but of much smaller size,
which originally was placed between the larger statues.

[17] This lack of success had not dampened all hopes: «Alexander décida de relancer
son attaque, mais, cette fois, aprés un bombardament digne de ce nom [sono parole sue]...
et non pas sans doute une simple démonstration comme celle du 15 février... 576 tonnes
sur moins de deux kilomètres carrés! Le général Canon commandant la aviation tactique
avançait qu'avec un peu de beau temps et en rassemblant toutes les ressources disponibles
en Italie, il devait être possible d'enlever Cassino "comme un vieux chicot"» (MORDAL,
127).

This time also, bad weather caused a delay of a few days. But on March 15 «dés 8 h.
30, les premières escadrilles de bombardiers lourds B 25 apparurent dans le ciel de
Cassino. De dix en dix minutes, se suivirent ainsi Mitchells, Forteresses volants et
Liberators. Chasseurs et chasserurs-bombardiers avaient pour objectifs, les emplacements
de l'artillerie ennemie, les ponts de la vallée du Liri, le terrain d'aviation d'Aquin, la gare
de Cassino, le Colisée, et les centres importants de Piedimonte, Pignataro, San Giorgio,
Pontecorvo, Ceprano etc. auxquels s'attaqueraient en outre quelques groupes de bombardiers lourds et moyens.

Pour ceux que ces chiffres intéressent, 775 avions furent ainsi engagés le 15 mars
1944, la plus forte concentration à coup sûr réalisée par les Alliés contre un obiectif aussi
limité dans l'espace. Six appareils seulement furent perdus, et pour midi, douze cents tonnes de bombes étaient tombées en trois heures et demie.

L'artillerie prit la suite aussitôt. Sept cent quarante-six pièces armées par les Américains du IIe Corps, les Français du C.E.F., et sourtout les Anglais et Néo-Zelandais,
declenchèrent brusquement à midi, sitôt le dernier avion disparu, un formidable tir de
concentration. Les calibres allaient du 37 au 240. Puis... les 144 pièces de 25 livres du
Corps néo-zélandais commencèrent un barrage mobile, avançant par bonds successifs à
150 mètres sur l'avant de l'infanterie, balayant Cassino d'une extremité à l'autre...

A l'abbaye, tout ce que avait résisté au bombardement du 15 février s'écroula, non
sous le poids des bombes, car, ce jour-là du moins, l'aviation alliée n'avait pas visé
Montecassino, mais sous le feu continuel des concentrations d'artillerie qui la réduisirent
progressivement en un amas de décombre». And in a note he adds: «D'après les évalua-
tions des officiers d'artillerie, il ne tomba pas moins de 300.000 obus sur Montecassino, la
plupart au cours des combats de mars; les restes, au cours de la préparations de l'offensive
de mai» (p. 133).

The monastery and Rocca Janula were defended by the 1st Battalion of the 3rd
Paratroopers Regiment and all the rest by the 1st Paratroopers Division entrenched between Cassino and Mt. Cairo. This division (I Fallschhirmjäger Division) was commanded
by Gen. R. Heidrich.

On March 15, according to Col. Böhmler, the defenders feared to be buried under a new bombardment of the abbey, which was supposed to facilitate the task of the attackers.

Instead, although they captured Rocca Janula, three sections of well placed machine guns blocked the advance of the 5th Indian Brigade towards the monastery.

«Le contre-attaque du 18 sur Rocca Janula fut lancée sans préparation d'artillerie».

What followed was a savage struggle: from the top of Monte Cassino the observers were able to follow it and: «s'achernaient sans résultats a déclancher l'artillerie... La crête de Rocca Janula fut bientôt une telle boucherie qu'Allemands et Néo-Zélandais se mirent d'accord pour une trêve de deux heures afin de reveler les morts et les blessés qui s'accumulaient sur le champ de bataille. Et l'on vit - spectacle extraordinaire - ces hommes, qui venaient de s'entretuer farouchement et s'apprêtaient à recommencer, s'aider mutuellement dans cette besogne humanitaire. Les Néo-Zélandais prêtèrent leurs brancards aux Allemands, distribuant aux blessés ennemis thé, chocolat ou cigarettes. Les parachutistes accueillirent les blessés dans leurs postes de secours, jusque dans l'abbaye, et le commandant du 1/4 laissa passer sans le moindre contrôle tous les blessés Gurkas qui descendaient de la côte 435... Aprés quoi le combat reprit» (p. 151).

«On monta pour le 19 un nouvel assaut qui devait être lancé sur le monastère à six heures du matin par les fantassins de l'Essex et par les Gurkhas, montant de Rocca Janula au-devant des charts américains et néo-zélandais venus de la région de l'Albaneta par une piste qui conduit au village de Caira. Mais, devançant ce proiet, des parachutistes du 4.e Régiment contrettaquèrent à travers le ravin qui s'étend au nord-est de l'abbaye, s'emparèrent de la cote et isolèrent les troupes alliées qui tenaient la colline du Bourreau de la cote 202. Les mines et la boue arrêtèrent les chars.

Toutes les attaques ultèrieures échouèrent de la même façon... Alexander, après longues hésitations en [de l'offensive] ordona l'arrêt le 23 mars... Avec quatorze bataillons, les Allemands avaient tenu tête a des forces alliées qui en comprenaient vingt-quatre. Dans le domaine de l'artillerie, la disproportion était plus écrasante encore, puisqu'on seulement 240 pièrces allemands contre plus de 700 aux Alliés. Ne parlons pas de l'aviation: la Luftwaffe en dix jours ne totalisa que 217 sorties, même pas le tiers de ce que les Alliés mirent en l'air dans la seule journée du 15. Pour les chars, la proportion était de l'ordre de 579 à 90 en faveur du Corps néo-zélandais... On avait, sans résultats, détruit une ville entière, enfoui sous les décombres les richesses accumulées depuis des siècles dans les murs d'une abbaye universallement célèbre. On ne avait pas gagné cent mètres de terrain, mais on avait justifié à l'avance cette phrase du critique militaire américain Hoffman Nickerson, que le "seul résultat de la plupart des bombardements est de destruire les choses pour la sauvegarde desquelles on est supposé se battre"» (p. 137).

In the May fighting the monastery was held by the 1st Battalion of the 4th Paratroopers Regiment. The operation of capturing m. 593 level, Albaneta and the monastery had been assigned to the Carpathian Hunters. After the attack of May 12 failed, the struggle resumed on the 18.

Böhmler (pp. 455-456 544-545) stresses the fact that the Poles were unable to take by assault neither Colle S. Angelo, nor Dosso «Fantasma». They occupied them only, after the withdrawal of the entire defensive line, forced the division of Heidrich to evacuate those positions. Of the company that had been in the focal point of Calvary, only an officer, a sergeant and a trooper survived.

On May 17, in fact, the English had arrived at Piumarola crossing the so long sought Casilina road, thus cutting communications and refurnishments of the Germans on Monte

Cassino. The French, meanwhile, were advancing through the mountains west of Monte Cassino.

«Et c'est ainsi que ce 18 mai 1944 à 10 h. 20, une patrouille du 12.e Lanciers vint hisser au sommet de décombres de l'abbaye de Montecassino» the Polish flag. Among the ruins and in the vicinities, seventy paratroopers with their captain, Beyer, were captured. Others were taken along thne mountain by the English. In the midst of the devasted and desolated plain, on the blighted mountain, on which only a few burned trees seemed to lift their horrible scarred trunks to the sky as in protest or imploration, the great abbey appeared in its real condition, a huge mass of rubble.

[18] This does not exclude the possibility of fighting among individuals or isolated groups.

BIBLIOGRAPHY

When the first edition of this volume appeared in 1947, the bibliography on the World War II period Monte Cassino involvement and its destruction, was almost nonexistent, since then several works have appeared which have, on the whole, confirmed the objective narrative of this work.

The first one to speak with competence and honesty on this subject was Gen. A. JUIN of the French army, who later wrote, «Pélerinage au Mont Cassin», in *Mercure de France,* 1947, pp. 1-11. Another voice from the opposite side was that of Gen. F. VON SENGER UND ETTERLIN, commander of the German forces in the Cassino sector, at the time of the destruction. After several articles, all his remembrances were gathered in the volume, *Combattere senza paura e senza speranza,* Milano, Longanesi, 1968. Gen. Anders, *Mémoires,* Paris, La jeune Parque, 1948, and Gen. M. CLARK, *Calculated Risk,* London, Harrap, 1951, to which may be added Gen. A. KESSERLING, *Memorie di Guerra,* ital. transl. by A. Zanchi, Milano, Garzanti, 1954, complete the testimony on the events by the commanders that operated in the Cassino zone.

The commander of the German paratroopers, who held the ruins of Monte Cassino to the bitter end, R. BÖHMLER, has left a precious testimony of the events in his, *Monte Cassino,* Darmstadt, Mitteler, 1956. J. SCHLEGEL has written about the evacuation, in which he had a large role, in several articles from: «Mein Wagnis in Monte Cassino», *Die Osterreiche Furche,* 1951, n. 45-49 to n. 50: «Monte Cassino, ein Ende und ein Anfang. Da Echo zu einem Tatsachenbericht».

Larger is the number of historians who have elaborated on these memoirs and military reports. The most reliable, except a few details, in J. MORDAL, *Cassino,* Paris, Amiot-Dumont, 1952. Completely unreliable, deplorable in fact, are: E. MAJDALANY, *La battaglia di Cassino,* Milan, Garzanti, 1958 and, A. Ricchezza, *La verità nella battaglia di Cassino e l'apporto del Corpo Italiano di Liberazione,* Torino, Pozzo, 1958.

L. A. ALECCI, *Incontro a Montecassino,* Roma, Albo, 1970, gathers the testimonies offered by veterans of all nations meeting at Monte Cassino. Most interesting the pages dedicated to German witnesses and that of the American M. Blumenson, who once again confirm our narrative. The volume includes also the more recent bibliography, which would be too long and rather superfluous here.

The most authoritative and documented statement on the events leading to the destruction has been written by H. BLOCH from Harvard, «The Bombardment of Monte Cassino. A New Appraisal», in *Benedictina,* 20 (1973), also available in separate off-prints.

The readers must also be made aware of the fact that many writers under the name of Monte Cassino confuse the mountain, the abbey which is on the mountain and even the town of Cassino, below the mountain.

About the vicissitudes of the material transported to Rome, cfr. E. RE, «L'Archivio di Montecassino a Roma», *L'Urbe,* 16 N.S. (1953), n. 6, 9-14.

The diary of the tragic days at the abbey, kept by E. GROSSETTI and don M. MATRANOLA, has been published with other documents by F. AVAGLIANO, *Il bombardamento di Montecassino,* Montecassino 1980, in Miscellanea Cassinese, n. 41.

IX.
THE NEW DAY

«*At cur sperare non liceat... fore ut... antiquissimum hoc Archicoenobium ad pristinum quam primum restituatur decus?*»*
(Pius PP. XII, Enc. *Fulgens Radiatur*)

1. THE DARK NIGHT.

The darkest hours are those that precede the dawn. And surely, one could not imagine a darker horizon than the one that met the eyes of the first people who hastened to Monte Cassino after the battle of May 18.

As soon as the fighting ceased in the vicinities, d. Ildefonso Rea, abbot of Cava, overcoming all sorts of obstacles, rushed to the abbey, accompanied by the then undersecretary for Public Education, Angelo Jervolino. A few days later, the Abbot of Cava left one of his monks there as a custodian. Only later, on July 3, a small group of Cassinese, two priests and a lay brother, were able to go there from Rome.

What squallor! This destruction was the last in order of time, but certainly the first for the intensity and extent of its violence. This time, the objective had been more important, the instruments of destruction more powerful and the will to carry it out more determined.

From the devasted plain, where all former lush vegetation had disappeared, to the torn up summit, the abbey offered a stark sight of its present condition.

In the place where the monumental, solemn cloisters had

---

* «But why it is not possible to hope that... this most ancient abbey be restored as soon as possible to its primitive splendor?»

been, one could now see vast and deep chasms, running down to the underlying wells. The monumental central stairway had disappeared. Above the nave of the church, covered by rubble over 13 feet deep in spots, one could barely see the huge truncated piers that had supported the dome. In fact, in that mass of ruins where everything was reduced to shapeless rubble and dusty debris, there were few things that could even still be clearly distinguished. The great central cloisters with the Loggia del Paradiso had completely disappeared; one could barely make out the perimetrical design. The great entrance stairway was still standing, and so were the two lateral chapels of the Crypt, those of the Cella, the chapels of the Holy Monks and of the Addolorata in the Torretta; the basement of the College and a few rooms here and there still remained, but all these were unsafe and called for immediate restoration.

Under those stones and the thick layer of dust, so many art treasures and so many memories lay buried. It was not merely the frightening crush of an artistic monument, it was, in fact, the break-up of a centuries old tradition whose continuity remained well-defined and in logical relation with the future.

The desolation that had descended all over the «Land of St. Benedict» in the wake of the terrible storm was no less. Churches and villages were destroyed, priests and entire populations deported with nothing except the clothes on their backs. On the sad and deserted landscape was not a drop of drinkable water, not a shady tree, not a blade of grass, only burned trunks that seemed to twist, as if in pain, and large pools of stagnating water which seemed to hide death under their brackish green.

As usual, human hyenas made the desolation and the difficulties worse. These, while the place remained unguarded before the monks came back, swooped through to rummage through the ruins and carry away all they could. Other devastations and depredations were the work of soldiers eager for booty and souvenirs. It was in this way that the marvelous choir of the basilica, whose higher stalls had survived the bombing, was lost, and in a similar manner all the silver, reliquaries, etc., disappeared. On the other hand, one must not forget the opposite behavior of the Polish soldiers under those circumstances; they not only refrained from any plunder but they even gave to the Holy Father a large Sunday collection of $ 1,000.00 for Monte Cassino.

It was a dark night indeed that received that first group of monks back. Nevertheless, the divine psalmody, silenced by the first onslaught of destructive fury, began once again to mount to heaven from the sacred summit. Taking shelter as well as they could in the same basement that had saved them from the bombardment, they worked among dangers and difficulties. In spite of the malaria which attacked all of them, leaving in some painful and lasting effects, the monks rapidly increased in number and resumed their life in work and prayer. While English authorities with great generosity alleviated the total lack of even the barest necessities, the Italian, with noble enthusiasm, offered needed help in clearing the rubble and providing guards to save what was left. Italian and Polish soldiers, who established on the slopes of Calvario a cemetery for their fallen comrades, provided a temporary access road, helped the monks with the water supply and facilitated communications with their trucks.

Meanwhile, when it became impossible to assemble the whole monastic community in the vicinities of Cassino, the larger part gathered in the abbey of Farfa, welcomed with love by the brothers there; only a few remained in Rome to take care of the complex paper work necessary under such abnormal conditions. The Abbot with the personnel of the Curia, who could not reside at Monte Cassino because access there was so difficult, were given hospitality by the Archpriest d. Gennaro Iucci of S. Elia Fiume Rapido; meanwhile the nearby sanctuary of Casalucense was being rapidly restored to allow accomodations for about twenty monks.

Thus, though the horizon was still dark and the future uncertain, at least some of the sons of St. Benedict had returned to watch over the house and the paternal inheritance, trying to revive the weak spark, to bring back light in the shadows of death.

2. FLASHES OF LIGHT IN THE SHADOWS.

Some gleams of light indeed began to appear in the darkness. First of all, the venerable tomb of St. Benedict, to the wonder of his anxious children, appeared to be intact. In spite of the enormous weight of the piled up rubble from the dome and the supporting piers, it had remained, prodigiously intact.

The main altar standing above, although heavily damaged, reappeared to the light with its artistic features preserved, and in the cell below it, where the copper plates of d'Arpino with the representations of the two remains were located, even the silver lamp was in its place.

Even more remarkable, an artillery grenade had lodged itself in one of the steps located right on the vault of the tomb without causing any damage.

Thus among such great ruins, only that tomb had survived unharmed, a testimony, together with the spiritual and cultural patrimony safe in Rome, of the continuity of the tradition, a lasting guarantee of its eternal life.

The love of his children soon built a small chapel above the tomb and the Host of peace was again offered over that miraculous grave. Soon pilgrims began to come again, the very first from the devastated «Land of St. Benedict» on March 21.

Interest, however, in the future of Monte Cassino had not died down. The Holy Father, who had tried everything to avoid «such a grievous injury to our holy religion, to the arts and to human civilization itself» [1], did not forsake Monte Cassino, and its return to its former splendor continued to be his most ardent desire.

At the same time, a committee under the chairmanship of the Abbot of Monte Cassino was set up by the minister for Public Works, Meuccio Ruini, «to study a general plan for the reconstruction of the abbey of Monte Cassino and to determine the directives to follow in its realization».

Thus the Italian government, because of the personal concern of the minister himself and of His Excellency Giuseppe

Spataro, bound itself to rebuild Monte Cassino. And with a significant gesture, it was decided to make Monte Cassino, a symbol of Italian life, the first step in the great task of national reconstruction.

On March 15, 1945, the anniversary of the destruction, the first stone for its reconstruction was laid. Eight ministers, several undersecretaries, ambassadors, and other authorities were present, including His Excellency Costantini, president of the Pontifical Commission for Sacred Art, as the representative of the Holy See.

On that day on which at Monte Cassino the anniversary of Pope St. Zachary, one of the strongest promoters of the first reconstruction, was commemorated, «the laying of the first stone was performed with a ceremony of austere simplicity». It was necessary to fall on one's knees like St. Benedict. After the benediction and the ritual digging of spades into the ground performed by the government representatives, the octogenerian Abbot, over the ruins of his fifty years labor, spoke the words of truth and evangelical wisdom: «even the destruction of the abbey is good because God willed it that way. Let us not attempt to understand the mysteries of Divine Providence. «These were the most moving and reassuring moments of that auspicious day [2].

On that first stone, as a preliminary to the great reconstruction, a small structure was built. This modest and temporary residence, a few yards from the wall of the monastery, where once the seminary of St. Joseph had stood, allowed the monks to get out of the unhealthy, dusty quarters beneath the ruins, which together with the malaria had caused so much hardship. Their new house, though quite inadequate, permitted them to keep an eye on the most important materials that surfaced during the removal of the rubble.

This was the first and necessary task. At the start, it was conducted with poor and rudimentary equipment, then with help from the Italian government, more systematically and rationally. The access road was also fixed as well as possible.

While, however, the walls of the small house were being raised, giving vent to new hope, Monte Cassino was again faced with a new trial. The Abbot, who had ruled for thirty-six years and who, during those painful days, was the symbol of unity and continuity with the future, died unexpectedly. With the death of d. Gregorio Diamare, as in the final act of great tragedy, an epoch definitively closed in the history of Monte Cassino.

One of the early memories of his long life at the abbey had been the millenary of the abbot St. Betharius in 1884. Just arrived from his native Naples and soon after putting on his new habit, he took part in the sacred rites in the humble function of thurifer. One wonders if there was then some obscure presentiment in the mind or some unusual trembling in the young monk, who was not yet twenty? Perhaps at that time the eyes of the unvanquished martyr cut down by Saracen swords were posed on him, the future heir of similar cares and sorrows. We do not know. It is a fact, however, that abbot Diamare was particularly thoughtful, during his late years, to increase the worship and to renew the memory of his glorious predecessor of the ninth century. Indeed, he resembled St. Bertharius more than any of his 186 predecessors, both for his emphasis during his governance on consolidating and developing the inheritance of St. Benedict and for the tragic catastrophe of the monastery and his death on the field of battle among all those losses and ruins.

We have already seen his long ranging activities during his long years of rule, surpassed only by abbot Aligernus, and how, especially during the terrible days of the desolation, while around him every form of civil behaviour was crumbling, while surrounded by miseries among the sick and the dying, he stood firm as a fearless bulwark and as the only source of Hope, divine and human, for his people.

After the storm which had driven him away passed, saddened but not beaten, trusting as always in God alone, he returned among his people, suffering and dying from privations and epidemics to his destroyed abbey to resume his work and to put the pieces together again.

In spite of the fact that he arrived in Rome with just the

clothes on his back, and notwithstanding the strained conditions at the abbey, he did not abandon his works of charity. Besides bringing help to thousands of refugees by instituting a secretariat in Rome to assist them, he shared with the poor large sums of money and other help placed at his disposal by the generosity of many people. With this help, and especially that of religious institutions, he managed to partially provide holy vessels and clothes to the sixty odd churches in his jurisdiction that had been damaged or destroyed in the fighting.

All his thoughts were concentrated now on the work of reconstruction which he wanted to be complete and, therefore, had to be gradual and timely in harmony with the demands of the centuries old tradition and, at the same time, answering the needs of the modern age. He was also anxious to see the publication of this volume; he desired this not only because in the new collection of the abbey's memories he saw the means to encourage and strengthen the resolve of his tired and scattered monks, but he also wanted to stimulate to the work of reconstruction all people of good will.

His days, however, were getting close to the end. He was in Rome on monastic business, but on the eve of the Assumption, he decided to return at all costs to Cassino to take part in the solemnities in honor of the Holy Virgin, whose celebrations were being resumed as a symbol of hope among all those ruins. There among those unhealthy stagnating waters, on the very night of August 15, he was stricken with the disease that was causing so many deaths in the area. At first, he seemed to have weathered it and was already planning to take part in the meetings of the ministerial commission in Rome, when he was stricken again. This time, his heart, weakened by so many sufferings and privations, did not resist. He fell asleep in the Lord, suddenly and peacefully, on the evening of Sept. 6, in his temporary quarters at S. Elia Fiume Rapido.

In that same village, which still showed clearly the deep scars left by the war, in the stark simplicity of a small parish church also damaged in the fighting, on Sept. 10, the funeral was held, solemn in spite of the exceptional difficulties of the times and the place. Rather than the golden pomp of the basilica and the majestic grandiosity of the Cassinese cloisters, this simple place appeared fitting for one who had died on the field of battle, a victim of the great storm.

On the afternoon of that same day, the remains were taken in sad but triumphal cortège to Monte Cassino, so that within those battered walls that were witness to his hard-working and tormented days, they would rest in peace with his fathers waiting for the glorious resurrection [3].

3. THE DAWN.

After declining for a long time the tremendous burden of the succession, d. Ildefonso Rea acceded finally to the wishes of the Holy See, which had accepted his nomination by the Cassinese community (Nov. 21, 1945).

On the day sacred to the Immaculate Virgin and as once St. Benedict had done on the ancient pagan shrine, his 188th successor boldly raised the cross on the summit, where among the shadows of death, rays of hope were beginning to appear. With this sign of victory, he confidently began his task of knitting together traditions that were over a thousand years old, returning to the house where he had first professed his vocation but which he had to leave in 1929 when called to assume the governance of the great abbey of Cava.

As his first official act, he established his residence at Casalucense, gathering there a small community, since the restoration works of that small monastery, though not completed yet, were well along. It was thus possible to restore within the inheritance of St. Benedict the full observance of the Rule. On the major holidays, the smaller community joined the group at Monte Cassino to celebrate the liturgy in a more dignified way over the tomb of their common father.

Abbot Rea, who succeeded Abbot Diamare also as president

of the ministerial committee, on Jan. 16, 1946, set forth his ideas about the ultimate goal of the reconstruction, which would be synthetized in the brief slogan: «Where it was, as it was».

The formula, which, based on a pre-existing architectonic plan, constituted neither an imitation nor a forgery, appeared to be a happy synthesis of a program aiming at preserving the monumental character, a featurè not easily changeable, and of maintaining that plan from which, in the words of Urban V, «constructionis aliorum monasteriorum forma processit» *, while tying together again the thread so violently cut. The plan met, therefore, with almost unanimous approval, which was also, above all, an act of faith.

The removal work, meanwhile, received a fresh impulse. The Allied Military Command placed at the disposal of the Abbot 100 German war prisoners who, provided with the necessary equipment, from March 1st to Sept. 15, freed from the rubble the central cloister and the area where were located the quarters of the monks, the Archives, and the library. At the same time the Italian Corps of Engineers rebuilt the great central well.

Meanwhile, the small temporary building of St. Joseph was completed, and on March 19, 1946, it was officially turned over to the Abbot in the presence of the minister of public works, Leone Cattani, high officers of the same ministry, and various illustrious guests. The Abbot had consecrated the altar in the chapel that very morning.

On July 11, the day that commemorates the efficacy of the protection of St. Benedict, the reassembling of the community at Monte Cassino finally became a reality.

In the morning, the Abbot celebrated the Pontifical Mass on the tomb of the Father, remarking that the children were gathering there on that day not, as in the preceding Feast in March, to disperse afterwards, but to remain there permanently.

Towards the evening, the traditional eucharistic procession from the «Torretta» to the Saint's tomb did not stop at the usual

---

* «the building model of all other monasteries originated».

place but continued to the new building dedicated to St. Joseph. Thus the first one to take possession of it was the Lord. Before his arrival no one was allowed to live there; in fact, no living quarters had as yet been prepared there. That very evening, however, taking with them the barest household necessities, the monks moved in.

During the first ten days of August the monks who had remained at Farfa to complete the necessary work at that college also arrived. Thus the reunion of the community was almost complete. This event, fundamental in the life of the abbey, was once again repeated, this time, in fact, sooner than on the previous occasions.

Meanwhile, the work proceeded to restore electric power and running water, and with the help of generous benefactors, the new house was properly furnished.

In the old house, after the aide by the Allied Command was terminated, the removal work was continued by the Italian Corps of Engineers. At the beginning of December, the recovery of the remains of the civilians buried under the ruins was completed. The excavations produced the entire skulls of only 148 people, of which only twenty could be identified. There is no doubt that there were other victims besides those who died in their attempt to escape from the mountain, but their remains were not found.

Some of the corpses were found in pitiful poses: a «Carabiniere» * was trying to make an opening for himself, attempting desperately to move the stones with his hands, and an old man was shielding a child with his own body. An entire family had been buried alive in a small room; only the father had been outside. After the first wave had passed, the wretched man had rushed to help his own, who were begging him with heart-rending cries. While he worked feverishly, however, a second wave buried him also. He was able to free himself once again and hurry to bring help, but new explosions made vain all his efforts, while the voices of his beloved ones gradually faded into eternal silence. All

---

* Italian army police.

the bodies were buried in the cemetery of Cassino.

Work then was started to free the church from the rubble. The damaged floor, the marble footing of the piers and the wall coverings, which reached on the average only twelve feet in height, were brought back to light. It was possible to recover, although it was badly damaged, the magnificient tabernacle of the Chapel of the Holy Sacrament; on the altar an unexploded bomb was found.

It is interesting to note that no relics of the Saints in the basilica were lost; even the urn of SS. Constantine and Simplicius, the first successor of St. Benedict, was found intact, although it was blown out of the Chapel of St. Gregory, in which it was kept, by the bombardment. Truly «custodivit Dominus omnia ossa eorum! Unum ex his non *est contritum*» *.

Another form of activity was resumed with the new academic year: the diocesan seminary was reopened at Casalucense for the gymnasium courses and at Monte Cassino for the first year of philosophy.

The real work of reconstruction began on April 1st, 1949, and was continued without pause through the interest of succeeding ministers like Tupini, Aldisio and Merlin, and various ministerial offices. Starting in 1947, some structures, such as the *Torretta,* the great refectory and the presbytery of the church had already been almost entirely rebuilt.

As soon as the decision was made to rebuild the abbey «where it was and how it was», the abbot gathered carefully «a wide documentation on the buildings destroyed, in order that the reconstruction would be as faithful as possible». Of fundamental help in this project proved to be the fact that, a few years before the destruction, d. Angelo Pantoni, an architect by profession, had had to make a planimetric and altimetric survey of the whole monastic complex upon request by the Italian authorities.

In fact, all the offices of the abbey, since the suppression

---

* «The Lord has protected all their bones, not a single one has been reduced into ashes» (Psalm 33).

decree of 1868, were listed as property of the state, entrusted to the custody of the monks. From the same epoch therefore, the maintenance of the buildings was assumed by the ministry of Public Works. To this one must add also the provisions now made by the state for the support of cathedral churches, seminaries, archives, and state libraries. The funds for the reconstruction, therefore, the cost of which, considering the size of the enterprise, was not excessive, came out of the budget of the public works ministry, which entrusted the Abbot of Monte Cassino with the drawing of the projects and the granting of contracts for the execution of the work. The work was divided into well-defined phases according to the availability of money.

The overall direction of the work was entrusted to d. Angelo Pantoni, who had already prepared various preliminary designs. The drafting of the plans for the various sections together with necessary technical and administrative assistance was commissioned to the architect Giuseppe Breccia-Fratadocchi. The building contractor, from the very beginning, was the firm of Gravaldi, which had already done work at Monte Cassino before the destruction. The work employed about 400 people, almost all from the area, and many craftsmen specialized in working with marble, stone, iron, wood, etc.

In carrying out the task great care was given in reproducing faithfully, on the base of the few surviving elements, what were the most characteristic architectonic features. Thus an original arch, pier, a column, or decorative fragment were incorporated in every cloister, as witnesses of the fidelity of the reconstruction [4]. A similar task was given to d. Francesco Vignanelli, a sculptor, for the decoration of the basilica in varicolored marbles. The monk sculptor worked closely with the experts of the Henraux Co., which did all the work. The owners of the company, the brothers Cidonio, donated the decoration of an entire chapel. The Gravaldi firm did the same, while the Cassa per il Mezzogiorno made some contributions for other chapels.

In carrying to the end this reconstruction, which it had pledged since 1945, and in reasserting its commitment with many solemn declarations, the Italian government showed its great care for the restoration not only of the material but even more of the moral patrimony of the nation.

On a scale naturally more limited, the interest of loyal friends has remained constantly alive, acting directly or through committees, like the ones which collected in the large cities as well as small villages the offering that the whole of Italy pledged for this purpose on Dec. 21, 1947. They also kept alive the memory and the problems of Monte Cassino [5].

To this universal concern, the Holy Father wished to add his august and commanding voice with the Encyclic «*Fulgens Radiatur*» addressed to the whole Catholic World in commemoration of the fourteenth centenary of the death of St. Benedict. Proclaiming *in medio Ecclesiae* the praise of the great patriarch of Western Christendom, he appealed for the prompt restoration of the most fitting monument to the Saint: his destroyed house [6].

4. THE DAY.

When the first part of the works was completed, the Cassinese returned to their house. They were led by the abbot, who carried with his own hands the same cross that his predecessor had borne among the deaths and the ruins in Feb. 1944.

The work of reconstruction proceeded with alacrity in spite of the unavoidable difficulties. With help from the Cassa per il Mezzogiorno it was possible to restore the ancient choir, to complete the decoration of the Crypt and of the artistic wardrobes of the sacristy, to restore the two sixteenth century tombs in the presbytery and also to complete the new marble seat of the Abbot, although still missing was the pictorial decorations which lent such suggestive atmosphere to the basilica.

With subsidies from the Fund for Catholic Worship, the statues of the Benefactors in the court in front of the church were restored and put back in place together with a marble inscription recalling the course of the history of the church down to the last consecration by Pope Paul VI.

In the «Torretta», to the frescoes of A. Pegrassi, which decorate the lower floor, Luigi Filocamo added those of the main floor in the main chapel, which evoke episodes in the lives of St. Benedict and St. Scholastica. More recently, the magic brush of maestro Pietro Annigoni, assisted by his disciples, has been restoring the pictorial decoration of the basilica.

The archives and the library were arranged in the new shelves provided respectively by the ministry of the Interior and that of Public Education. The generosity of the latter has allowed the library to make up, in part, for losses with contributions coming also from the Accademia dei Lincei and from the Dean of Winchester, the Rev. E. G. Selwin. The Accademia asked for donations of books from universities and academies all over the world while dean Selwin promoted similar contributions from the Anglican Church. The bookseller Blackwell from Oxford sponsored a similar drive among his colleagues.

Among the art works, which, alas have only come in small quantity to take the places of the old ones, we want to remember the bronze doors designed by Canonica, with the casting arranged by the president of the Italian Republic, Luigi Einaudi; the Way of the Cross donated by the same Canonica; the group of St. Benedict dying in the arms of his monks, work of the sculptor Selva, a gift from the German chancellor, Conrad Adenauer; the silver front of the main altar, Selva's last work made possible by contributions by the Cassa per il Mezzogiorno; the new statues of St. Benedict and St. Scholastica in the Crypt, cast on models designed by d. Francesco Vignanelli through the generosity of Mr. Ettore Moretti; the group of St. Martin by the same Vignanelli, who also worked out the models for various mosaic compositions; the group of the Pietà, an uncompleted work of Selva; and many paintings purchased or received as gifts from friends.

The mountain, completely ravaged by the enormous amount of explosives rained on it, was completely restored and given back its green cover by the ministry of agriculture and forests, while the «land of St. Benedict» once again was dotted with its hundred white churches and ecclesiastical buildings. Life at the abbey became normal again, and so in 1957 it was possible to reopen the college for lay students next to the Diocesan Seminary.

A memorable date of this same period was marked by the deposition of the Holy remains of St. Benedict and St. Scholastica in their original site of rest under the main altar. The precious urn of silver and bronze was placed there on December 1, 1955, in the presence of numerous bishops and abbots.

Another date to remember is May 24-25, 1961, when the remains of St. Gregory VII paused at the tomb of St. Benedict on their triumphal journey to Rome.

To crown the work of reconstruction, the Holy Father John XXIII raised to the episcopal dignity, with the title of Corone, the man who gave life and strong direction to the project, Abbot d. Ildefonso Rea. He was solemnly consecrated on March 12, 1963, by the Card. Carlo Confalonieri, secretary to the Holy Consistorial Congregation [7].

At the start of the difficult task, the Abbot himself, in the appeal he had read over the radio on Feb. 15, 1946, had hoped that the abbey would rise again «as an expiatory monument of the devastating violence of war, a temple of peace, from which St. Bendict once again would launch his appeal, his motto for future generations: Peace...!»

A monument to peace, love and brotherhood among all men». And which, after being «an altar of sacrifice», would become the *ara pacis novae*, «the altar of the new peace».

The invitation was translated into reality by the movement of the «Lamp of Brotherhood», inspired by the apostolic soul of the late mons. Ferdinando Baldelli. Around the tomb of St. Benedict, fourteen lamps keep the vigil, brought there by seven mothers and seven widows of war victims of the once hostile countries. It was also decided that every year a pilgrimage of war veterans and authorities would gather there to aliment with a symbolic offer of oil the flame of concord [8].

Another movement under the patronage of St. Benedict was

that of agrarian renewal. With the letter *Sanctum Benedictum Abbatem,* John XXIII on July 12, 1961, proclaimed the Holy Patriarch patron Saint of the Agencies for Land Reform, of the Committees for Land Reclamation, and of all Italian farmers. This proclamation was solemnly celebrated on May 21, 1964, in the presence of the minister of agriculture, the Hon. Ferrari-Aggradi, other members of parliament, and authorities.

But the new day was soon to be blessed by a new and even brighter light.

5. THE GLORIFICATION OF ST. BENEDICT AND THE CONSECRATION OF HIS BASILICA.

Monte Cassino was still a pile of rubble, but the figure of its founder, as once before after the first destruction, was drawing universal attention, radiating with new splendor.

The commemoration of the fourteenth centenary of his death appeared to bring St. Benedict back not only among the ruins of his house but also into the midst of the material as well as the moral ruins of Europe to encourage and inspire new hope for the future. Although his mind always longed to remain fixed in the contemplation of the eternal truths, he had however, set a vigorous example on how to act among the ruins of the ancient world, how to deal with the darkness of a frightening present, and how to nurture the hopes of a hidden and uncertain future.

Drawn by this example, many were moved to renew his memory and invoke his patronage on those nations that once were religiously formed or strengthened by his teaching. He was invoked as patron of a Europe painfully rising from her ruins with a greater awareness of its unity.

The difficulties of mutual understanding, then still existing among European countries, did not allow the echo of similar requests to reach everywhere so that it would produce that unanimity which alone would have persuaded the Apostolic See to accept them.

The man who was seated on the chair of Peter during those difficult years, Pius XII, was sensitive and alert in accepting and evaluating the signs of the times, and he did not remain deaf. Soon after raising, as he alone knew how, a great hymn of glory to St. Benedict in the Encyclic *Fulgens Radiatur,* in the solemn reunion held at St. Paul's in Rome, he did not hesitate to declare «Europae pater S. Benedictus est». And a few years later, in the message that he sent to Norcia for the solemn celebrations of August 1958, he confirmed the declaration at St. Paul's: «We must find it a pleasant duty to point to the sweet figure of the great Patriarch, the Father of Christian Europe... We ask the Lord, under the auspices of St. Benedict, that the divine grace which guided the Saint in the prayer and the action of restoring peace and unity in Europe may assist those who have heavy responsibilities, in order that their concerted efforts may be crowned by success, thereby tying all the people of Europe in a bond of true brotherhood».

This was a clear reference to the movement for European unity which was, with the support of distinguished Catholic statesmen, gaining some ground in spite of the unavoidable conflicts. Among those who strongly shared this view with Pius XII was the man who was going to succeed him.

Since his youth, d. Angelo Roncalli had learned to love St. Benedict and Monte Cassino through his devotion to the study of history. When he came to give a brief retreat to the students of the college, he summarized his impressions while writing to a friend: «O quam bonum est nos hic esse» *.

When he returned on a pilgrimage to the tomb of St. Benedict on the 13-14 of January 1955, card. Roncalli was deeply affected by the enormity of the catastrophe which had taken place and by the awareness of the new life which again seemed to spring up from the rediscovered remains of that Patriarch of whom he, as Patriarch of Venice, styled himself «humilis cliens».

As soon as he returned to his See, he wrote to the Abbot: «in

---

* «Oh, how good is for me to be here!»

the restored monastery, everything appeared to me worthy of admiration, and I experienced spiritual emotions quite unexpected
to the point that I am convinced that the direct intervention of the
Father and master of monastic life in allowing the destruction to
make the reconstruction more splendid is truly a prodigious
event».

When he was elected Pope John XXIII a few years later,
among the first wish and design that he formed was that of placing the apostolic seal to the reconstruction by consecrating the
resurrected basilica.

The execution of the plan, following the example of his
predecessors, was subjected, however, to various delays. The
leading cause for these was the need to prepare for such an event.
It was the Pope's desire that this should have a most solemn
character; in fact, he came to consider it as a manifestation of
Vatican II, both to offer a worthy homage to St. Benedict and
also to give, in modern times, a memorable recognition of the
mission carried out by the monastic movement in the life of the
Church.

The poor health of the pontiff contributed to the delay, but
until the last days, he would not let this change his mind. Among
his annotations, one was found that read: «I wanted so much to
go to Monte Cassino, and who knows?».

The exclamation was caused by the events which had brought
delays and limitations to the program. Even after he was unable
to keep the date, marked on his personal appointment book for
May 23, he kept his interest in the Cassinese journey, on the regal
gifts to be offered to St. Benedict, and on the Bull that had to
commemorate the consecration, giving no thought to the state of
his health. He was ready to remain, even if he was ill, in a monk's
cell under the protection of St. Benedict! Then he would, undoubtedly, fulfill also his other vow, the one he expressed while
he was still a cardinal: «Without any arguments St. Benedict
deserves it: Protector of Europe and western civilization».

The designs of Providence, however, were different. Pius
XII had strongly desired the resurrection of Monte Cassino but he

did not live long enough to see it accomplished. John XXIII
wanted to consecrate its basilica, and besides (it is not a secret
even if his wish remained unfullfilled) he wanted to make of
Monte Cassino a place of rest from the demands of his pontificate [9].

It fell, however, to the man who followed in the path of both
to boldly develop the plan and perform the consecration and to
issue the proclamation.

In the *Osservatore Romano* of October 15, 1964, one could
read:

«THE HOLY FATHER AT MONTE CASSINO: On the morning of
Saturday Oct. 24, the Holy Father Paul VI will travel to Monte
Cassino to consecrate the rebuilt Church of that abbey and to
proclaim St. Benedict the Protector of Europe».

For a few months the movement to proclaim St. Benedict the
patron of Europe had gained new life and, to the old requests,
many other authoritative petitions were being added; this led Paul
VI to grant the request of such a large and popular appeal, which
political conditions also seemed to favor.

In the audience of October 17, 1964, for the participants to
the General Assembly of the Townships and Local Communities
of Europe, the Supreme Pontiff was able to declare, «Is your
presence in such large number at this gathering not, in fact,
another sign of the vitality of this new Europe which is seeking
herself and which knows well that the future demands its
unity?...»

You know that the Catholic Church has always been in-
terested in this capital problem. Pope Pius XII, of revered
memory, often spoke in favor of the unification of Europe. In
1947, on the occurrence of the fourteenth centenary of St.
Benedict, and again in 1958, our Predecessor presented the
founder of the Benedictine Order as the Father of Europe and
asked for his help so that the Lord would come to the assistance
of all those on whom heavy responsibilities lay, so that they could
see happy results in their common efforts to unite the people of
Europe in bonds of true brotherhood (*Oss. Romano,* August 29,

1958). John XXIII, gentlemen, was of the same opinion. As for us, we intend to renew this patronage at the end of this month, when we shall consecrate the basilica of the monastery of Monte Cassino, devasted during the last World War.

You should see in this act the Church taking a firm position in this problem. The Church does this in a manner which is fitting to her, which stems from a spiritual point of view and with the firm desire to respect the temporal domain which is the province of the citizens of the various countries, of the governments and the several institutions, born from the desire to «make Europe one». This attitude of respect does not come from a lack of interest in the problems of Europe. Quite recently, we gave an audience to the members of the Democratic-Christian group in the European Parliament, and we renewed to them our encouragement and our prayers for the realization of a project, indeed quite complex, but the need of which is vital for the Europe of tomorrow, and, perhaps, the world».

One commentator declared: «Solemn words that reveal the seriousness of the aim that the Holy Father proposed in willing that the Father of Europe would be recognized and implored as its Patron».

On the day after the first announcement of the journey to Monte Cassino, the *Osservatore Romano* had further added, «The Holy Father, desiring not to provoke disturbances in the flow of traffic and to avoid excessive duties to the forces of public order, will travel to Monte Cassino by helicopter». The departure from the Vatican, probably from the court of St. Damasus, would probably take place at 8:00 A.M. of October 24, and the return at about 1:00 P.M.

Meanwhile, the preparations which had been under way for a few days, within the limits that discretion and secrecy imposed, assumed a feverish pace to utilize as much as possible the very short time available. On the afternoon of October 23, everything seemed to be ready for the beginning of the celebrations.

The responsible ecclesiastical authorities had, in fact, disposed that the first two parts of the solemn rite of consecration would take place that evening and had chosen as principal celebrant His Eminence the Benedictine Cardinal Anselmo Albareda, while, on the following day, the third, essential, and conclusive part had been reserved for the Holy Father.

Together with the main altar, all the other altars of the main church were to be consecrated, except that of SS. Sacrament (already consecrated by the Abbot in 1956) and the three in the Crypt: altogether 12. The bishops for those ceremonies were chosen on the basis of the ancient ties of their dioceses with Monte Cassino, with an eye at having all continents represented as well as membership in the Benedictine order.

The bishops, who began to arrive on the 23rd. were joined in the late afternoon by the cardinals Tisserant, Dean of the Sacred College, Aloisi Masella, Camerlengo of the Church and a native of the nearby city of Pontecorvo; Cicognani, Secretary of State; Giobbe, Datary of His Holiness; Antoniutti, Prefect of the Holy Congregation for Religious; and Albareda, a Benedictine with long ties of friendship to the abbey.

After the preliminary office of the Vigil of all Saints whose relics were to be deposed in the altars was conducted in the Chapter, at 6:00 P.M., the first two parts of the solemn rite were initiated.

Unfortunately, adverse weather conditions, which had begun to appear during the night and which continued into the morning, forced the cancellation of the helicopter flight for His Holiness; many other people feared to leave for the same reason.

In spite of the bad weather, however, from the very early hours of the morning the road leading to the monastery was invaded by cars and buses which were coming up the mountain; the cloisters began to fill with the faithful who wanted to make sure that they would be able to see the Pope.

The cardinals who had arrived the preceding evening were joined by the four Cardinals Urbani, Patriarch of Venice; Castaldo, Archbishop of Naples; Cento, Major Penitentiary; and Heard. Card. Wyszynski, Primate of Poland, who had announced his participation, was unable to come at the last moment but sent an enthusiastic message. Other members of the sacred College, equally desirous to attend, were prevented by other obligations.

There was a very large number, over two hundred, of bishops, superiors general of religious orders, Benedictine abbots from many and far away centers of the order, pastors of the diocese with members of their congregations as well as nuns, officials of the provincial and town government, reporters, institutes, and faithful from all walks of life. The bishops and the major authorities were seated in the basilica; the people crowded into the cloisters and under the shelter of the porches.

Soon it was announced that His Holiness had left by car from the Vatican at 7:00 A.M. and was on his way on the highway of the Sun. He travelled privately with a motorcycle escort; the trip was uneventful, but the Pope was warmly acclaimed by the faithful who waited here and there for him, and he, in turn, lovingly blessed them. Near the gate of the monastery, a great crowd gave him the first warm welcome, and he answered with fatherly benevolence. As the Holy Father stepped out of the car, he received the filial and joyous welcome from His Eminence the Abbot of Monte Cassino and all the officials.

At his appearance in the basilica, there was a strong applause and an eruption of festive acclamations from a crowd that had been waiting for that moment patiently for hours, in spite of the inclement weather. At the entrance, His Eminence Card. Tisserant, who was there waiting for him with the other cardinals, offered him the aspergillum with which he blessed all present, while the choir with a mighty voice sang the *Tu es Petrus,* intercalating the Psalm *Laetatus sum.*

The Holy Father sat on the throne and after accepting the initial homage proferred by the Father Abbot, began immediately the most essential rite for the consecration of the church. While the other bishop consecrators approached the piers that each had respectively to anoint, the Holy Father with his following went to anoint and incense the cross of the pier next to the chapel of the Pietà, then he stepped down to anoint the two jambs of the central door, and finally he walked along the entire nave and anointed the pier next to the chapel of the Assumption. At the same time, the bishop consecrators mounted, in concerted unison, the predisposed ladders and anointed the crosses of the other piers.

The *Schola* accompanied the functions with antiphonies and psalms and with the hymn *Urbs Jerusalem beata,* which in its beautiful original form and sweet melody proved to be a superlative lyrical comment on the suggestive ceremony.

Thereupon, the Supreme Pontiff moved on to the consecration of the main altar, anointing it with the chrism and blessing the grains of incense which were burned on it, while the *Schola* and the voices of all present sung the *Veni Creator Spiritus.* At the same time the bishops performed the same rite on the other altars.

The ceremony of consecration thus concluded, the Pope took off the cope and put on the chasuble to prepare himself for the Mass; at the same time, the altar was covered with a precious linen cloth and decorated with many flowers.

At the recited Mass, the Pope was assisted by his secret Almoner, His Eminence Mons. Venini, and by his Sacrist, His Eminence Mons. Van Lierde. The timbre of his voice and his calm and measured rhythm guided the recitation in which all present participated.

At the conclusion of the Holy Sacrifice, after the Holy Father returned to his throne, four monks took positions in front of the main altar and began the appropriate *acclamations,* of which the children's choir sang the various invocations and the audience answered with the *Tu illum adiuva.*

When the singing ended, the Supreme Pontiff read from the throne his admirable speech, which was not a passing, occasional panegyric, but an authoritative, paternal program. The concluding announcement that St. Benedict was declared heavenly Patron and Protector of Europe, was greeted by the whole assembly with a vigorous and enthusiastic applause.

The Holy Father then received from the Chancellor of Pontifical Briefs, His Eminence Mons. Camagni, the «Brief», that is, the solemn document that confirmed his will and the act with which Paul VI had proceeded to the declaration. Drafted in elegant Latin, the text of the document was written in the traditional calligraphic style on a parchment which was adorned at the edges with four very fine miniatures.

The Pope placed the documents in the hands of the Most Reverend Abbot Primate, d. Benno Gut, who immediately proceeded with the reading. The conclusion of this document also received the warm applause of all present. When the Abbot Primate came to the foot of the throne to thank the Pope in the name of the whole order, he was warmly embraced by him. The gesture was renewed when the Abbot of Monte Cassino expressed to him the gratitude of the community. The two embraces by Pope Paul were followed by the applause of all.

The Pope then intoned the *Te Deum,* which was sung with great joy by the *Schola* and the crowd.

To the glory of St. Benedict the Pope also wished to add a gesture of Christian charity: the offer of six lamps, the magnificent work of the sculptor Enrico Manfrini, destined to the town cemetery of Cassino and to the five war cemeteries of the area. He had ordered them himself and had the name of the donor and the date engraved on the bases. On the shaft each had four figures of angels in bas-relief, on the four panels that covered the lamps, the symbols of the Evangelists, and on the top, the pyramidal volutes of a flame.

Approaching the steps of the main altar, on which the lamps had been lined up, Paul VI blessed them and then lit them for the first time.

After he returned to the throne, the Pope had the mayor of Cassino, Sig. Gargano, summoned and handed him a small case which contained three commemorative medals of his pontificate as a gift to the city. The mayor, quite moved, thanked the pontiff for the beautiful and unexpected gift. When the Pope, accompanied by the Cardinals and the Abbot, started to step down from the throne, all the faithful present crowded around him to kiss his ring.

He expressed, meanwhile, the desire to go down into the

oratory of St. John, beneath the main altar, for a brief prayer. While the cardinals waited outside, the pope entered the small chapel with the Abbot and stopped in prayer next to the grating leading to the underground area of the tomb of St Benedict. He came up to the nave again, and through the efforts of many who opened a passage for him through the crowd, he entered the monastery followed by the abbots, the monastic community, the pastors of the diocese, the nuns, and many faithful.

After a brief rest, he graciously granted a special audience in the small throne room of his private apartment to the monastic community alone.

His Eminence the Abbot, with great emotion, expressed to him the feelings of gratitude and respect in his and in the name of the entire Cassinese family and begged him to accept a few modest gifts: a gold medal for the «Supporters of the Reconstruction of the Abbey», a plate with a bas-relief of the Glorification of St. Benedict, a relic of the Saint in an artistic reliquary, a collection of the volumes published in those years by the monks of Monte Cassino, and a parchment, with miniatures made at Monte Cassino for the occasion, signed by all the members of the community.

The Pope listened amiably to the words of the Abbot and accepted with pleasure the gifts, which he wished to examine one by one. Then he wished to present his personal gift to the library, a copy of the photostatic edition of the Bible of Borso d'Este. He had already donated to the abbey the beautiful chasuble and the precious chalice which he had used at the mass. The inscription that he had had engraved under the base of the chalice showed his kind thoughtfulness; it read:

Paulus VI P.M. — aedi sacrae principi Archicoenobii Casini — die quo eam rite dicavit et S. Benedictum — Europae caelestem renuntiavit Patronum — A.D. IX Kal. Nov. Anno MCMLXIV.

Not satisfied with such august generosity, he also wished to reminisce with fatherly pleasure about the fond memories he had of previous visits; and he also added warm exhortations for the spiritual life.

With great kindness he said, first of all, how much he valued not only the homage and the devout expressions of the Abbot, but also the significant gifts that he had received, which he would always hold dear as precious reminders of that hour truly blessed and the filial grace with which the Cassinese community had welcomed the Vicar of Jesus Christ. And those gifts were to him even more welcome, because they would be for him a lasting memory of the pledge of prayers to the Lord that would always be said on his behalf in this «City on the Mountain», by the children of St. Benedict who live in his house.

The joy of being there that day also renewed the sweet memory of other brief stays that he had made there in his youth. The first one was in Sept. 1919, when he was a theology student but was not yet wearing the ecclesiastical habit. He had joined a large group of university students who, led by Mons. Giandomenico Pini, gathered there to make a spiritual retreat as preparation for the reconstitution of the University Federation of Catholic Students after the war. He noted amiably, that besides the meditations and the prayers, there was a certain amount of noisy student uproar, which was tolerated with comprehension and indulgence by the Rector of the College who was given charge to assist the numerous company and by the other fathers at the abbey who followed the example of the revered abbot Diamare.

The second time (he remembered it well) that he came up the mountain was in 1930, on the tenth anniversary of his ordination, for another retreat, undertaken with quite different maturity and seriousness, together with father Giulio Bevilacqua. Glorious days, he commented, of long silences, meditation, and colloquy with God.

He was glad that he had been able to visit not only Monte Cassino but many other Benedictine abbeys in Italy as well as abroad; he had found the experience to be always edifying. The Benedictines knew then, the Holy Father remarked, that they had in him one who understood, respected, and loved them.

He was, therefore, happy to voice for his beloved Cassinese monks his most fervid hopes that, as the buildings of their monastery were happily resurrected, so would their religious perfection soar higher and higher. To grow in numbers, that comes by the grace of God; to grow in virtue, however, comes not only through God's grace but by everybody's efforts in harmony with the monastic vocation.

To these pious exhortations, Paul VI graciously added a friendly request, that the dear religious of Monte Cassino would continously ask from their Patriarch the protection of the church of God. The tone of his voice became graver, though he remained calm. The Church, he advised, was feeling the troubles, the struggles, and the difficulties of the present; many were the problems and of long range; therefore the monks, like Moses on the mountain, must implore from the Lord help for the activities, the mission, the life of the Church and for the triumph of the kingdom of Christ in the World. The Holy Father wanted to offer his thanks to these children from whom the Church already expected so much, and he blessed them all with love and the Christian wish which is so beautifully summarized in the greeting «Praise and Love to Lord Jesus Christ».

The loving speech was greeted at the end by a vibrant applause of gratitude from the Community. The Abbot renewed his thanks to the Holy Father and announced that, starting the following day, all the monk priests would celebrate the Holy Mass, for the intentions of the Pope, each in turn with the chalice that he himself had consecrated, a filial thought that Paul VI seemed to appreciate very much. He imparted then the apostolic benediction and allowed all to kiss his hand.

When the Pope left his apartment, because it was a bit late and the inclement weather continued, he was unable to follow the great hall and the outside stairway, so he was taken by elevator to the entrance gate, there too he was greeted by acclamations and applause.

After getting into the waiting car, he had the top taken down and standing up, protected only by an umbrella, he continued to salute and bless the faithful crowding the avenue outside the gate as far as the chapel of St. Agata.

Again at the start of the descent, as soon as he was in sight of the Polish cemetery, he stopped the car for a brief prayer for the repose of the souls of those dead and for all other soldiers fallen in that area. Then, preceded by the Abbot and followed by the cars of his retinue, he started for Cassino, where, welcomed enthusiastically by the people, he spoke in the church of St. John and concluded his itinerary with a short visit to the cemetery, where he stopped again for a prayer.

Thus ended that day of October 24, 1964 which has passed in the eyes of the readers in a synthesis perhaps too rapid, but which marks in the long series of the centuries the highest summit, the one covered with more light: not for worldly greatness or acclaim not for temporal power or wealth (by now a faint echo, although, historically, noteworthy and beneficial) but for purely spiritual affirmation, for a triumph of the world of the spirit. *Post nubila Phoebus — Post fata resurgo — Succisa virescit* these are the well known affirmations that we have seen many times realized in Cassinese history. Still even remembering and adding them all, the events of that day surpass them all.

The 24th of October 1964 marks not only another victory of life over death [10], but it confers a divine chrism to this new resurrection, the sign of that hand «which destroys and revives, which brings pain and consoles». It is, once more, the charismatic recognition of the validity and vitality of the work of Benedict.

With the blessing of the newly rebuilt house, the ancient Father saw his fatherly protection reaffirmed on the generations which have followed and continue to follow each other «*per ampla mundi climata*» [11].

A first sign of the public and official recognition came on the feast of March (1965) following his proclamation. The ambassadors of almost all the countries of Europe, the representatives of the European Economic Community, together with numerous bishops and political leaders, gathered to observe it solemnly around Card. Carlo Confalonieri, who carried a message from the Holy Father exhorting «all men of good will, concerned about Europe's future, to work with diligence for the affirmation of those moral and religious values which, preached by the children of St. Benedict, have contributed so much to the progress and to the spiritual unity of the peoples of Europe» [12].

In closing his admirable speech at Monte Cassino, Paul VI had, in fact, said: «Two important points make us, even now, sorely miss the austere and sweet presence of St. Benedict among us: the faith that he and his order preached to the family of the people that is called Europe, ... and the unity which the great social monk, who loved solitude, taught us, and through which Christianity made Europe one. Faith and unity: what better could we wish and invoke for the entire world and in a particular way for that important and chosen part, which, we repeat, is called Europe? What is more modern and more urgent, what is more difficult and conflicting? What is more necessary and more useful for peace?

And it is, indeed, in order that men of today, those who are free to act and those who wish they could, who want to achieve the intangibile and sacred ideal of the spiritual unity of Europe, may not be lacking help from above to realize it in practical and provident ordinances, that we have proclaimed St. Benedict Patron and protector of Europe».

6. THE CHANGING OF THE GUARD.

Unfortunately, after such intense building fervor, after such high accomplishments, the new day saw also the passing away of the man who had been the relentless animator of the recovery: the Abbot-bishop d. Ildefonso Rea.

On the 23rd of September, a few days before the fiftieth anniversary of his ordination to the priesthood (Oct. 5, 1921), he finished his earthly journey. The mission to which he had been destined had been faithfully brought to conclusion. His days were not many — he was born in Arpino Jan. 14, 1896 — but they were full of operosity, suffering, and accomplishments.

He had laid down the abbacy a few months before. Pope

Paul VI had allowed him to retire on April 17 because of the gravity of his condition. The Holy Father also sent him a laudatory letter on the occasion of his fiftieth year in holy orders; it arrived, however, only after he had expired.

The few months that he lived were filled with suffering and preparation, until answering the Father's call, he reclined his weary head and passed on to the reward that surpasses any desire, leaving behind great regret and an overwhelming feeling of emptiness [13]. His name remains forever connected with Monte Cassino, which was his great love. «I loved it more than my life», he used to say. It was the ideal to which he dedicated his life. On May 22, d. Martino Matronola, by vote of the community with the approval of the Supreme authority, had succeeded him in the governance of the abbey [14].

A native of Cassino, at the time of his elevation he occupied the office of Claustral Prior. He had worked therefore, side by side with his predecessor in both the government of the monastery as well as in various duties in the diocese. He had been very close also to the abbot Diamare, helping the revered old man, especially in the last tremendous events of his life.

He was also elevated to the episcopal dignity by Paul VI, to the title of Torri in Numidia (March 21st 1977), and was consecrated by Card. Sebastiano Biaggio, prefect of the Holy Congregation for Bishops, on May 8 of the same year. Thus the importance of the diocese of Cassino for the preservation and the restructuration of which the new Abbot had worked very hard, was duly recognized.

NOTES

[1] Encyclical, *Fulgens radiatur,* March 21, 1947.

[2] G. GONELLA in «Il Popolo», March 16, 1945. St Benedict also, in the narrative of Gregory the Great, had praised in the first destruction the will of God, recognizing that it had happened «omnipotentis Dei judicio».

[3] This is how a service of the newspaper «Tempo» commented on this death: «Death has come for the eighty years old Bishop. He had survived something that certainly was

dearer to him than his life; he has passed away now that a merciful field of crosses has risen on the slopes of his Monte Cassino, almost inviting him also to the final peace. But among those ruins, his spirit still lives; there remain the words of hope of one who knows that to build and rebuild is the eternal law of the spirit. Those words remain there, where a decade ago provoked the moving meditation of Harnack. It is the millenary Benedictine motto and it should be that of the world if it wants to rise again: *ora et labora* (Carneade)».

To the memory of the Abbot, the Italian government awarded the Gold Medal to Civilian Valor, His Excellency Spataro officially delivered it to Monte Cassino on Feb. 15, 1952. This was the second gold medal awarded to him, the first one coming after the first world war. Cassino has named a square after him and placed a bronze statue of him; a school also has been named after him.

His work to promote Christian education of the youth has been recalled in particular by A. GAETANI, *L'Abate Mons. Gregorio Diamare. Educatore della Gioventù Cassinate,* Cassino, 1966.

⁴ Cfr. *L'Abbazia di Montecassino. Precise notizie circa la conduzione e lo stato dei lavori* in «Documenti di vita italiana» 17, 1953 aprile, 1305-1306, editi dal Centro di documentazione della Presidenza del Consiglio dei Ministri della Repubblica Italiana. The communique has been reproduced by a few dailies, like the *Osservatore Romano.*

S. JANNETTA, in *Trionfo della vita. Distruzione e rinascita di Montecassino,* 1960, and in the English translation, *Triumph of Life. Destruction and Restoration of Montecassino,* gives an exact and brilliant synthesis of the destruction and reconstruction, accompanied by numerous illustrations.

⁵ Because of the inexact claims, still current, one must repeat here again that no foreign government has contributed to the work of reconstruction, in fact, even the sums collected, directly or indirectly under the name of Monte Cassino, e.g. by the association of the «Sons of Italy» in the United States of America, have been used for different purposes. One must, also, remember here the name of the Prefect Guido Letta, who devoted all his mind, heart and energy to the service of the committees «Pro Montecassino».

⁶ So that this document also might not be missing from this volume, we report here the passage from the Encyclic in English translation.

«The war, when in its recent conflagration reached the shores of Campania and Latium, struck most lamentably, as you Most Venerable Brothers well know, also the sacred summit of Montecassino; and although we tried everything in our power, praying, exhorting, imploring to avoid that such great injury be done to our holy religion, to the arts, to human civilization itself, it has, nevertheless, destroyed and obliterated that famous center of studies and piety, which as a light piercing the darkest shadows had emerged from the waves of the centuries. Therefore, while cities, hamlets, villages all around were turned into rumble, it seems as if also the Cassinese archiabbey, the Mother House of the Benedictine Order, had wanted in a sense to be part of the mourning of its children and share their misfortunes. Of the monastery, nothing is left standing except the hypogeum, in which, with great veneration, are kept the mortal remains of the holy Patriarch.

At the present, where once great works of art gleamed there are only tottering walls, rubble and ruins that the brabble mercifully covers; only a small house for the monks has been recently built nearby. Why should we not, however, be allowed to hope that, while we commemorate the fourteenth centenary of the day in which our Saint gained heavenly happiness, after starting and completing such a great enterprise, why, let us say, we cannot hope that with the participation of all good people, and especially the more generous and more affluent, this most ancient abbey be restored to its former splendor? Modern civilization certainly owes to St. Benedict such an act of generosity, it is in great part due to him and his hardworking family, if it shines with the light of so much knowledge and possesses so many documents of the civilizations of the past. We trust, therefore, that the results correspond happily to our expectations and our vows; and let this task be not only a duty of reconstruction and reparation, but an omen of better times in which the spirit of the Benedictine order and its ever more necessary teachings may flourish more and more every day».

[7] Gratitude for the work of reconstruction was solemnly expressed, on the twentyfifth anniversary of its start, Dec. 8, 1970, with unanimous and very large manifestation. Participating in it were also the Holy Father Paul VI, who sent a long letter expressing his pleasure, the President of the Italian Republic conferred on him the title of Cavaliere di Gran Croce dell'ordine di merito della Repubblica Italiana and H.M. Umberto II, the decoration of Cavaliere di Gran Croce dell'Ordine dei SS. Maurizio e Lazzaro. To the commemoration of such acknowledgements a special issue of the *Bollettino Diocesano* was dedicated.

[8] The ceremony of May 15, 1960 was especially solemn. Almost seven thousand veterans came, representing the sixteen nations that had fought in the most painful battle on the Italian front, also the leaders and the main protagonists took part in it.

[9] In the beautiful volume of CURTIS BILL PEPPER, *Un artista e il Papa*, at p. 194, among the reasons given by mons. Capovilla to convince the Pope to give up his journey to Monte Cassino, because gravely ill, there was that «the Benedictines, to whom the abbey beloged, had not kept an old promise made to the Pope, and, therefore, he had no obligation to go there».

Now, aside the more or less exactness of the reference, it is a fact that Monte Cassino had given the Pope no cause for regret, in fact Pope John to the end was very kind to the abbey. If some other monastery failed to maintain its promise, this cannot be imputed to Monte Cassino or other monasteries, because Benedictine institutions are constitutionally autonomous, and thus not responsible for the actions of others.

[10] How could one forget that it was on October 24th 1943, the nineteenth Sunday after Pentecost that the last conventual Mass had been offered in that Church now reborn? In the light of the new, and at that time unsuspected event, the words of that introit «Salus populi ego sum... de quacumque tribolatione clamaverint ad me, exaudiam eos», assumed a particular meaning, almost the fulfillment of a promise.

[11] Another motive of great comfort is to note that the memory of that day had not faded from the Pope's mind, though pressed and distracted by so many cares and preoccupations. To all the Benedictine Abbots assembled in his presence on Sept. 30, 1970, he said: «A splendid day, unforgettable for us, when we went to Monte Cassino, the mountain sacred to your memories, for the mortal remains of St. Benedict and St. Scholastica, for the footprints left by the Founder, for the richness of the spiritual, religious, cultural and artistic life which always flowered again in spite of the bloody wounds left by events, which passed like a storm, in the course of the centuries over that famous abbey, a true beacon which illuminates your order.

[12] To the select group the Abbot offered brief augural words: «You have gathered today around a tomb, but do not cry or commemorate a dead, enjoy instead and celebrate a life. That life which his mortal remains, entrusted to these few inches of soil, have always inspired and even now sustain and which, if in the course of the centuries appears sometimes

to grow weak and become extinguished, it soon recovers more vigorous than ever.

It is this vital spirit, which started from these mountainous cliffs, the moving force which gave form to our ancient «fatherlands» and helped to press them together into an ideal unity, that of Christian Europe.

Just following the last catastrophe, which had turned our continent into a mass of mortal and deadly ruins, a Pope, who had given all of himself to keep away the storm and then did everything to alleviate the innumerable evils, as a comfort and a remedy, chose him, who established here his last abode, the common Father of those who had barely ceased tearing each other ferociously.

Did not this Father, in the darkest years of our common history, build his city on the mountaintop, challenging almost, with his gaze fixed on the eternal truths, the oncoming evils and those threatening his very existence from all sides? And were not his humble sons, who worked silently and tenaciously, with their eyes always looking up high, to alleviate the wounds, to rebuild, strong and faithful workers, that vast city, in which ancient Rome had transformed the world, and extend it where the eagles of the Caesars had never arrived?

Not many years have gone by since Pius XII invoked the gracious favor of the ancient Father of Europe, and Europe has risen again, for the greater part at least, from her prostration. With the recovery there has been also a growing awareness of her unity, a stronger need is felt to face «viribus unitis» the difficulties that still abound and will never unfortunately disappear. It is not a question to erase those limits that God himself has marked on nature, but rise above them with love and mutual help.

And now, on these noble ideals, on this enterprise which promises many mutual benefits, but which also presents many difficulties, Paul VI takes up again the vow of his predecessor and invokes the protection of the ancient Father. He and his children can no longer work directly for this goal, but He, now one of the clearest heavenly pearls, can sponsor it «in that last sphere, where all desires find fulfillment».

What did the Holy Father, on that memorable 24th of October, ask for the whole world and Europe especially? What are we all asking today, Your Most Reverend Eminences, who represent the spiritual leaders of all our countries, You, official representatives of these noble nations, You, who are working at creating among them ties of good will, and we humble custodians of this sacred palladium? Our vow is one: Let Europe find again her faith and unity, those two principles which have made her mother and teacher of contemporary world civilization and which still have force and vitality to continue in this mission for universal peace and prosperity.

And He, who as we shall hear in today's liturgy, with words inspired by the ancient prophets, once "curavit gentem suam a perditione et praevaluit amplificare civitatem", will be, we pray and hope for, still "quasi stella matutina in medio nebulae, unitatis pacisque dona concedens" ».

[13] One can find an echo, albeit weak, in the publications: *Recessit Pastor Noster. In Memoria di D. Ildefonso Rea Abate di Montecassino,* an off-print from the «Bollettino Diocesano di Montecassino», 1971, n. 4; *Luci di un'anima. D. Ildefonso Rea.* Montecassino, 1972.

[14] Cfr. *Eredità perenne: D. Martino Matronola nuovo Abate di Montecassino,* Montecassino, 1971.

BIBLIOGRAPHY

It is not possible to report here all that has been written in newspapers and periodicals on occasion of the coming of the Holy Father to Monte Cassino. Besides the official *L'Osservatore Romano,* we are limiting the list to the two publications published by the Abbey of Monte Cassino: *Pacis Nuntius,* which, besides the complete chronicle of the events, includes articles of various authors, to comment and explain the celebration and numerous illustrations; *Beata Pacis Visio,* a special issue of the «Bollettino Diocesano», this too with a chronicle and illustrations. Our narrative is based on this chronicle.

X.

THE FIFTEENTH CENTENNIAL OF
THE BIRTH OF ST. BENEDICT

«All you people, come to Monte Cassino. Come to meditate on the past history and understand the true meaning of your earthly pilgrimage».
John Paul II

1. JOHN PAUL II AT MONTE CASSINO.

Paul VI was allowed to accomplish what his predecessor had so greatly desired, that is, the consecration of the Cassinese basilica, but it was not given to him to participate in another form of glorification of St. Benedict.

Already during the last year of his pontificate, thought had been given to the not too far off anniversary of the fifteenth centennial of the birth of the Patriarch, remembering, especially the preceding centennial of 1880, which had marked a memorable date. The Abbot of Monte Cassino, who had been given the task of preparing the program had already spoken about it to the Holy Father, who, however, on account of his declining health, could not be sure about his participation. And, in fact, his death, followed by the rapid and unexpected death of this successor on top of change taking place in the highest political ranks and in the monastic communities themselves, caused many delays and uncertainties in the initiative.

It fell to the Archbishop of Cracow, who used to withdraw to the monastery of Tyniec from time to time to follow its claustral life, to add special luster to the Benedictine celebrations.

He had already been at Monte Cassino in 1970, and on a rainy afternoon had officiated in the Polish cemetery with two hundred priests, survivors of the concentration camps of Dachau and Mathausen. As a Pope, he wanted once again to return to Monte Cassino on the eve of his return to Poland, as if to gather the voices of all those who slept in the shadow of St. Benedict and take their echo back with him to the fatherland.

This time, however, it was a radiant sunny day, May 18, 1979, and the anniversary of the Polish conquest of Monte Cassino marked also the birthday of the great son of the Polish nation.

Preceded by half an hour by the helicopter of the prime minister, the Hon. Giulio Andreotti, the Holy Father arrived also by helicopter, landing in an area set aside in front of the house of St. Joseph, and then in an open car proceeded, among a festive throng, to the Polish cemetery.

At the entrance, the Hon. Andreotti, together with the Abbot of Monte Cassino, welcomed the Pope and addressed to him, in the name of the Italian government, a warm greeting. In doing so, he recalled with gratitude the sacrifices made by the Polish soldiers thirty-five years before during the liberation of Italy and offered best wishes to the Pontiff on his birthday.

After thanking Andreotti for the noble words that had been addressed to him, the Holy Father explained the purpose of his journey to Monte Cassino. He said he had come «to visit these places sacred to human pain and Christian hope», to listen to and to transmit to everybody the message of those who rest in these cemeteries». And he concluded, «In this perspective my stop at the abbey of Monte Cassino acquires a symbolical meaning; destroyed by the fury of war and reborn from its ruins, it continues to be for Europe and the world a center of spirituality and culture».

The Holy Sacrifice followed, offered in the center of the sacrarium, during which the Pope gave the homily, in Italian, which he then summarized in Polish. Besides the dignitaries, there were, in fact, present about five thousand Polish pilgrims who had come from every country.

The Pope returned then to the monastery and stopped to pray near the tomb of St. Benedict. Afterward, together with the prelates that were accompanying him and the Prime Minister, he shared the monastic fare.

In the afternoon, he received the Community in a private audience and was given a few altar sets for the celebration of the Mass, destined to be given to the poorer churches of Poland, during his visit there. In separate halls, the Pope then greeted the Bishops of Latium who had gathered there with Card. Ugo Poletti, the mayors of the Cassinese diocese, introduced to him by the Hon. Andreotti, and, finally, the clergy of the diocese.

On his way to the basilica, he was welcomed in the ambulatory with great enthusiasm by the nuns of the diocese. He stopped briefly in the Chapter hall to examine some mementoes exposed there, especially those which had to do with the relations between Monte Cassino and Poland.

Passing through the basilica, the Pope reached the top of the stairway of the central cloister, where, in front of the main door, the throne had been set up with the dignitaries and the prelates arranged along the sides while the loggia and the porticoes were filled to capacity with an exhuberant crowd. The Abbot of Monte Cassino addressed him with brief words of homage, to which the Holy Father, after reading a passage from the Scriptures, answered with a speech outlining a program for the future of Europe that in St. Benedict had her Father.

In closing, he exhorted the assembly to pray that «the search for a more united Europe be based on the Benedictine spiritual tradition and on the Christian Catholic meaning "universal" tradition.

It is only in the name of that tradition, he added, that now, in this place, today, the son of a people of a different language and history can come as Bishop of Rome; because he is rooted in the same foundation, in the same spiritual tradition, in the same Christianity, he can come among you as a member of the family, and also as your pastor».

His final thought, as usual, was for the Holy Virgin, remembering that a group of the soldiers who had captured the summit of Monte Cassino had built a small chapel to her in the area where the new church was now built. «Under her protection», he continued, «let us go forth with faith and courage, saying with St. Benedict: "ora et labora et noli contristari" ».

«In this perspective», he said repeating the words of his morning message, «my stop at the abbey of Monte Cassino acquires a symbolical meaning: totally destroyed by the fury of war and reborn as a center of spirituality and culture. On this most solemn day, in the name of God and man, I repeat to all: "do not kill! do not prepare destructions and exterminations for men! Think of your brothers, who suffer hunger and misery! Respect the dignity and the freedom of everybody!" »

With this heartfelt call from the summit of Monte Cassino, the memorable gathering ended, and the Holy Father returned to Rome by helicopter.

2. THE CENTENNIAL.

The preceding centennial of the birth of St. Benedict, in 1880, was indeed a noteworthy event for the time, but while it left an indelible mark on the history of monasticism, due to the conditions of the time, it had a character prevalently if not exclusively ecclesiastic.

The other centennial that of the death of St. Benedict, falling in 1947, was celebrated among the still smoking ruins left by the war. This time, however, the participation of the world turned out to be unanimous and much larger, almost a choral hymn of thanksgiving for the work of St. Benedict.

This participation of dignitaries and people took place according to well-organized programs; besides the solemn liturgical celebrations, at which, often, the bishops of many nations officiated, there were conferences, scholarly meetings, concerts, art shows, scientific publications and informative ones, — even commemorative stamps — all activities designed to illustrate the various fields in which, during the course of the centuries the history of Benedictine institutions had moved.

Given the multiplicity of such activities it is not possible to give details. For Italy alone, one might remember, a ministerial commission was formed in which all major cultural institutes were represented; the regions also showed great interest, and so did the local agencies of tourism.

The first of the cultural events was held on the Capitol in Rome on March 28, with a plenary session in which Prof. Raffaello Morghen, president of the Italian Historical Institute for Medieval Studies and a member of the Accademia dei Lincei, spoke about the figure and the influence of the work of St. Benedict, «which are aspects of a tradition which runs, like a life-giving fluid, through the whole formative process of the established patrimony of human civilization».

It would be impossible to mention here all the events held in almost all the regions of Italy, and especially in those where Benedictine monasteries are located; here, only the main activities which took place at Monte Cassino will be reported. The Abbot, as president of the International Committee established for the celebration of the Centennial, in an audience held on Jan. 4, 1980, informed Pope John Paul II about the program. In the «Land of St. Benedict» on January 6, the «*peregrinatio*» of the Saint began. It was a triumphal procession, which often, whenever it was possible, was joined by the Abbot. The first phase of it closed on March 16, but it was resumed on September 13 until December 7.

February 10, the feast day of St. Scholastica, twin sister, according to the tradition, of St. Benedict, was celebrated in her monastery of Cassino. After the liturgical functions of the morning, in the afternoon Abbot d. Enrico Baccetti, general procurator of the Vallombrosani, commemorated her figure to a crowded audience, which also enjoyed the singing of the polyphonic choir of Pontecorvo. This was the first event co-sponsored by the Latium region, chiefly through the support of the alderman Guido Varlese, and the tourist agency of Cassino, which promoted and supported a number of other initiatives.

The bicycle race of the two seas selected Monte Cassino as its first leg on March 9. The flame, carried by relays of runners which left Rome the previous day, after being blessed by the Pope, reached Monte Cassino the 20th of the same month.

But these were only the prelude to the activities of the celebrations of the centennial, which started with the feast of St. Benedict on March 21st. On the eve at Monte Cassino, a solemn concelebration joined the diocesan clergy with the monastic community at the tomb of the Patriarch. Mons. Gaetano Bonicelli, Bishop of Albano Laziale, who presided, besides giving the homily during the celebration, held a conference for the priests and in the afternoon spoke to the people in the liturgy of the word held in the mother church of St. Germanus in Cassino.

The day after, on the anniversary of the *dies natalis* of the Saint, the Cardinal secretary of State, Agostino Casaroli, who brought a vibrant message from the Holy Father, in the presence of the ambassadors of Europe, including those of the East and other nations which had embassies in Rome, underlined in his sermon the significance of the centennial.

In the afternoon the well-known editor of *Civiltà Cattolica,* father Bartolomeo Sorge, spoke to the illustrious audience on the actuality of St. Benedict in the current conditions of Europe.

From that day on, events followed each other at a steady pace; here, unfortunately, they can only be briefly reported.

The series of conferences began with the one held in Cassino on February 7, when Professor Raoul Manselli of the University of Rome spoke on the theme, «Montecassino e la crisi della civiltà europea». The conferences continued, alternating between Cassino and Monte Cassino, with the following speakers: Father Trape and Father Spiazzi, the professors Manselli, Vallauri, Leonardi, Cilento, Cavallo, Grègoire, Pratesi, Malatesta, Lipinski, Gedda, the regional alderman Varlese, and the director general of Academies and Libraries, Prof. Francesco Sisinni; the last two gave great support to all the activities of the centennial.

The series of professional meetings had begun on February 23 when the artists of Rome and Latium gathered at Monte

Cassino under the chairmanship of Mons. Giovanni Fallani.

On March 22, it was the turn of the Lions Clubs of Cassino and Formia, which were also commemorating the 20th anniversary of their establishment. There was a very special meeting on March 25. About 360 nuns came from every corner of Italy. The gathering was presided over by the Benedictine Archbishop, Mons. Agostino Mayer, secretary of the Holy Congregation for the Religious and Secular Institues; he was assisted in the celebrations by the Abbot of Monte Cassino and the Bishops of Piedimonte Matese and Fabriano, who had accompanied their respective communities. The liturgy of the afternoon was followed by a conference of Sr. Aquinata Boeckmann, Professor at the Pontifical Institute of St. Anselm in Rome, who commented on the Marian aspects implicit in many parts of the Benedictine Rule.

There were several other gatherings of communities of nuns at Monte Cassino: on July 2nd, seventy came from Sicily and Perugia; on October 7, the nuns of Alatri came with their Bishop, Mons. Umberto Florenzani; the following day, the sisters of Tarquinia arrived.

On September 2, hundreds of Benedictine oblates held a daylong reunion at Monte Cassino. On November 22, about one hundred university students from the Florentine center «Giorgio La Pira» arrived. On January 12, all the principals and didactic directors of the province of Frosinone gathered around their superintendent at the abbey.

The most important conference, from the cultural point of view, was the one organized by the Italian Center of Studies on the High Middle Ages, which, after the meetings of Norcia and Subiaco, closed its itinerant cycle at Cassino and Monte Cassino on October 2-5, 1980.

Meetings and conferences were almost always accompanied by concerts and musical presentations, promoted mainly by the Latium region and the Tourist Agency of Cassino. Besides the performances by individual, very valid artists, one will want to remember here the concerts held by the Opera Theatre on May 1, 18 and 25. By initiative of the same region, and with the collaboration of the Theatre of Rome, on September 5 and 6 in the central cloister of the monastery, recitals of the «Mystery of the Nativity, Passion and Resurrection of our Lord» on a text by Silvio d'Amico, drawn from the Laud of the thirteenth and fourteenth centuries, were held.

The PANARTIS of Rome offered a concert on March 15, 1981, feasturing music of A. Scarlatti and G.M. Trabaci.

Polyphonic choirs arrived from Munich, West Germany, (May 22), from the cathedral of Luxembourg (June 3), and from Argentina (Sept. 8).

It is impossible to keep count of all the pilgrimages that arrived, even when led by famous personages. For their very particular character, one must remember here the pilgrimage of the Penitentiaries of the Roman Basilicas (April 21), that of the Holy Congregation of the Religious and Regular Institues (June 20), and that of about one thousand pilgrims from Slovenia, accompanied by four bishops and thirty-one priests.

For their ecumenical character one must mention here the visit of the Patriarch of the Syrian-Antiochene Church with seven bishops and accompanied by Cardinal de Füstenberg, and the visits of the Patriarch of Armenians, the eight bishops from Taiwan, and the ten from Korea.

For the benefit of the visitors, a number of exhibits were offered at regular intervals. The very first one was that dedicated to Sacred Art, which was sanctioned and inaugurated by the president of the Italian Commission for Sacred Art, on July 10, with a talk on «L'Arte Sacra e Liturgica». About 150 works were exhibited. It was followed on December 1st by that of the *Codices* and the editions of the Rule of St. Benedict, sponsored by the Direction of the Academies and Libraries, whose director, Professor Sisinni, gave a formal address on December 19. A special catalogue was issued for the occasion. On December 7, a modern art show was added with the participation of the senator Amintore Fanfani.

The last exhibit to arrive at Monte Cassino, on April 26, 1981, at the conclusion of the Centennial, was the one sponsored by the Latium region and inaugurated at Rome on January 14 in the foyer of the Argentina Theatre. It documented the activity of the «scriptorium» of Monte Cassino, which was illustrated by Professor Alessandro Pratesi with a special catalogue. To this was added an exhibit of goldsmith and ivory works illustrated by Professor Angelo Lipinski.

The high point of the centenary celebrations was reached and marked on Saturday, September 20. In 1880 Pope Leo XIII, due to the conditions of the time, was only able to send his legate to Monte Cassino, who, in May, consecrated the restored «Torretta» in his name; in 1947 Pope Pius XII chose to take part personally in the celebration of the Holy Patriarch but, since Monte Cassino was still a mass of rubble, the Holy Father had to preside in the papal chapel of the basilica of St. Paul in Rome, and it was then that he exalted St. Benedict as the Father of Europe. This time, however, John Paul II took an active part and, in his inimitable style, came personally to the places sacred to the memory of the Patriarch, whom he celebrated repeatedly in speeches, messages, and in a letter sent to all the communities following the Rule of the Saint.

On September 20, he returned to Monte Cassino, where 460 abbots and superiors of monasteries and about 100 abbesses were waiting for him. He arrived in a helicopter on the esplanade of St. Joseph and went on foot with the Abbot of Monte Cassino to the main gate and from there went directly to the church. At the altar he was flanked by Cardinal Pironio, prefect of the Holy Congregation of Religious, and Cardinal Hume, Benedictine Archbishop of Westminster. All the superiors present concelebrated in Latin with Gregorian chant. The Pope gave his allocution also in Latin. The Abbot of Monte Cassino had offered him a brief message of homage after the incensing of the altar; the offertory prayers were then read in the various languages: Spanish, English, Italian, French, German and Latin. The dinner, for 560 people, was blessed by the Pope himself, who afterwards, however, withdrew to the small refectory with the monastic community and the prelates who were accompanying him.

After a brief interval, he granted a private audience to the Cassinese community and then greeted individually all the superiors who had lined up along the great hall and the abesses who waited for him in the ambulatory.

After a brief visit to the Polish cemetery, once again by helicopter, the Pope went down to Cassino, where he was welcomed by an enthusiastic crowd. In the mother-church he spoke to the clergy and the sisters; then blessing groups of sick people he went to the Curia, where he spoke to the young people assembled in the coutyard; finally he was driven to De Gasperi square. There he was greeted by the mayor, Domenico Gargano, and by the minister Signorello, who represented the government. Here the Holy Father gave a very important speech in which he stressed those points so fundamental during his papcy: Respect for the rights of man, among which the right to work, the exhortation and the invocation to peace, «the sweet word», he said, «that I must pronounce especially at Cassino, theatre of an incredible and absurd struggle among nations».

It was 7:40 P.M. when the helicopter lifted off from the old Cassino sports field to take the Pope back to Rome. Thus this memorable day came to an end; it had marked with the gathering around the tomb of the Patriarch, as the Holy Father said, «almost the greatest of all centennial commemorations».

The day, however, did not mark the closing of the Cassinese celebrations. Some have already been mentioned, and since the 21st of March 1981 had been set aside for the papal function in St. Paul in Rome, the official closing was postponed to Sunday, April 26. Cardinal Pericle Felici, who presided at the ceremonies, was the bearer of another message from the Holy Father. The government of Italy was represented by the Hon. Franca Falcucci, undersecretary to Public Education; with the dignitaries were also present the mayors of the towns of the diocese with their respective gonfalons and many faithful. In the afternoon there was the opening of the scriptorium exhibit already mentioned above.

Thus the cycle of festivities was closed and, one hopes, that some good was left behind, like the continued appeal to the teachings of St. Benedict, to his actuality in the contemporary world; may they long live and contribute to the revival of European unity.

3. ANNIGONI AT MONTE CASSINO.

A more lasting echo of the centennial commemoration, besides the publications in part mentioned in the pages of this volume, is entrusted to a painting of exceptional value. The hope of returning its old painted decoration to the reborn basilica seemed like an impossible dream. The concourse of many artists dominated by the figure of Luca Giordano, had made the old basilica a veritable picture gallery of the contemporary Neapolitan school. There seemed to be great contrast, however, between sixteenth century forms and modern art.

Still, even here the miracle of the resurrection took place; the program, «where it was, like it was» was realized. A master who even in his use of modern techniques represents a link with the great old tradition offered himself, spontaneously, to initiate a new decorative cycle. Pietro Annigoni, who had already achieved so much glory, came with his disciples from the city on the Arno river, to mount to the top of the Cassinese acropolis.

And so on the background of the renovated aula Dei, a new great fresco, which covers the whole wall, reappears. It is no longer Giordano's scene full of movement and the costumes characteristic of his time, but a vision of peace which opens like «the longing of man for the empyrean and the glory of the Saints». At the center is the Patriarch and «around him a crown of brothers who have convened from far away in history, from the Benedictine Martyrology and Calendar... in the form of a garland, from a semicircle (where light and shadow contend for space and the character of the individual faces) in that crowd of abbatial miters and monks where one moves in depth, in new planes scanned by the shapes of the figures and the intertwining of the gestures, towards the central luminosity» [2].

The scene (27.3 by 20.34 feet) is surmounted by the figures of the two patriarchs whose spirit St. Benedict was an heir to, Abraham and Moses. The great work was finished by Nov. 1978 but was solemnly presented only in the afternoon of Saturday March 31, 1979. Before a large and learned audience, after a brief introduction by Abbot, the work of Annigoni at Monte Cassino was brilliantly illustrated by the president of the Commission on Sacred Art in Italy. His eminence Mons. Giovanni Fallani, also announced the participation of the Holy Father in the memorable event.

The eminent master had not finished yet at Monte Cassino and gave another proof of his noble generosity. In two sessions in 1980, he painted a great fresco in the cupola. To the sight of one entering the church, a whole series of figures soar in the high luminosity of the beautiful dome. In the center, the Holy Virgin, whom Pope Benedict XIII named cotitular of the basilica, stands out, and kneeling in veneration in front of her are the other two cotitulars, John the Baptist and Benedict.

All around the scenes of the memorable vision of Benedict the reception of the remains of his sister and his passage through the arms of the disciples recount almost all the conclusive parts of the cycle of the earthly life of the Patriarch, while all around his tomb, the founders who received from him the rules of life keep vigil in their great medallions. Just above the four piers, the four fundamental vows are symbolized as the pillars of Benedictine life and institutions.

To the work of the master, one must add the great industry of his disciples. Ben Long donated three paintings for the chapel of St. John the Baptist, Silvestro Pistolesi gave one canvass to the chapel of St. Peter, and Ugo Ugolini and Nando Bernardini began the series of Benedictine popes moving toward the sacred area of the tomb of the Patriarch.

And as Mons. Fallani stated, «The fresco in a church is like an open book and represents the popularization of an idea through a synthesis; Pietro Annigoni, so great in his artistic humanity, was entrusting to Monte Cassino the gift of a new document». And «if the symbologies and the realities of faith assume the form of artistic image, a glimpse of the eternal images», it is up to us to receive them «as a gift of the truth» [3].

NOTES

[1] G. FALLANI, *Annigoni at Monte Cassino,* p. 38.
[2] *Ibid.*
[3] *Ibid.* pp. 35, 43.

BIBLIOGRAPHY

On occasion of the coming of the Pope to Monte Cassino May 18, 1979, a special issue of the *Bollettino Diocesano di Monte Cassino,* richly illustrated, was published.

For the celebrations of the Centennial, a complete account is still missing. The *Bollettino Diocesano* has faithfully reported all that took place at Monte Cassino, while for the memorable day of Sept. 20, one should consult especially the *Osservatore Romano,* which devoted to it the nn. 218-220 of Sept. 20-22. A special issue of the *Miscellanea Cassinese* has been devoted to the conferences.

The work of Annigoni has been illustrated in many magazines and particularly in the two volumes *Annigoni at Monte Cassino,* Rome: La Gradiva, 1979, and *Annigoni,* Roma: La Gradiva, 1981.

The Basilica as it was

As it was

As it was

The vault as it was - Frescoes by Luca Giordano

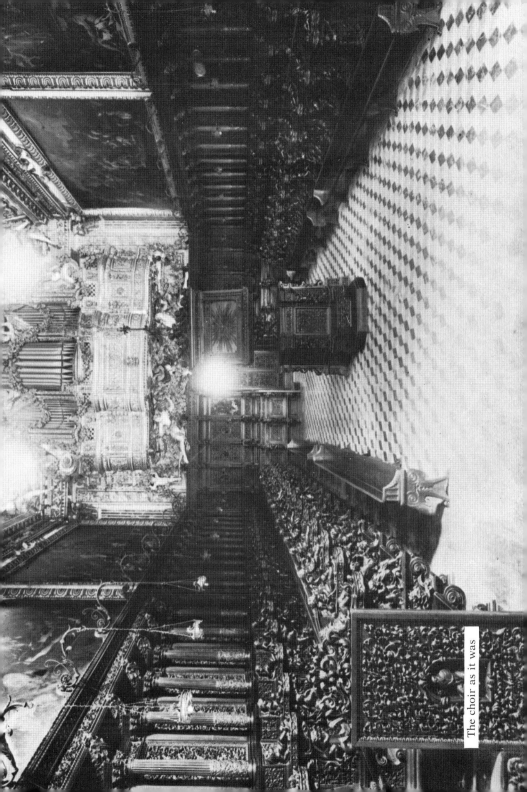
The choir as it was

The crypt as it was

Central altar of the crypt as it was

The sacristy as it was

Detail of the sacristy

The ancient capitular hall

The ancient museum

The great corridor as it was

Paintings of the Beuron's School, now disappeared

Montecassino that is lost

St. Benedict's Cell as it was

PART II

The labors

I.

«...THAT WARMTH WHICH BRINGS TO LIFE FLOWERS AND HOLY FRUITS»

(DANTE, *Paradise,* XII, 47-48)

«Haec domus est similis Synai sacra jura ferenti
Ut lex demostrat hinc quae fuit edita quondam.
Lex indi exivit, mentes quae ducit ab imis
Et vulgata dedit lumen per clymata saecli» *.

1. THE SAINTS.

The lines of the sweet Cassinese Vergil, gleaming in the golden apse of Desiderius, present in lapidary style the principal mission of Monte Cassino, that which constitutes its chief dignity and gives the institution an almost hieratic character. It was there, in fact, that from the «heart of St. Benedict, as from a heavenly spring» rushed out the regal river of the Rule. And although the autograph codex was lost in the fire at Teano, the spirit stayed alive and was the flame that warms, illuminates and supports life.

All the life at the abbey in its multifarious variety is like a commentary to the Gospel, the answer to the cry that is perennially repeated on this mountain top, from Benedict's to our own days: «ecce nos reliquimus omnia et secuti sumus te» **. And this in spite of obstacles and adversities. Every life entails a struggle and, therefore, the necessity of going through evil times and temporary deficiencies. No monastery, perhaps, has been put to the proof by external factors more than Monte Cassino, and yet life has never died without always being reborn still more splendid

---

* «This house is like the Sinai, where the law of God was issued and this is demonstrated by the Rule that from here was long ago published. From here comes the law that raises the mind from moral depths and, diffused far and wide, spreads its light through all time and places».

** «Now we have forsaken everything to follow you».

and warm. The Domus excelsa Casini therefore remains fundamentally the «domus terrena, per quam infinitae animae conscenderent ad caelestia*» [1], the community for God's service where they work to make themselves beautiful for eternity.

Its basilicas resplendent with marbles and gold, its solemn and silent cloisters, the wide, severe lobbies, the small cells, the mountain itself covered with convents and hermitages — S. Matteo dei Servi di Dio, S. Maria dell'Albaneta, S. Angelo in Fortunola, S. Nicola della Cicogna, S. Salvatore, Ss. Cosma e Damiano — they all seem to watch over jealously the mysteries of a life hidden in Christ, which has continued for fifteen centuries. They all seem to repeat the echo of the peaceful, inner victories for loyalty to the evangelical ideal. Of the majority of its inhabitants, unavoidably, no precise memory is left and yet there are not a few whose names have survived the vicissitudes of the centuries. Their memory has been preserved for us, first of all, in the *Dialogi* of abbot Desiderius, which are held with a make-believe interlocutor named Theophilus. Many are also mentioned in the *Chronica,* but the work of Peter the Deacon, *Ortus et vita iustorum coenobii Casinensis,* is more complete.

The golden chain begins, naturally, with the common father and master, Benedict, and his virgin sister Scholastica. It continues with the first disciples, Maurus, Placidus, Augustin and Paolinus and with their successors, Constantinus and Simplicius, whose remains rest in the special chapel of Vitalis and Bonitus in the Cassinese basilica. The chain continues after the restoration by Petronax, with the already well-known Carloman, whose remains, brought back from France in a golden casket, still rest in the chapel once built again for him. Ratchis continues to give his name to the locality where tradition places his vineyards, though his chapel is no longer there. Deusdedit, the holy abbot, died in jail and is invoked, especially, against the fever. Bertharius remains the unconquered martyr. Apollinaris crossed the Liri River with dry feet and, after his death, announced to the abbot

---

* «Earthly house, through which countless souls may ascent to heaven».

Bassacius the liberation of the monastery from the imminent danger of a Saracenic devastation; his remains also rest in the chapel dedicated to him in the Cassinese basilica.

In the third vital recovery, the following stand out above the rest: Guinizzone, who with the help of an angel freed himself from the hands of his persecutor Teodinus, exiting through the closed gates of the church and Gennadius, who confused the evil thoughts of a smith by taking a red hot iron in his bare hands without burning himself. Both of these men rest under the splendid altar, where the holy Eucharist is kept in the sumptuous pyx made on a design by Canevari. Dean John was able to cure the sick from afar, even, according to the testimony of Alexander II, with the water he had used to wash his hands after Mass. Other illustrious names are Liuzio, the founder of S. Maria all'Albaneta, John the disciple of St. Romuald, Teodomar and Elbizzone, Benedict, abbot Peter, Felix, Gebizzone, Gaiderisius, Fortunatus, Leo, Obizzone, Gregory, Azzone, Stephen, Aldermarus, splendid for his miracles while he was still alive and much venerated even today in the Abruzzi region, Frederick, who later became Pope Stephen IX and Victor III. To them, one must add Lindanus, the Saint worshipped at Sezze, Amicus, the hermit of S. Pietro Avellana, and according to some, Stephen, the Bishop of Caiazzo. It was then not without reason, considering the virtues of these and others unknown to us, that the austere Peter Damian heaped so much praise on the Cassinese community of this time.

And the list continues to the successor of Desiderius, Oderisius I, who by many authors is given the title of Blessed; to Bruno of Segni whom no one denied the honors of the altar; to Gelasius II, well-known for the many sufferings he endured during his brief pontificate; to Berard, bishop of Teramo, who is still venerated there. Azzone, Albert, and Berard, bishop of Marsi, are all saintly men who lived in the same period.

In spite of the misadventures and the troubled climate of the following centuries, the flame of holiness did not extinguish itself. On the mystical Cassinese slopes the great soul of Thomas Aquinas began to soar towards infinity in his longing search for

God, while the abbots Bernard I and Andrea left behind examples of holy lives.

The flame burned even more vividly when in the new order, the abbey resumed its serene industriousness with Angelo Sangrino, in whom contemporaries venerated «priscae coenobitarum sanctitatis redivivum exemplar» *; with Zaccaria Petronio, admired for his virtuous life and the singular graces illustrated to us in the life published by the monk d. Casimiro Chzarnowski; with the Englishman d. Thomas Preston, a witness for the faith, held in harsh imprisonment for twenty-four years, and d. Bernard, who shone for his care of the sick and the pilgrims; with d. Martino Orilia, whose soul was seen right after his death soaring to heaven like an arrow; with d. Tommaso Eusebii and d. Francesco di Militello; with the humble lay brothers Bro. Gregorio, Bro. Bertario. Bro. Mauro Rainone and with the Polish Bro. Girolamo, we have several other men, eminent for virtue whose memory has been preserved for us by the jealous, pious diligence of contemporary historians and chroniclers.

Without doubt, however, the exact number of the souls who in the solemn silence of the Cassinese slopes have walked in «sanctitate et justitia», in the hidden exercise of Christian and monastic virtues under the eyes «superni spectatoris», can only be known to God. Their vigilant and blessed spirits are in heaven forming a worthy and glorious crown for Father Benedict, as the superb artistic vision of Belisario Corenzio had drawn them, soaring above his tomb. Sharing the Father's triumph, they had reached it through the luminous and triumphal road, first seen in a vision by the disciples, which St. Peter Damian with the eyes of faith again saw opening from Monte Cassino towards heaven: «Beati siquidem vobiscum vivunt, beati qui inter vos et in sanctis operibus vestris moriuntur. Pia nimirum fide credendum est qui scala illa, quae de Casino monte olim in caelum videbatur erecta, adhuc palliis strata lampadibusque coruscat. Sicut tunc excepit

---

* «A reborn model of ancient monastic holiness».

ducem, ita nunc, exercitum transmittit ad caelestia subsequentem;
nec ab eius glorioso tramite exorbitant declinantes jam defuncti,
cuius, dum in hoc exilio viverent, vestigia sunt secuti. Hoc est in-
timi fervoris incendium illud quod mihi inextinguibiliter flagrat in
corde, haec perpes fabula quae meo versatur in ore *» [2].

2. THE FOUNDATIONS.

Under danger of death, however, life cannot wear off in
itself alone, but must radiate outside. What the sweet doctor said
of St. Benedict can in a sense be applied to his family: «Pascit
vita, pascit doctrine, pascit intercessione **».

It is true indeed that St. Benedict, like all the ancient
monastic leaders, did not set nor indicate particular aims or external activities.

Still the «Dominici schola servitii», by placing, with
evangelical protection, solid bases to the inner life, makes the
disciples fit for the most disparate tasks to which Providence will
call them. Their activity, however, «currendum et agendum est
modo ***», will always aim only at «quod in perpetuo nobis ex-
pediat ****». Not just the prayer of entreating and propitiating
will rise up from the sacred mountain, but from it will also des-
cend the light of the example, of learning, and hard work.

«An immense eagle's nest, the refuge of holiness and learning», thus a contemporary Canadian bishop defines Monte

---

* «Blessed those that live with you, blessed those that die with you, practicing the holy life, because one must justly assume that the ladder once mounted to the sky from
Monte Cassino is still covered with tapestries and bright with splendid lamps. As once the
leader passed through it, even now it allows a way to heaven to the army of his followers,
because it is inadmissable that, dead, they may follow a way different from the glorious
one that he followed, when they had followed his footsteps while living down here in exile.
This is the conviction that burns in my heart with inextinguishable ardor, this is the continuous topic of my speeches».

** «It nourishes with its life, it nourishes with its teaching, it nourishes with its intercession».

*** «Today it is necessary to run and to work».

**** «What will benefit us for eternity».

Cassino, «the cradle of Western religious life. Here lived the greatest legislator of the Christian era, the Moses of Europe; the Rule that he wrote there is still practiced there, as it has been practiced and will always be practiced in other monasteries. Here the invading barbarism found its master, from here the civilizing influence of the religion of Christ descended to penetrate through all directions in the West, softening the harsh customs in the formation of new people» [3].

«Lombard and German monasticism of the High Middle Age... Carolingian emperors and Roman Pontiff», will, in fact, recognize in Monte Cassino, «the starting point of the spread of Benedictine monasticism in the world» [4].

Already begun at a very early period and then violently interrupted by the Lombard destruction, the expansion of Benedictine monasticism resumed with renewed vigor after the restoration of the eighth century. There is, in fact, evidence of a colony of twenty-two monks with an abbot Opportunus who, even at the time of Petronax left for Austria at the request of the Duke of Bavaria, Utilio (748). Not long after (759 ca.), it is King Desiderius who establishes for the Cassinese monks the famous monastery of Leno, near Brescia.

And while new foundations were appearing in most regions of Italy, while cells multiplied in the steadily increasing possessions, other groups crossed the Alps to go to France by request of Charlemagne to abbot Teodemar; into Poland upon request of King Boleslav; and into Hungary, asked there by St. Stephen. They were called to Sardinia by Barisio, where they gave life to a marvellous flowering of Benedictine monasticism; they also went to Lithuania, Dalmatia, Constantinople, and, it seems, to Jerusalem.

Baronio, impressed, commented on this movement, which appeared quite strong in the eighth century: «Mirum dictu quanta ex nova plantatione Petronacis fuerint propagata eo in loco genimina monachorum, et aucta ipsorum examina instar apum quae ex turgescentibus alveariis prodeuntes in diversa loca ad foetus multiplicationem volaverint *» [5].

Gattola is of the opinion that more than one hundred and fifty monasteries depended on directly from Monte Cassino, without counting the numerous houses, which in turn depended from those, and the various churches. And when, in the political climate of the regional states the Italian monasteries felt the need for unity, Monte Cassino became the moral leader from which the union took its name, and thus the appellation «Cassinese», from the original monastery and its dependencies, was extended to many other and famous convents.

While it is possible, however, to give a general sketch of this movement, it is not easy to furnish the details, because the vicissitudes of the times have caused so many memories to disappear. On the other hand, as it was noted by Amelli, the Cassinese historians have always preferred to devote themselves to events of national interest, caring little or nothing at all about the relations of Monte Cassino with the outside world.

One should not leave out, however, the memory of some events in time closer to us. A brief mention has aready been given of the relations with the Meleda and some French congregations. More important are the ties that Monte Cassino had in the seventeenth century with Poland.

After the witness to the faith d. Feckman died in jail, the only survivor of the ancient monasteries was d. Sigebert Buckley of St. Peter of Westminster. While he was still alive in prison, some young Englishmen joined the monastic life in the Cassinese congregation; others, afterwards, joined that of Valladolid. Among the first at Monte Cassino — Gregory Sayr (1589), d. Thomas Preston (1592), d. Augustin (1592) — were the promoters of the Benedictine English congregation, to which from the last survivor, mentioned above, were transferred the rights and privileges (1607-1612) which Paul V recognized in 1612. Some years later, d.

---

* «It is indeed, marvelous the multiplying of the monastic foundations derived from that of Petronax; they grew like bee swarms which, leaving behind the overpopulated nest, fly to settle and multiply themselves in other places».

Michael, a nephew of Preston, who died in jail in London, also came to Monte Cassino with d. Bernard. All considered, the beautiful prayer composed by Tosti and engraved on a rock at the foot of a cross on the slope of the mountain seems to be very appropriate: «Our Father, Who are in Heaven, make us brothers with the English, in the unity of Faith». The words, of course, commemorate the victory of grace in a soul, but they also express the constant fraternal desire for the noble island which was brought into Christendom by the children of St. Benedict [6].

The count Palatine Carlo Kepec, who stopped once at Monte Cassino for two months in 1622, built in the diocese of Vilna the monastery of Castrocassinese. The first abbot of this community, was the very pious d. Placido Wasnienscki, a monk of Monte Cassino, and the Vilna monastery was considered its dependency. All these arrangements reflected the desires of king Michael (1669-1673).

Like the count Platine, Prince Michael Casimir Radziwil also founded the monastery of the Holy Cross *ad Nervisium,* which was also joined with Monte Cassino. Later, in 1709, these two abbeys, with the permission of the Abbot of Monte Cassino, joined with others to form the congregation of the Holy Cross in Poland.

3. INFLUENCES AND RELATIONSHIPS.

Besides this penetration that one might call direct, it is impossible to calculate the impact that Monte Cassino had on the monastic movement in so many different ways through the course of the centuries. We have seen how the house of Benedict was a crossover point where varied tendencies came pouring in and flowed out again in new directions. In addition, from Monte Cassino came many bishops and high church dignitaries, and we shall see how far the influence of its school ranged.

There was, besides, a long established custom, mentioned already in the eleventh century by the Cassinese: «... plerique nostrae consuetudinis nostraeque conversationis cupidi, de suis quem congnoscunt ingenii, unum huc transmittunt, quo non solum auditu, verum etiam ipso visu pro quibus mittitur perspiciat; eoque modo quasi unus ex nobis, hic quidam per integrum annum, quidam etiam diutius manent; tandem, onmibus perspectis, ad sua certus cum gaudio redit *» [7]. St. Boniface, in fact, did not send Sturmi to any of the nearby monasteries of France or England, but «ut in monasterio quod beatus pater Benedictus instituit, disciplinam regularem et vitam moresque monasticos agnosceret **» [8]. He later introduced that discipline at Fulda, the first Benedictine foundation in Germany. St. Willibald, who had contributed to the restoration of Petronax, brought to his monastery of Eichstätt «in usum prioris vitae , quod videndo ad S. Benedictum ***» [9]. St. Pirminus, a bishop, came from Germany and so did St. Anselm from his convent of Nonantola. One has also seen that Charlemagne asked the Abbot of Monte Cassino for the very bases on which to establish the monastic unity in the empire; while his son, Louis the Pious, invited the abbot to take part in the famous synod of Aix-la-Chapelle (817), together with the abbots of Farfa and S. Vincenzo al Volturno; he was asked there only because of the importance of the monastery, since the synod's legislation would have no effect in Italy.

Almost all monastic reformers travelled eagerly to the mountain of Father Benedict to draw, like the hero of the fairy tale, strength and inspiration from contact with mother earth. St. Peter Damian stopped there for an entire season of Lent and declared that he was leaving only corporally such an angelic company. St. Romuald, as it has already been seen, presented himself

---

* «... many desiring to became familiar with us and our way of life choose one of the more intelligent among themselves and send him here to learn not only by hearsay but by direct experience the things that interest them. Thus they live among us as one of ours, some for a year, some longer, and after having examined everything well, they return happily back to their country».

** «But to study the legislation, the observances and monastic customs of the monastery founded by blessed Father Benedict.

*** «In conformity to the ancient monastic customs, which he had seen in Monte Cassino.

at the monastery humbly riding an ass. Odo, the great abbot of
Cluny, full of reverence for him who was full of the spirit of all
just men, got off his mount and came up the steep mountain on
foot. We must remember also St. Nilus and William, John of
Gorza and Adalbert, and St. Bernard, bare-footed, in company
with emperor Lothair. Pope Leo IX, at the beginning of the great
reform of the Church, came to Monte Cassino and took part in
the life of the community, even in participating in the weekly
«mandate» to wash each other's feet. With these, through the
centuries, came a long line of monks, saints, up to the latest great
exponents of the monastic order, men eminent for virtue like
father Ludovico da Casoria, a reborn St. Francis, whom God
called in ecstacy to himself for the first time on this mountain and
cardinal and popes who did not mind living with novices and
monks.

The currents of religious as well as artistic and literary reform
end up crossing and merging with each other on the sacred mountain; they came from the area of Byzantine Italy, from the East,
from the banks of the Saone and the Moselle, from the country of
the Anglo-Saxons like rivers which, to repeat Manzoni's phrase,
return unceasingly to the ocean to obtain renewed waters.

Like the saints, all past generations, drawn by the memory of
Fr. Benedict, have come to his house. Royalty also came, from
the Ostrogoth king Totila to Victor Emanuel II, king of Italy, and
the Norman William II; from King Desiderius to Charlemagne
and Lothair, barbarian and Lombard rulers, Carolingian and
Saxon emperors, Norman to Bourbon kings. Today, contemporary rulers often come with their wives to visit and venerate St.
Benedict. And with these kings come nameless crowds.

Another typical proof of the attraction that this mountain
has exercised is furnished by the insistence with which its inhabitants have continually been requested to allow participation
by others in the merits and suffrages available at Cassino.
Emperors, bishops, priests and the faithful as well, always
coveted the mention of their names in the commemorations for
the dead. St. Boniface recommended his missions to Germany to

the prayers of the Cassinese; St. Peter Damian, St. Hugo of Cluny, the emperor Alexis of Constantinople, Charles II of Anjou, and so many others up to our days wanted to be named in the prayers of the monks. Many made provisions for their burial in the land sanctified by the works of St. Benedict, as the pious Sikelgaita, the widow of Robert Guiscard, and in recent years, the cardinals Bartolini and Capecelatro. Many monasteries are remembered in the ancient Cassinese necrologies as being attached to Monte Cassino with particularly strong ties of piety: St. Stephen of Vercelli, Hildesheim and St. Martin of Hungary, whose ties made during the abbacy of Adenolf (1212) are still maintained today. Others were Altdorf, Weingarten, Kremsmünster, Cluny, Metten, St. Mary of the valley of Josafat, St. Mary of the Scots in Vienna, Reichenau, St. Paul in Rome, the Hospitalers of St. John in Jerusalem, and those of the Lateran.

Considering such far-ranging penetration of a river-like flow from an inexhaustable spring, one can well understand the description of Monte Cassino by Leo XIII as the «Blessed mountain from which the true spirit of the great Patriarch, who like a hearth ignited everywhere the torch of virtue and civilization, issued and spread throughout the world» [10].

And it is, in fact, due to consideration on the dual aspect of this monastic and civilizing spring, which is synthesized in the apologetic mission exercised within the Church of Christ, that the supreme pontiffs, as the emperors in the temporal sphere, have bestowed on Monte Cassino praises and ample privileges. It is a great moving chorus of voices which rises from the apostolic seat towards the mountain of Benedict. They are voices of joy, affection and protection for the monastery which they say is «Universorum per Occidentem monasteriorum caput a Domino institutum; vitae monasticae principale gymnasium; totius inclyti ordinis caput *». With special care, as it has been seen, they keep watch on its conditions, raising it if fallen, supporting it if in

---

* «Established by the Lord as head of all the monasteries of the West, principal school for the monastic life, leader of the whole glorious order».

danger, consecrating the basilica many times. They recognize its providential mission, and they praise its attachment to the Holy See, noting how many times they share the same history: «Per longam annorum seriem, monasterii Casinensis fastos Romanae Ecclesiae historiae magnam esse partem *». They show their loving gratitude for the help received in difficult moments: «is enim locus nostrorum pauperum relevatio fugentium, refugium fessorum, Sedis Apostolicae filiorum requies indefessa permansit et permanet; vestro nos loco plurimum debere cognoscimus **».

From papal benevolence the abbey derives many privileges; the popes recognized, from the early history of the monastery, the legal succession of the Abbot of Monte Cassino to the jurisdiction formerly held by the Bishop of the ancient Cassino and later extended it to the whole feudal patrimony; they reserved to themselves the blessing of the new Abbot, conferring all the privileges of the episcopal dignity, and in fact, when times and circumstances allow it, elevating him to the episcopate and the cardinalate. And always «pro reverentia tanti loci» from where came the Rule, they establish, unanimously (this was confirmed during the papacy of Leo XIII) that the Cassinese abbot, as the house, should «in omni conventu episcoporum et principum superiorem omnibus abbatibus sedem tenere et in conciliis et judiciis priorem ceteris suis ordinis viris sententiam proferre ***» [11].

---

* «Through a long series of years the annals of the Cassinese monastery are in great part the history of the Roman Church».

** «This place has been and it is a place of rest for our poor fugitives, the refuge of the tired, the safe resting place of the children of the Holy See; we recognize ourselves to be much in debt to your monastery».

*** «In all reunions of bishops and princes should have the first place among the abbots and in councils and trials express his vote before all the others of the same rank».

NOTES

[1] URBANO V. *Monasterium Casinense,* May 10, 1370.

[2] PETRI DAMIANI S., *Opuscula,* XXVII in Migne, *Patr. Lat.,* CXLV, 621. How important he considered his pilgrimage to Monte Cassino, he makes it clear in *Opusc.* XXXIII, *ibid., 562.*

[3] J.M. EMARD, *Au congrès eucharistique de Malte,* Valleyfield, 1913.

[4] I. SCHUSTER, *Subiaco o Montecassino?,* in «Rivista Storica benedettina», XIII (1913), 105.

[5] *Annales,* a. 717.

[6] Tosti himself tried to favor the renewal of ties through Gladstone; see LECCISOTTI, *Aspirazioni all'unità dei Cristiani nella corrispondenza Tosti-Gladstone,* in «Rivista di Storia della Chiesa in Italia», XVII (1963), 115-125.

[7] This document, published first by Mabillon, *Vetera Analecta,* IV, Paris, Billaine, 1675, p. 462 and then several times, is addressed to the Abbot of Herstfeld, Hartwig (1072-1085).

[8] *Ex vita Leobae,* MGH, Ss. XV, 1, 105.

[9] *Ex Vita Willibaldi,* in MGH, Ss., XV, 1, 105.

[10] *Fulgens radiatur, cit.,* calls Monte Cassino «princeps S. Patriarchi domicilium ac praecipuum eius virtutis sanctitatisque theatrum», whence «novum refulsit lumen».

[11] This precedence, even above Abbots Generals of monastic orders, has been recognized and kept nel Motu proprio *Pontificalis Domus* of March 28, 1968.

BIBLIOGRAPHY

The work of Peter the Deacon is in Migne, *Patr. Lat.,* CIXXIII, 1063-1116. *Ibid.,* CXLIX, in 963-1018 are the *Dialogi* of Desiderius, whose last edition is by G. SCHWARTZ-A. HOFMEISTER in MGH, Ss., XXX-2, 1111-1151. For more recent times, lost now the *Elogia Monachorum...* ms. of. C. Ceraso, it must be remembered, M. ARMELLINI, *Bibliotheca Casinensis,* III, Assisi, Sgariglia, 1733.

To the saints of Monte Cassino, A. LENTINI has dedicated a summary and a work of popularization, *Fiori e frutti santi a Montecassino,* Montecassino 1929. For the later centuries, one can find echoes in A. PANTONI, *Asceti, penitenti e mistici della congregazione Cassinese nei secoli XVI-XVIII,* in «Benedictina», XVI 1969, 244-282, which published also two letters from St. Charles of Sezze, commenting on his visit at Monte Cassino.

News about the English monks at Monte Cassino, can also be found in Y. CHAUSSY, *Les Bénédictins anglais refugiés en France au XVIIᵉ siècle,* (1611-1669), Paris Lethellieux, 1967.

The relations with the Pontiffs were the object of two articles in the *Osservatore Romano,* April 27 and 28, 1929 by T. LECCISOTTI; the relative documents, until 1197 are examined by P.F. KEHER, *Italia Pontificia,* VIII, Berlin, Weidmann, 1935, 109-193.

Those with the Orient were examined by M. INGUANEZ, *Montecassino e l'Oriente nel medioevo,* from «Atti del Congresso nazionale di Studi Romani», 1938 and by M. BLOCH, *Monte Cassino, Byzantium and the West in the ealier Middle Ages,* «Dumbarton Oaks Papers», III, 163-224, Cambridge MA, 1946. The Benedictine monasteries in Poland have been the object of B. ALBERS, *Zur Geschichte des Benedictiner-Orden in Polen,* in, «Studien und Mitteilungen, XV (1889), 194, 226-227.

The right of precedence of the Abbot of Monte Cassino has been studied and reported again by T. LECCISOTTI, *Sul diritto di precedenza dell'abate di Montecassino,* in «Benedictina», VI (1951), 143-147.

II.

THE INTELLECTUAL LIGHT

«Dum tot ac tantos viros in hoc sacratissimo coenobio liberalibus disciplinis plenos aspicio, oneris fasce devictus succumbo» *.
(PETR. DIAC., *Chron. Cas.,* IV, prol.).

1. THE STUDIES.

In the words of his biographer, the great legislator Benedict, «scienter nescius et sapienter indoctus» ** in the learning of his time had escaped the corruption of the schools of Rome by withdrawing and hiding in a barren gorge of the Simbruini mountains. Neither he nor his disciples, however, lived in ignorance.

The Rule that St. Gregory rightly defines as «discretione praecipuam, sermone luculentam» ***, in the classic rhythmic cadence of the *cursus* reveals a student «whose ear was instinctively attuned to the various closings of periods and meters, in which he had been trained in school since his early youth» [1]. The author must have, therefore, finished, at least, the courses of grammar and rhetoric.

He had, however, «too clear a perception of the reality which surrounded him to be able to give to learning the same importance as his contemporary Cassiodorus. History has proved him right; the learned academy of Cassiodorus at Vivarium was completely swept away by the migrations of the people... while the sacred reading of Benedict has later become... the custodian of ancient learning and mother not only to theology but of all the intellectual

---

* «When I think of the many great personage who excelled for high cultural achievements in this sacred abode. I feel overcome under this weight so far above my strength».

** «deliberately unaware — according to his biographer — and wisely ignorant».

*** «noteworthy above all for discretion and most clear in exposition».

culture of the Middle Ages» ².

The Cassinese Rule prescribed that in determined hours the monks had to do some reading, sometimes done in common for the benefit of those who did not know how to read. Right from the beginning there was a library in the monastery furnished with books of such quality and quantity to be enough for the use of all. The books that were distributed to every monk must obviously have been part of the library. Besides, among the objects that had to be issued to everybody, the Rule prescribed «codices, graphium, tabulas» *. Young boys also were admitted to the monastic life, and these, to acquire a sufficient knowledge of the Holy Scriptures and the complex liturgy, had to be schooled in the basics of secular learning: therefore, the monastery, among the other necessities, had to be furnished with a school, even a rudimentary one, so that the monks should not be forced to wander outside the monastery to get educated.

Among the first inhabitants of the mountain, whose names have come down to us through the mists of centuries long traditions, there is no lack of educated people. There were two brothers, for instance, who were later sent to Terracina, Specious and Gregory, and Mark the poet, who is still today credited by many with the fine verses in praise of St. Benedict which go under his name; there were also that Sebastian, author of a life of St. Jerome, and the third Cassinese abbot Simplicius to whom are attributed the verses that celebrated the praises and the success of the Rule.

It is also probable that medicine was cultivated there, perhaps only empirically, though following a definite direction. Proof of this can be derived from that part of the Rule that strongly enjoins the care of the sick, especially those who, because of local circumstances, were unable to receive any prompt and real help from the outside. On the other hand, one knows well that the healing art was always held in high honor among the Cassinese.

As has already been seen, however, the life of the monastery

---

* «books, metal pencil and waxed tablets».

was violently cut by the Lombard destruction.

When the abbey was finally restored, in the wonderful fervor of the renewal, literature and the arts also gained a new life to which men of every social condition and from every part of Europe contributed influences and brought tendencies sometimes unknowningly.

And while buildings were being raised by the monks even in distant regions, the course of studies at Monte Cassino was firmly regulated by norms which were mainly the work of Paul the Deacon. Born between 720 and 724, he probably followed his sovereign, King Ratchis, to Monte Cassino when he had already become famous for his great learning. If he was, indeed, «one of the highest representatives of the Romano-Christian culture of the Carolingian age» [3], he appears also as the advocate of the universal mission of Monte Cassino in the splendid and peaceful achievements of the culture of the times. Even far away at the court of Charlemagne, who honored him «as one of the greatest men of his age» [4], Paul longed for the quiet of the Cassinese cloister, and he finally returned there (799?) to compose his major work the *Historia Langobardorum*. Given his personality, it is no wonder that the fame of the Cassinese school, which his disciple Ilderic admired so much, led the bishop of Naples, Stephen II, to send some of his clerics there. In addition «almost certainly, it was Cassinese influx that led to that dawn of grammatical studies which opened at Benevento in the ninth century, especially through the work of bishop Ursus» [5]. The Cassinese were probably also responsible for that learning which, in spite of the calamitous times, is found in the principate of Salerno, at Capua and Naples.

While in Italy, the hymns of Paul spread more and more and «Monte Cassino triumphed with the Benedictine hymnal, used everywhere», one must also remember that «to the *Ars Donati* explained by Paul, in a commentary requested by Charlemagne, French culture also owes a great deal» [6].

Cassinese influence also began to range far and wide in the intellectual realm: numerous were the Cassinese colonies which went to the various regions of Italy. In Germany and in France, the diverse relationships which kept forming with the abbey led to the propagation not only of the Benedictine spirit but also of the fruits of the school and the art of Monte Cassino.

What subjects and what methods were used to teach in this school can be inferred, in a way, from the commentary to the Rule attributed to Paul himself. Even if not written originally by him at Monte Cassino, it still remains a source and a document of the direction that Paul's powerful personality and name imposed on the community. We read in it that the masters, «must fulfill promptly their duties, instructing the pupils in grammar, computation and the arts». The expressions are generic but one can see in them the clear sketch of the complete course of the *trivium,* which together with singing and computation formed the ordinary intellectual education of the Middle Ages. In particular, the grammar included the study of the classics with relative exercises, but without doubt, this study was not restricted to Latin only but included also Greek. This language, in fact, was then used currently by a large part of the population of southern Italy which still kept very close ties with the Byzantines. We find clear reflections of this situation which the abbey, on account of its dependencies — the territorial patrimony and later its political influence — had to have with the numerous Greek colonies and even with the empire of Byzantium itself, as it has been already mentioned, since the time of Petronax the Laud to God were sung in both Latin and Greek. Conversely, the familiarity with the language of Homer allowed the monks to write Latin verses in Greek letters and permitted abbot Bertharius to impose on his city the name, rather unpleasant in our days, of Eulogimenopoli.

Besides, Paul the Deacon himself, when he was called to the court of Charlemagne, found that not the least of the tasks he was given was that of teaching Greek to the clerics chosen to accompany the king's daughter, Ratrude, who had been promised as a bride to the emperor of Constantinople.

In the arts that the commentary mentions one can see the rest of the *trivium;* in computation, the elementary notions of the calculus were added to the complicated method used to master the intricacies of the calendar.

Paul was, indeed, the most illustrious of the Cassinese teachers of the time, but not the only one or the first. Even before his coming to the house of Benedict, there were many learned men there and, from the commentary of Paul, we learn that the monks devoted to the education and instruction of the young disciples were several, at the ratio of three or four for ten pupils, with whom they read in the hours that the legislator had prescribed for reading.

The way that the students showed their progress in the studies was somewhat different from our practices. Besides the ordinary examinations, they sometimes had to read in public, as, for example, during the holy services or in the refectory in the presence of the whole community. These readings are mentioned in several passages of the commentary; when a learned guest (the commentator calls him *sapiens*) came to the monastery, the prior, that is, the first of the monks allowed to deal freely with guests, had to choose and carefully prepare one of the disciples to discuss with the stranger topics studied at school. And the prior, the commentator, adds, «debet quasi non videns videre»; in other words, he must pretend to be unaware of eventual mistakes, limiting his role to that of mere spectator, but «post discessum hospitis debet... monere ubi negligenter interrogavit vel respondit... ut possit postmodum petentibus responsum reddere» *. And, of course, prizes were awarded, like public praises and the partaking of the choicer foods prepared for the guest; these were ways to stimulate fair competition.

To judge from what has come down to us, the school bore good and numerous fruits. The disciples of Paul, in fact, wrote verses and composed speeches without neglecting religious studies. They also followed in this the example of the master,

---

* «but, after the guest has departed, he will point out to him the questions and answers that were incorrect, so that in the future he will be able to answer in a satisfactory manner».

who, in the peace of the cloister, composed a collection of homilies by order of Charlemagne, which the sovereign officially adopted throughout his domains.

Among the disciples of Paul, Bassacius stands out prominently. He was later elected abbot and is remembered for his knowledge of sacred scriptures and dogmas and for his poetry. The deacon Theophanes was a poet like him. Peter the Deacon called him the author of «mirifici» verses on St. Benedict, on the foundation of the basilica of S. Salvatore, and on the construction of S. Maria a Plumbariola.

Even more important, as one of the few surviving documents that «describe to us the activity and the scholarly pursuits of Paul the Deacon», is the work, already mentioned, of Ilderic *magistri eruditissimi viri.* In his *Ars grammatica,* we note a current «completely Latin, based directly on the ancient tradition of classical grammar and unrelated altogether to any influx of the Carolingian-Alcuinic renaissance» [7].

Bertharius, the successor of Bassacius as abbot, as already mentioned, wrote a great deal. Ausilius, who supported the party of pope Formosus in works that even today are of great historical interest, is generally considered to have been a Cassinese monk. John Imonides, a deacon, on request of Pope John VIII, wrote a life of St. Gregory the Great which is still the most complete and detailed. Novati [8] attributes also to him the adaptation of the *Cena Cypriani* into rhythmic verses quite elegant and festive in form.

While wild bands of Arab marauders devasted the plain below and threatened Monte Cassino, the *Chronica S. Benedict Casinensis,* compiled information on contemporary events in a style terse and unrefined, and partially, completed the work of Paul. «In each of three parts» which make them up, «Monte Cassino is, of course, the center of observation; the outlook, however, extends to the whole of southern Italy» [9].

Monte Cassino, however, was once again destroyed in 883, and with it, the larger part of that immense treasure that the cultural movement had generated was also lost. The vivid remembrance of those painful days finds an echo in the *Historia Langobardorum* by Erchempert, a Lombard from Benevento who had a troubled life. He also wrote poetry, some still unpublished, the Martyrology of Bede, and other works which have been lost.

During the abbatial rule of John I, besides the great care devoted to works of art and miniature, the *Edictus* of the Lombards was transcribed to help the monastery in its litigations. Thus in spite of the adversities, traditional scholarly work saw no interruption. Pope Victor III is indirectly a witness of this; in fact, he remembers in his *Dialogi* a monk, Antony, well-known in almost the entire province. Some years later, it was the turn of Lawrence, bishop of Amalfi, who was the author of sermons and Saints' lives, and who was also the teacher of the future Pope Gregory VII.

The tenth century, therefore, although saddened by the invasions and the exile, was not altogether a sterile one for the Cassinese community as well as for other Italian cloisters. Like «the earth, that even under its mantle of snow quivers with renewing life», even then among the deep mist, the harvest was preparing. Witnesses to this, is the appearance in the decisions and judgements still held in the archives of Monte Cassino (960-963) of the earliest monuments of the Italian language forming in the region. The witnesses called to give depositions state in their habitual language, «Sao ko kelle terre per kelli fine que ki contene trenta anni le possette parte sancti Benedicti» *. The same testimony is repeated many times with only the slight variations required by the different cases.

It is also at Monte Cassino that we find the earliest use of rhyme in Latin verses and, while the *scriptorium* and the library flourished, we can also see that astronomy and music were cultived.

Thus begins the golden century in which the abbey, a real city

---

* «I know that those lands and the boundaries that hold them were held for thirty years by St. Benedict's side».

on the mountain, draws the attention of the whole universe. «No other place in the world could compete at that time with Monte Cassino in the various fields of learning or in cultural and artistic splendor» [10]. In the century old struggle, Monte Cassino had become a fortress of refuge for the popes who were often received within the safety of its strong walls. V. Balzani writes that at this time «the monks often came out of their stronghold as knights of Christ, and, as soon as they had left the tranquility of their cloister, they plunged enthusiastically in the whirlwind of the political and religious wars to fight their battles with the pen and the word» [11]. The hope of victory smiled more brightly on those fighting with moral weapons than on those fighting with material ones, and those cenobites, besides the glamor of the holy life, had also the added advantage of culture.

In the monastery, which right at that time had become the most beautiful in Christendom, learning continued to make progress. To all the abbots of this century one can attribute, within certain limits, what the *Chronicon* states about Desiderius: «Ex diversis mundi partibus eiusdem... diligentia vel iam eruditos aggregaverat, vel in hoc ipso cenobio erudiri studiosissime fecerat *» [12].

A great part of the merit for this scientific movement must be given to Frederick of Lorraine, an abbot and then Pope Stephen IX. Because of his skill in the theological sciences, as seen before, he had already been sent to Constantinople as one of three legates charged to bring to an end the controversy with Cerularius; he had also served as chancellor in the Roman Curia. As it has already been seen, many other Cassinese were raised to the cardinalate at this time and some of them had also the office of chancellor; the immediate successor to Frederick as abbot, Desiderius, also became pope under the name of Victor III. Of the works that he, an expert in medicine, poetry, and music, composed, we have three books of his *Dialogi* and some verses.

---

* «He used all possible means to attract to the monastery from various parts of the world men of great learning or had them instructed there with the greatest care».

Desiderius' beloved friend Alfanus (ca. 1010-1085) had studied medicine with him at the celebrated school of Salerno and had followed him to Monte Cassino; later as Archbishop of Salerno he was present at the death of Gregorio VII, who expired in his arms. For his great ability and the sweetness of his verses he was called «the Cassinese Vergil» and, «more than anybody else in Italy, had great familiarity with Greek and Roman antiquities». His love for the Muses, however, did not keep him away from the study of philosophy and medicine: his *De quattuor humoribus corporis humani, De pulsis,* and *De unione corporis et animae* were works that had very great importance at the time. In addition, what was of great importance then was that he did not lack the knowledge of the ancient authors, from whom he translated the περὶ φύσεως ἀνθρώπου of Nemesius.

These three men and their works, which received even greater resonance because of their high offices, made a great contribution to the increase in splendor and fame of the Cassinese abbey and to the disciplines taught there. It is good to note, as Giesebrecht [14] did, how each of them impressed on those studies the characteristic of their own personality: Frederick, the sharp vigor of theological disputation and controversy; Desiderius, monastic rigor and austerity; and Alfanus, the form and the beauty.

While these men deserve first place, they were not the only contributors to such great intellectual wealth. Constantinus Africanus was much more experienced in medicine and had greater importance for the influence he exercised on the development of western philosophy. After an adventurous life and a past master at Salerno and secretary to Robert Guiscard, he obtained the monastic habit from Desiderius and in the cloister he continued to enrich all those who wished to profit from his vast scientific knowledge. Among his disciples we find the monk Atto, who later became the chaplain of Empress Agnes. Constantinus had travelled very far to acquire his knowledge in India to Ethiopia, and among the Chaldeans, Arabs, and Persians, he was hailed as a new Hippocrates and master of the East and the West. He used his vast learning to reveal to the West several Greek and Arabic works, among them the treatise of Isaac Israel on the elements, some works of Galen, Hippocrates and others. These translations had considerable importance in the formation of eleventh century thought. It was in this way that western science was able to add notions and elements drawn from the Arabs to its own philosophical speculations. More limited to local importance, but far more widespread and deep was the influence of Constantinus on the school of Salerno. The origins of this are lost in the mists of the centuries, but from very ancient times Salerno had close and frequent relations with Monte Cassino which in that city possessed the monastery of St. Benedict. The old relations became tighter in the eleventh century when several disciples of the famed medical school, amongst whom Alfanus and Constantinus were the greatest, came to Monte Cassino.

At any rate, this was just the continuation of an ancient tradition. While the *scriptorium* provided the manuscripts necessary to study, the pharmaceutical laboratory, as the *Chronicon* informs us, had a well furnished *armarium pigmentorum*. Alfanus himself, going with Desiderius to visit Pope Victor II, who, then in Florence, had brought some medicinal codices and pharmaceutic preparations that he had made up, to offer them to the pontiff. It was in recognition of these ancient merits of the abbey that the international Congress for the history of medicine, which had gathered in Rome, offered to Monte Cassino a bronze plaque designed by Mistruzzi.

Another distinguished Cassinese poet of this era was Guaiferius, a compatriot of Alfanus, of whom his lines echo the classical taste and the nobility of expression.

A young boy from Settefrati, Alberic, was accepted at Monte Cassino by abbot Gerard (1111-1123). He should not be confused with the other Alberic, his contemporary, the author of a *Chronologia,* and a priest and vicar of S. Maria dell'Albaneta. This Alberic from Settefrati was the author of that very famous Vision which, rearranged by Peter the Deacon and perhaps others, appears superior to those of the same genre which abounded in the Middle Ages.

Desiderius had wanted to introduce Alfanus to historical studies also, so that he could prepare himself to write the history of the abbey; this task, however, was reserved for somebody else. Leo, from the family of the counts of the Marsi, who was received in the monastery by Desiderius himself when still a boy of fourteen, undertook the task to raise this monument to the glorious traditions of the abbey. Abbot Oderisius asked him to write a life of his great predecessor Desiderius, and from this original design the *Chronicon monasterii Casinensis* was born. Leo carried his narrative to the year 1075; there were, however, various compilations, and other hands enlarged the story and added notes. Thus it was continued to 1139. Created cardinal bishop of Ostia by Pope Pascal II, Leo had a very important role in the Lateran council of 1112. He had conciliar tendencies and in 1111 found himself present at the famous fracas in St. Peter from which he fled disguised as a peasant with another cardinal. Born in 1046 ca., he died May 22, 1115 (1117). His work distinguished for loftiness and impartiality, richness of detail, and for the greater part reliable, places him among the more noteworthy historians of the Middle Ages.

In the same epoch, Bishop Amatus florished at Monte Cassino and dedicated his famous history of the Normans in eight books to Desiderius; the original, unfortunately, has been lost, and we have only a poor French translation of it.

The continuator of the work of Leo, resuming, however, the work of his master Guy, was Peter the Deacon (1077-1159). An extraordinary and restless mind, he left behind many works that deserve notice. He was wrong, however, in falsifying the sources and the traditions; thus all his work has come under the pall of suspicion.

The *Ars dictandi* had a very important place in the Cassinese school. It goes back to another Alberic, a monk at Monte Cassino before 1060 and one who turned out to be of singular importance for his times. The treatise *De Corpore Domini* testifies to his theological knowledge. The tract was written against Berengarius on the occasion of the Roman council of 1079, where he was responsible for having the exact word «substantialiter» included in the formulary submitted for signature to his adversary. He composed, besides, *De Virginitate Mariae* and was skilled in poetry and the sciences, especially astronomy.

His work, however, is especially noteworthy for the *Ars dictandi,* on which subject he composed several treatises. The most important among them are *Breviarium de dictamine* and *Flores rhetoricae (seu dictaminum radii).* The first, dedicated to Gundifrid and Guy, his Cassinese disciples, was written as a textbook for beginners. The *Flores rhetoricae,* instead, was written for those who had already good training, and so it proposes examples drawn from the Latin classics and other sources. The renewal of the *Ars dictandi* was followed by that of the Latin language and, particularly, that of the *cursus* rhythmic, the chief ornament of speech. Alberic himself had wanted prose to be «sonora et distincta, id est quasi current» *, and his disciples followed his instructions so well that Albert of Samaria reproaches them as «scholasticos seu grammaticos dictatores, qui dictamina more metrorum seu rithmorum... claudicare coegerunt» **.

Among the faithful disciples of Alberic one must place John of Gaeta, who embraced the monastic life and pursued his studies at Monte Cassino, where his uncle by the same name was also a monk. As an example of the considerable progress that he made at the monastery school, one should consider his *Vita Sancti Erasmi,* written undoubtedly as a school exercise; it remains one of the earliest examples of the new style. When Pope Urban II, shortly after his election at Terracina on March 12, 1088, came to Monte Cassino, he noted the intelligence and the ability of the young monk from Gaeta and made him his secretary. As his biographer Pandulf, Cardinal of Pisa, adds, he decided to make him chancellor so that with his rhetorical skills, he could restore to

---

* «sonorous and distinct as a running stream».
** «writers bound by the rules of the school and the grammar, who gave to their prose a halting pace, like meters and rhythms».

the apostolic see the ancient elegant style, now completely lost, bringing back the rhythm of the Leonine *cursus*. Thus his elevation to the chancellorship was the direct result of his knowledge of the language and his rhetorical skills, both of which he had mastered, according to his own testimony, in the Cassinese school. One can thus safely conclude that the movement of renewal of the papal chancery had its origin in Monte Cassino. The new norms established there were later confirmed by John of Gaeta himself, when he became pope under the name of Gelasius II.

Even after it penetrated a center of world importance like the Roman chancery, the movement did not stop. Perfected even further, it was used at the royal courts of Sicily, France, and Germany, contributing everywhere to restore the damage suffered by the Latin style. The movement started at Monte Cassino must with good reason be credited with the advancement of literary culture in Italy and in Europe. Besides, it made its way into the university of Bologna, where the study of rhetorical arts was so intimately joined to that of the law that gradually the *Ars dictandi* became part of the notarial style. Furthermore, the vigor of the Latin language, renewed by the work of the *dictatores*, accelerated the formation of the new neo-latin idioms and of the new humanistic culture.

One must see, therefore, a providential significance in the fact that even now in the house of St. Benedict are kept two key documents from the history of Italian: the first clear linguistic documentations of the renewed Italic people in the already mentioned judicial decisions of the tenth century, and the celebrated *Ritmo*, which goes perhaps to the twelfth century and which is one of the most important documents of the new language. Anyway, the fact that the Italian dialect was used very early at Monte Cassino is confirmed by the poem of the crying of the Virgin in a Passion play which used to be presented there [15].

The resurrection of the *Ars dictandi*, with its felicitous and important consequences, was not, however, the only glory of the Cassinese school of that epoch. While the abbey, however, in the

century of the first Italian renaissance, represented on one of its
more active centers, new trends coud also be felt in the course of
its political activities, in the arts, in the sciences, and in the law.

The numerous codices preserved there bear witness that
juridical studies were cultivated at Monte Cassino. One should
not be surprised by this; in the Italian schools, legal precepts were
included in the *trivium* and especially in rhetorics, when «de
genere iudiciali» was studied. This, of course, was just the continuation of the ancient method reported by Quintilian, then by
Isidor and Martianus Capella. Novati [16] even formulated the
hypothesis that the compiler of the collection of Lombard laws
known as the *Liber Lombardae*, which was so important in the
history of legal studies, was a Cassinese monk named Pietro da
Teano. In any case, this collection kept at Monte Cassino,
although not of Cassinese origin, testifies to the fact that in the second half of the eleventh century law studies were undertaken at
the abbey. In this epoch, in fact, besides Byzantine influxes,
codices of Justinian were brought there by the intervention of
Desiderius.

It has already been seen that the monks dedicated themselves
actively to the sacred sciences; in fact, literary studies were a
preparation for them. To those already mentioned one must add
above all Bruno di Segni, a Bishop and Abbot of fearless zeal,
who «for biblical exegesis has no equals in Italy from the sixth to
the twelfth century» [17]. In his agiographic, polemic, and
theological works, he is closer to the scientific approach of the
school of Anselm of Aosta than the dialectical school. One
should not forget the monk Paul, of Ligurian origin, who,
although blind from infancy, applied himself with so much pa-
tience and perseverance to his studies that he deserved to be called
Didimo, with clear allusion to the blind Alexandrine writer of the
fourth century. He also took part in the debates over unity with
the Eastern Chuch at the time of Pope Pascal II.

This rapid survey, obviously, is not and could not be complete. From contemporary sources one realizes that those deserving to be remembered for their learning are much more

numerous. It is enough here to bring back the memory of the request of Barison of Sardinia. In 1182 he asked the Abbot of Monte Cassino to sent him twelve monks to take possession of S. Nicola *de Gurgo*, a monastery that he had founded; out of them he asked to have three or four «ita literati, ut, si necessarium fuerit, in archiepiscopos et episcopos possint eligi, et etiam regni nostri negotia, sive in Romana curia, vel in curia imperatoris et ubique valeant tractare*» [18]. The king was certain he could find such men in a monastery that had to provide for more than one hundred and fifty dependent houses scattered as far as Dalmatia, Lithuania, and Constatinople; he asked such men from a community that had already given many of his members for the governance of the Church universal.

In spite of the enormous difficulties that the times imposed, the studies kept their pace in the thirteenth century, and the school followed its traditional path as well from the didactic point of view. Some monks were sent to the new scientific centers to be sure, but it was always some exceptional case and only to acquire further specialization in disciplines already mastered.

It was at this time that St. Thomas Aquinas was educated in the Cassinese school. According to Tolomeo di Lucca, he made good progress «in logicalibus et naturalibus», studies which, as it is well known, indicated a superior degree in the arts. Various causes, besides political happenings, led the young Aquinas to break his bond of «oblate» with Monte Cassino; the signs of his early formation, however, remained evident, not only in the general orientation of his mentality but in particular in his love for poetry, even in Italian perhaps, and his mastery of Latin.

Later on, completely absorbed in his speculative studies, Aquinas did not have the leisure to devote himself to works of poetry, of which he seemed quite capable. Thus he left Monte Cassino well prepared intellectually, while the balance and medita-

---

* «Trained well enough that if it were necessary could be elected archbishops and bishops, and also capable to deal with the affairs of our kingdom at the Roman Curia, the Emperor's court and everywhere else».

tion of the monastic life helped by the enchanting setting of the
stupendous natural surroundings, contributed to mature the wonderful qualities with which his incomparable soul was endowed.

Pietro di Atina was born toward the end of the twelfth century; he became chancellor of the Church under Gregory IX and
composed the *Glossae ad decretum Gratiani*. Pandolfo di Santo
Stefano, later Abbot or better «administrator» of Monte Cassino,
also wrote on various topics; in the same ranks one must mention
Richard, Abbot and Cardinal; Bernard of Castrociclo, later cardinal and vice-chancellor; and Stephen Marsicanus, Abbot from
1215 to 1227, called by Riccardo di S. Germano «vir non minus
studii quam honestatis amator *»[19].

Mention should also be made of the monk Alexander, who
dedicated his *Exameron* in Latin verses to «prudentissimo viro
virtutibus et sapientia insigni magistro J(ohanni) **». This
Johannes must be distinguished from the other Cassinese, John
of Salerno, who was Cardinal of St. Stephen on the Caelian.

Magister Erasmus came to Monte Cassino when he was
already an adult. His scientific formation, close to that of
William of Auxerre, was originally Parisian with tendencies
towards the new scholastic orientations. His reputation earned
him a chair in the recently established university of Naples, by
concord invitation of both masters and scholars. It was there,
perhaps, that he had the opportunity to influence even more the
formation of St. Thomas Aquinas[20].

From the men and the words quoted, one can deduce that
studies at Monte Cassino kept pace with scientific advances. The
Glossae to Gratian's *Decretum* indicate progress in juridical
studies. Notice of Abbot Bernard has already been taken.

The intellectual depression becomes noticeable, although not
total even then, in the following century, one so tragic for Monte
Cassino because of wars and earthquakes.

At the beginning of the century there was Nicholas of Frat-

---

* «completely devoted to the studies no less than to the virtues».
** «To master John, man of exemplary virtue and great wisdom».

Montecassino destroyed (15th February, 1944)

South-west side

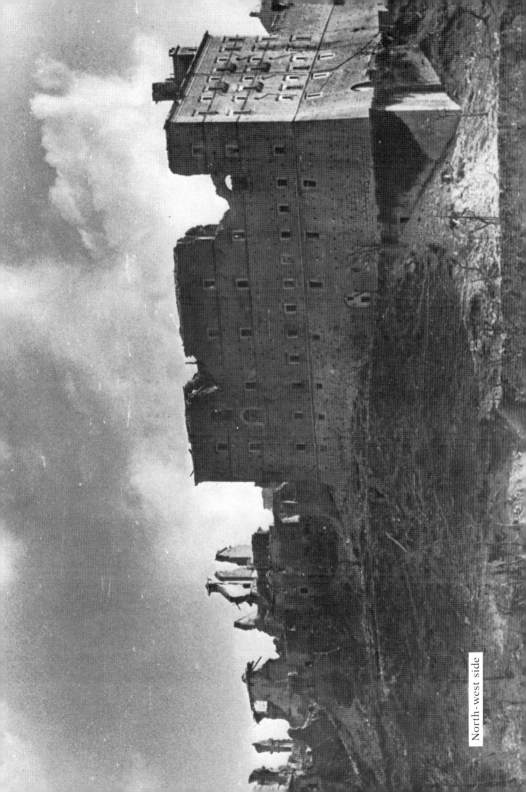

North-west side

West side

Middle cloister

Entrance cloister

Lower cloister

Corner of the schools

Façade of the Basilica with the statue of Tertullo

Where the Basilica was

The destroyed Basilica

The vault of the choir

Pillar of the Basilica

West side

West side

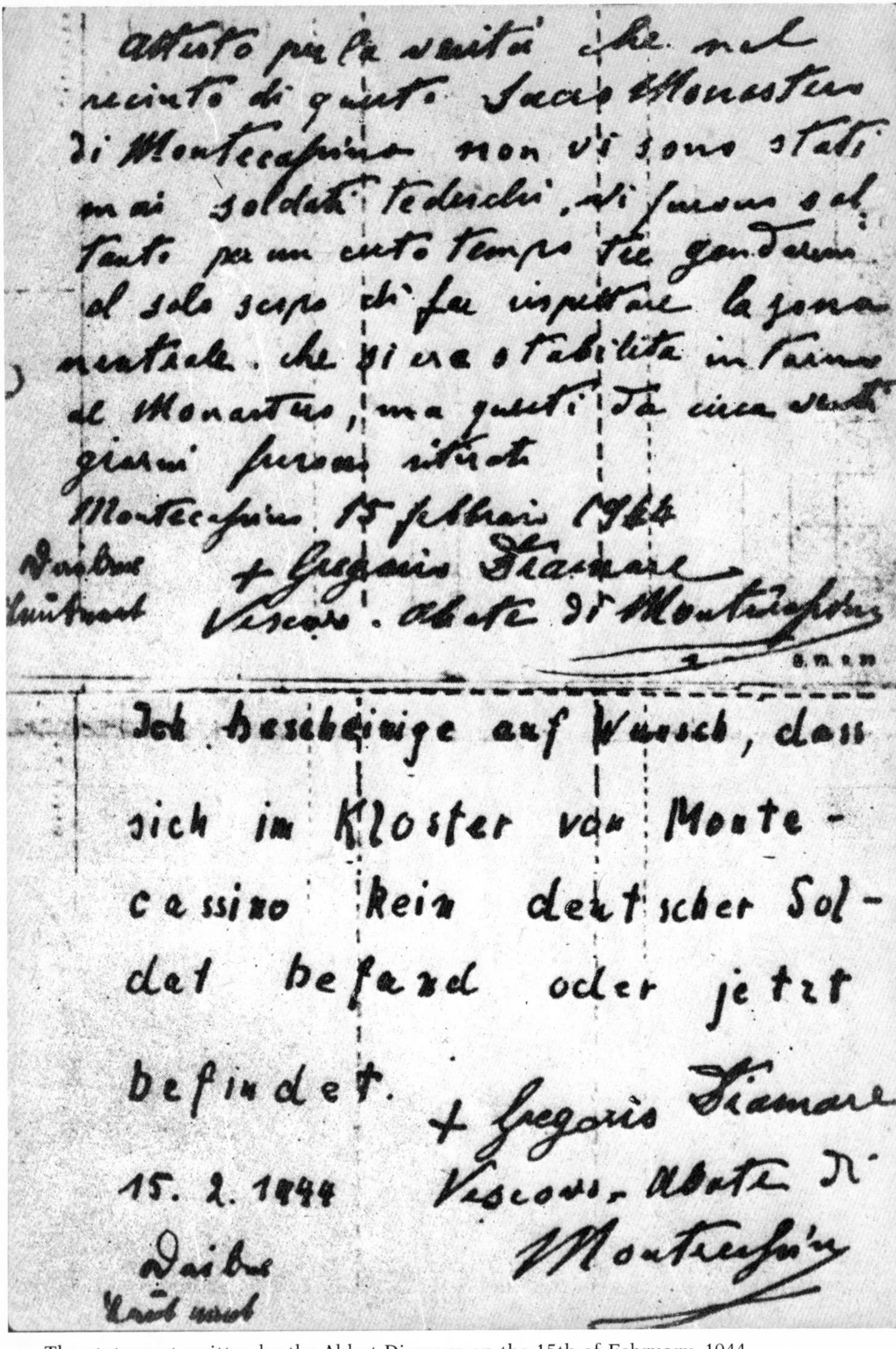

Attesto per la verità che nel
recinto di questo Sacro Monastero
di Montecassino non vi sono stati
mai soldati tedeschi, vi furono sol-
tanto per un certo tempo tre gendarmi
al solo scopo di far rispettare la zona
neutrale che si era stabilita intorno
al Monastero, ma questi da circa venti
giorni furono ritirati.
Montecassino 15 febbraio 1944

Daiber
Leutnant

+ Gregorio Diamare
Vescovo-Abate di Montecassino

Ich bescheinige auf Wunsch, dass
sich im Kloster von Montecassino kein deutscher Sol-
dat befand oder jetzt
befindet.

+ Gregorio Diamare
Vescovo-Abate di
Montecassino

15. 2. 1944

Daiber
Leutnant

The statement written by the Abbot Diamare on the 15th of February, 1944 tura, who in 1307 lectured on the Decretals in the university of Naples with a yearly salary of ten ounces. After he became Abbot of S. Vincenzo al Volturno, in 1317 he held there an important synod, and in 1318 he was among the envoys of king Robert of Anjou at Genoa. The Cassinese archives still have one of his manuscripts, a commentary on the Rule. Equally unpublished is the commentary of another learned jurist of the time, Riccardo di S. Angelo.

As it appears from the surviving codices of the period, grammatical, moral, dogmatic and scriptural studies were followed there, including the natural sciences, according to the Aristotelian scheme, following the trend of the time.

The famous codex 512 of the *Divine Comedy* also belongs to this century; it has marginal glosses attributed to Zanobi da Strada, the vicar of Angelo Acciaroli, Bishop of Cassino. History has only one humble representative in the anonymous but brief *Chronica* from the beginning of the century.

Not long after the great earthquake of 1363, the school was reorganized by Bishop Angelo Orsini who invited to teach there the monk Marco di Alvito, then vicar of S. Martino d'Alvito, S. Nicola della Valle Sorana, and S. Benedetto da Pascusano. One must consider as alumni of the school that Gregory the Spaniard mentioned in an extract of a charter of 1377 by Pietro de Tartaris as «a learned expositor of the Decreta», Guglielmo delle Marine di Fondi, who in 1378 had the title of baccalaureate and Gugliemo da Sessa, who is also mentioned in 1380 as a Licentiate in the Decretals.

The depression continued in the following fifteenth century so that while the whole of Italy wsa captured by the humanistic fervor, Monte Cassino, because of the misfortunes it was suffering, remained almost completely out of the movement.

It is true, of course, that the usual studies like medicine, metaphysics, morals etc. continued as in the preceding centuries; John the Deacon wrote verses in honor of the Holy Virgin, and Ignatius of Prague, prior and librarian, wrote a brief life of St. Bertharius.

This activity, however, limited and following traditional schemes, lacked the clear, characteristic humanistic mark.

The decision of Card. John of Aragon was destined to yield more abundant fruits. As already mentioned, in 1481 he reopened, this time in the vicarage of Albaneta, the school for the oblates: «ut et nostris et futuris temporibus monacorum numerus augeatur et regularis observantia facilius observetur et divinus cultus sine gravi labore adimpleatur, instituimus et etiam nunc ordinamus ut post hac reciperentur et recipiantur pueri qui secundum instituta prefati pii patris Benedicti, sub regulari nutrendi institutione a parentibus offerentur *».

As we know, however, at the beginning of the following sixteenth century, a new era opened for Monte Cassino. Almost as if to compensate for the preceding meager cultural activity, the spirit of the renaissance, in its sound, true essence affected it profoundly, renewing it completely in the exterior aspect of its buildings and reforming it in the life of the spirit and the intellect.

The principal personage of the century was, under every aspect, d. Angelo de Faggis, who was called Sangrino.

Named after his birthplace, Castel di Sangro, where he was born in 1500, he came to Monte Cassino when he was 16 or 18 years old. In a short time he mastered both Greek and Hebrew, while polishing his Latin in company of d. Onorato Fascitelli and d. Leonardo degli Oddi, a classical poet from a noble family from Perugia, who came to live at Monte Cassino after some sad misadventures. Besides his great learning, Sangrino lived a very saintly life and proved to have the skills of a statesman. He served as Abbot for a long time, and the fathers of the Council of Trent wished to have him amongst them, while Pope Pius V entrusted special missions to him. As it will be seen, his artistic activity was intense, and the abbey owed to him the grandiose and monumen-

---

* «in order to increase in our time and in the future the number of the monks, to maintain more easily the regular observance and to carry out without excessive labor the divine worship, we establish and command that from now on the children offered by their parents to be educated to the life of the Rule, according to the prescription of the Holy Father Benedict, be received».

tal scale that it has shown in the last centuries; still his intellectual activity was no less intense.

Most of his poetry constituted «an harmonic and solemn song» [21] and it was partially published in a few volumes. He died at an advanced age in 1593, and his corpse was found completely intact eight years after the burial.

D. Onorato Fascitelli, in contrast, was mostly a classical poet «the more Horatian and Catullian among the Cassinese, in the spirit of his poetry as well as in the form». He had close ties with Card. Bembo in the Roman Academy, with the Aretin, and with other humanists. Born from an illustrious family of Isernia in 1502, he came to Monte Cassino in 1519. He was named Bishop of Isola in Calabria and was a member of the Council of Trent who distinguished himself there as «the most elegant humanist» [22]. He died in Rome in 1564. He edited for the famous Renaissance press of A. Manutius the works of Pontano, Lactantius, Sannazzaro and, together with Angelo di Costanzo and Bernardino Rota, of Petrarch (1546). Very little of his own poetry was published, and the greater part has been lost; a few of his epigrams and some letters are still unpublished.

D. G. E. Mormile is noteworthy for the abundance of his literary output, and his works have been judged «among the most beautiful and felt of the vast humanistic production» [23]. He belonged, probably, to the noble Neapolitan family of the same name and came to Monte Cassino about 1563.

Of great renown was also d. Benedetto dell'Uva, of a noble family from Capua, who was already at Monte Cassino in 1562. A friend of Torquato Tasso and Annibale Caro, he was «among the best didactic poets of the end the sixteenth century» [24]. His work, *Le vergini prudenti,* was reprinted five times in a period of twenty-six years.

Around these major figures, mostly humanists, besides these poets who rise above the rank of local personages to assume national importance, many other learned men illuminated the *Cinquecento* at Monte Cassino both in the sacred and the natural sciences. Just to mention a few, we have d. Gregorio da Viterbo

(1530), quite versed in law and the author of homilies on the Gospel of St. John, and d. Benedetto Canofilo of Castel di Sangro, a famous jurist, among the best of his time. Canofilo was created a knight of the empire by Emperor Maximilian in 1512, but in 1525 he joined and became a monk at Monte Cassino and died there in 1550. His works were published in five volumes in Venice in 1542; the most famous was *De foro Fori et de foro Poli*. D. Crisostomo da S. Geminiano, from Calabria, supervised the reform of the Benedictine congregation of Meleda in Dalmatia and was the Bishop of Ragusa when he died. A jurist and a great theologian, he took part in the Council of Trent; he knew Hebrew and did translations from the Greek. D. Saverio d'Aversa (1530) and d. Luca delle Fratte (1534) were learned in the Holy Scriptures and philosophy. D. Paolo d'Altavilla (1541) was a great expert in Hebrew, Greek, and Latin. D. Basilio Millani (1541?), a jurist and a Latinist, also translated works from the Greek. D. Benedetto da S. Germano († ca. 1600), one of the major philosophers and theologians of the entire Cassinese congregation, was skilled in Latin, Greek, and Hebrew and left behind several works that later were lost. D. Antonio Petronio (1546), well-versed in law as well as Greek and Latin, reorganized the archives after the era of the commendataries. D. Bernardo of Genoa (1545) was quite learned in philosophy and Sacred Scriptures, while d. Luca Antonio of Fermo (1552) was well read in philosophy and medicine. D. Teofilo di Marzio of Siena (1586) was called the «*ammirabile*» for his profound knowledge of mathematics and astronomy, which were also followed then at Monte Cassino by the Abbot Brugia and by d. Angelo Pria. Teofilo worked on the reform of the calendar at the time of Gregory XIII and was also well read in theology, philosophy and the liberal arts. D. Tommaso of Eboli (1556), the author of various books, was also an adviser of St. Philip Neri. D. Placido Petrucci (1570) was archivist and historian of the abbey. D. Onorato de' Medici (1571) continued the work of Petrucci, whom he succeeded in the direction of the archives. D. Felice Passero († 1626) published many volumes of poetry. The English d. Gregorio Sayr, jurist and moralist, left numerous works of dogmatics, morals and canon law; he died, still young, in 1607. D. Tommaso Preston, another Englishman, was the author of a treatise on theology. D. Zaccaria Sereno, a knight of Malta who fought in the battle of Lepanto, became a monk at Monte Cassino in 1575; he composed several works, among them the *Commentari alla guerra di Cipro.*

Around men like these, and the list is by no mean complete, the school again lived up to its better traditions, but with the new character required by the times. Monte Cassino was one of the teaching centers of the congregation, and the curriculum was prescribed by the Church and the general chapters of the order. Public debates and meetings, especially on solemn occasions, besides the traditional examinations, served to give public demonstrations of the work that was done there, while the scholarship and the skills of the men mentioned above constituted the visible fruits.

Particular mention must be made about the institution of the diocesan seminary which, following the dispositions of the Council of Trent, at the end of the century was placed side by side with the old school, although clearly distinct even in administrative matters. The Abbot d. Andrea da Sessa (1589-1590) asked Pope Sixtus V for permission to built it. The approval came with a papal bull of May 20, 1590, which, to keep the monastic community free from any burden, mandated that only the Abbot and the Vicar general had to have care of it. When the Abbot d. Andrea died, the seminary was opened by his successor d. Girolamo Brugia (1590-1595) on Dec. 29 of the same year, 1590, at the church of S. Maria della Pietà near the collegiate church of S. Germano. In the eighteenth century, a large and imposing building was constructed in the area of the ancient amphitheater, but the unhealthiness of the site combined with the difficult political situation that then developed did not allow the transfer. Only later, in the ninteenth century, as a result of the new conditions of life, the seminary was moved into the buildings of the abbey. This too contributed its share to the revival of studies and the formation of many good men.

Towards the middle of the century, Monte Cassino and other monasteries of the congregation contributed to another notable enterprise, the revision of the Vulgate, that is, the text of Holy Scriptures currently used by the Catholic Church. To the trust placed in them by the Holy See, the monks of Monte Cassino answered by providing variations to twenty-four codices, which was more than two-thirds of all the codices consulted to prepare for the colossal task. The work was not carried out by the supreme authority, which only recently has entrusted it again to the Benedictine monks.

In the seventeenth century intellectual and scholarly activities followed a similar pattern. There were theological debates and literary gatherings attended by illustrious personages. In 1620 we find in attendance Card. Gaspare Borgia, viceroy of Naples; in 1630 the Cardinal Archbishop of Naples, Francesco Boncompagni; and in 1695 the Card. Giuseppe Sanchez de Aguirre. Mabillon, who was there with his travel companion d. Michel Germain, in his book, *Iter Italicum,* wrote as follows: [25] «Interfuimus et disputationibus publicis, quae apud Cassinates nostros frequentissime fiunt de rebus theologicis et philosophicis, maxime moralibus necnon etiam de scripturis sacris. Eiusmodi collationes passim conditae orationibus et poematibus, ut hospitibus suis gratificarentur. Sane apud Cassinates praeclare instituuntur iuvenes qui per sex annos continuos sub accurata magistri disciplina in novitiorum conclavi privato degunt, ubi in officiis pietatis atque in litteris accurate exercentur» *. This was the custom of the congregation, and several monks from Monte Cassino were also sent to teach in other monasteries. Among

---

* «We have also taken part in public debates that our Cassinese hold very frequently on theological and philosophical arguments especially moral as well as on the Sacred Scriptures. These conferences are also adorned with speeches and poems in honor of the guests. Among the Cassinese, in fact, the young are extremely well educated; they remain for six years in the local novitiate, separate from the rest of the monastery, under the vigilant eye of the master, and there they exercise themselses with great diligence in their religious duties and in literary studies».

those who taught elsewhere, there were d. Simplicio Caffarelli, a disciple of the above mentioned d. Gregorio Sayr, professor of philosophy and theology; d. Severino Pepe, whose special method of teaching theology was introduced through the various abbeys of the congregation by the students that he had over a period of fourteen years; and d. Andrea Deodati, who later led to the establishment of St. Anselm in Rome and was destined to receive and form in Rome the best intellectual hopes of the congregation.

Among the learned monks who were authors of works on various topics, the following should be remembered: d. Girolamo Petronio, d. Bernardino Saivedra, d. Antonio da Napoli, d. Paolo Agostino de Ferraris, d. Paolo Andrea Gualtiero, and the Englishman d. Ratchisio Gennaro of Durfram. Above all, one must note the Abbot d. Angelo della Noce, who became Archbishop of Rossano and died in 1691. An eminent figure of erudition an archeologist, philosopher, theologian, orator and poet, he was a professor both at Monte Cassino and the Sapienza in Rome. He loved to talk almost exclusively about scientific subjects and always remembered that during his abbacy, in the afternoon recreation period, he used to propose to the monks the solution of doubts. A new edition of the *Chronicon Cassinese* is owed to him; it was not the first but certainly more noteworthy than the two preceding ones. In Rome, where he spent his last years, he shone among the major theologians and scholars, was dear to popes, cardinals and queen Christina of Sweden, and it was only because of maneuverings by mischievous people that he did not receive a cardinal's hat.

Intellectual activity became even more intense in the following century. From the very beginning of it, the abbots were very diligent in perfecting even more the educational process. D. Ippolito della Penna (1697-1704) gave greater importance to canon law; d. Gregorio Galisio (1704-1717) never considered the cost in order to obtain the best teachers of literature; d. Oderisio Pierio di Chio, a visitor and apostolic vicar of the Greek rite Mainoti, left various writings also in his language; d. Cornelio Cerasio, besides an interesting short work on Gaeta published in several editions under other name, and the history of S. Liberatore alla Maiella, this too under an assumed name, left several unpublished treatises, among them, the *Elogi* of the monks and the most minute description of customs at Monte Cassino in his times. D. Pier Maria Giustiniani, Bishop of Sagona in Corsica and then of Ventimiglia, and d. Angelo Longo, Bishop of Teano, were also learned monks deserving mention.

Famous above all, however, was d. Erasmo Gattola from Gaeta (1662-1734), who with his *Historia Abbatiae Cassinensis* continued the great tradition of the Cassinese, leaving behind a work which has never been surpassed. A noble, scholarly figure, in Italy as well as abroad, «there was no one who, getting involved in a topic having to do with the Middle Ages, would not want to consult him» [26], from the great Muratori to Fontanini and the famous monks of the congregation of St. Maur, who kept with him a long and active correspondence which was published a few years ago. Besides the prefecture of the archives, to which he devoted tireless care until his death, he also held for a long time the office of Vicar general of the diocese, directed the works of embellishment of the church done at the time, and put much work into defending the rights of the monastery in the frequent juridical challenges of that epoch.

With Gattola, one must also remember two other Cassinese erudites of the eighteenth century, the brothers Federici, G. Battista (1736-1800) and Placido (1739-1765). The first wrote the history *Degli antichi duchi o consoli e ipati di Gaeta* and, in manuscript form, the large *Codex diplomaticus Casinensis;* the second brother wrote the *Storia di Pomposa* and, in manuscript, the *Codex diplomaticus Pomposianus,* besides an important catalogue of Cassinese codices. Both were in communication with the more noteworthy intellectuals of the period and d. Placido had a particularly close friendship with Pindemonte and Monti, who donated to him some of his Latin and Italian poems, which recently have been published [27].

One must place in this group, which represents worthily

Monte Cassino in the great century of Italian erudition, d. Giuseppe M. Franchini and d. Sebastiano Campitelli, both learned archivists; the Irishman d. Giuseppe Macarty, a Latinist and archeologist; and d. Casimiro Correale from Sorrento, author of a *Lexicon Hebraeo-Caldeo-Biblicum* in ninty-nine big volumes, of which the death of the author (1774) allowed the publication of only the first number.

Worthy heirs of this erudite tradition in the ninteenth century were the prefect of the archives, d. Ottavio Fraja-Frangipane (1763-1843) who continued wisely the collections of the codices and discovered in the codices of the archives unknown sermons of St. Augustine; d. Sebastiano Kelefati († 1863), an expert in Graeco-Byzantine documents; and d. Andrea Caravita, author of the work in three volumes, *I codici e le arti a Monte Cassino.*

The flame of scholarship, indeed, did not die down because of the ominous winds which threatened the very existence of the abbey. On the contrary, the work resumed with renewed vigor in the second half of the century. As the *scriptorium* had been at one time, the typography and the chromolithography were set up not for commercial purposes but to facilitate the publication of Cassinese works, and these served to spread for a long time the fruits of such great intellectual activity. The *Biblioteca* by Ferraris was newly published (1843) in seven volumes and was adjourned with scholarly notes by the monks. Other publications included the *Codice inedito di Dante,* 1865, and the *Bibliotheca Casinensis,* 5 vols., 1873-1896; the *Spicilegium Casinense,* 3 vols., 1893-1901; the *Codex diplomaticus Cajetanus,* 2 vols., (1887-1891); the *Paleografica artistica di Monte Cassino,* 1876-1877; and *Le miniature dei codici cassinesi,* 1887. These are the principal collections, begun with cooperative efforts at the urging of Abbot De Vera, and here one wants to recall names like Tosti, Quandel, Piscicelli, Caplet, and Amelli.

Tosti (1811-1897), who came to Monte Cassino when he was still a child, is famous for his great historical, poetical, and patriotic works. A man of great intelligence, granted his exuberant imagination, he called for immediate peace between the

Church and the newly established kingdom of Italy, which would
have avoided the fatal conflict of the Italian *risorgimento,* which
he, indeed, had strongly desired and promoted with the word of
faith and his activity as an historian. To him also, as vice-archivist
of the Holy See, Monte Cassino owes a great deal for its preservation.

Of the two brothers Quandel, Giuseppe, the first one, who
died as abbot of Monte Cassino in 1897, left interesting evidence
of his activity as an official in the Engineer Corps of the Bourbon
army in the campaign of 1860 in his *Lavori del genio napolitano
nelle posizioni occupate dall'esercito dietro il Garigliano fino al
termine dell'assedio di Gaeta.* He was a man of tireless activity
and a loyal and constant collaborator with Abbot d'Orgemont,
whom he succeeded in the governance of the abbey. He was rector
of the college and the administrator of the monastery, he always
found time for studies and important work. He directed the excavations and the restoration of the ancient monastery, of St.
Benedict, and in three manuscript volumes, he diligently gathered
the memories of building activities at the abbey. Resuming a work
which had already been started, and with the cooperation of some
fellow monks, he published the two large volumes of the *Codex
diplomaticus Cajetanus,* a valuable collection of documents
about the ancient duchy of Gaeta. He also left in manuscript form
the fruits of other research. He was also the founder, with advice
from Quintino Sella and M.S. De Rossi, of the metereologic-
geodynamic observatory, which was quite well known into the
present, when, through the dedication of d. Bernardo Paoloni, it
was the location for several years of a special radio atmospheric
service and also the editorial center of a journal.

The younger Quandel brother, d. Cesare, who came to
Monte Cassino at a very young age, was in charge of the archives
for some time and was preparing a history of Gaeta when he died
quite young (1880) with the work still incomplete; he was,
however, able to make ready for publication the *Commento alla
Regola* attributed to Paul the Deacon.

D. Oderisio Piscicelli-Taeggi (1840-1917), who as the great

prior of Bari blessed the wedding of the royal princes Victor Emmanuel and Helen, future king and queen of Italy, was the editor of a valuable illustration of the Cassinese miniatures which received large praises and prizes. Unfortunately, the government positions that later were entrusted to him did not allow him to complete the series, and he was also unable to finish his careful researches on the basilica of St. Nicholas in Bari, on the Cassinese congregation, and on other topics to which he applied himself in his hard-working life.

D. Anselmo Caplet, a Frenchman († 1916), was one of the Benedictines who under the direction of Tosti, by request of Leo XIII, had to bring forth an edition of extracts of the documents in the Vatican archives. Besides publishing the *Regesto di Clemente V,* he also took care of the publication of the *Regesto di Bernardo I* of Monte Cassino and of the *Commento alla Regola* written by the same Bernardo. For many years a professor at the international college of St. Anselm in Rome, he was endowed with an easy poetical vein, of which examples may be found in some of his writings.

D. Ambrogio Amelli, the last in time of the glorious group, came to the Cassinese cloister after fighting for the restoration of the sacred chant and after establishing the Italian association of S. Cecilia. Disciple of the great Ceriani in the management of the Biblioteca Ambrosiana of Milan, he found at Monte Cassino a wide area to devote his energies to. A prefect of the sacred studies, especially the patristic and scriptural ones, he closed his long and noble life († 1933) as vice president of the pontifical commission for the revision of the Vulgate, the establishment of which he himself had suggested to Pius X. Born during the struggle for Italian independence and ordained a priest on Sept. 20, 1870, he was able to see the realization of that ideal of conciliation which he had shared with Tosti, from whom he had also inherited the strong, passionate love for his country [28].

There are, however, many other Cassinese who deserve to be recognized in other fields of studies. D. Gaetano Bernardi, an experienced teacher, was the first who came to Monte Cassino to embrace the monastic life after the suppression of 1868. A man of letters of excellent taste and a major authority on Manzoni, Bernardi was first teacher and then very dear friend of D'Ovidio, with whom he kept up a quite interesting literary correspondence. His literary theories were collected in the best known of his works the *Avviamento all'arte del dire,* which, after the first edition of 1868, has been printed several times, even recently. Director of studies at Monte Cassino, he was chosen by Leo XIII to work with Card. Dusmet in the reconstruction of the college of St. Anselm on new bases. He died at Monte Cassino as president of the Benedictine congregation in 1895.

D. Luigi Vaccari from Calabria worked strenuously for the dogmatic recognition of the Assumption of Mary. His principal work was in fact, the one that in its second edition received the title *De B. V. Mariae morte, resurrectione et in coelum gloriosa Assumptione,* Ferrara, Taddei, 1881. He died on Dec. 17, 1887, with a reputation of great virtue, as titular Bishop of Sinope, coadiutor with right of succession, and administrator of Nicotera and Tropea.

The Abbot d. Carlo De Vera (1863-1871) was not only the promoter of a new intellectual movement, but himself «the purest writer, who, had he been free from the cares of government, would have been among the major in Italy» [29]. His successor, the Abbot d. Bonifacio Krug (1909), who came to Monte Cassino from the monastery of St. Vincent in Pennsylvania, had the soul of an artist and left behind some noteworthy musical compositions and, as a prior, directed the rearrangement of the Pomposian collection. Also worth remembering are d. Constantino Postiglione (1898), a famous surgeon and a former professor at the university of Naples, and d. Agostino Latil from Lyon (1926), a marvelously versatile mind.

The tradition has continued to the present. The continuation of scientific collections like the *Spicilegium,* the description of the codices, the pubblication of miniatures and the registers, the various contributions in journal and separate publications, all bear witness to an activity never interrupted. Omitting those who are still alive, one must remember especially the archivist d. Mauro Inguanez (1955) who, although busy with various other tasks, has left behind a deep and lasting imprint on Cassinese studies with the publication of the *Catalogus* of the codices, various registers, and numerous other documents from the archives entrusted to him.

Meanwhile, another form of intellectual activity had been set into motion after the fearful days of the 1848 revolution, the establishment of a school of classical studies for young laymen, to which the Cassinese tradition gave a special appeal. It was, undoubtedly a novelty for Monte Cassino, yet it soon proved to be a realistic enterprise which seemed to answer an existing need. This was proved by the great success that it had among the foremost noble families of central and southern Italy, and the reputation it soon earned as one of the better colleges in Italy, especially for its emphasis on serious scholarship. Abbot Bernardi, who developed the curriculum, and the abbots Quandel and Diamare as rectors were most solicitous about the success of the enterprise. Other monks, helped by priests and laymen, provided the teaching faculty. The school was located in the old guest house, which was completely modernized and furnished with all the necessary equipment, including well-supplied science laboratories.

The diocesan seminary, which after the perturbations of the eighteenth century had been transferred, as already mentioned, within the abbey itself, also required a great deal of attention. At the end of the last century, in fact, it split into two separate institutes for some time, St. Benedict and St. Joseph. The schools, which used to be joined with the college, had been separated after the first world war, and they were almost all run by the monks.

The Cassinese monastery has always been kept as a fertile field in which the injunction to work has also found ways to yield intellectual fruits.

Together with holiness, learning gave life, in the Cassinese cloister as well, to that dual light which, according to the exhortation of Innocent IV to the Cistercians, had to serve to enlighten mankind, and at same time, earn greater glory to the monks in heaven.

2. THE «SCRIPTORIUM».

Such intellectual activity would have been impossible without the necessary means.

We have seen already how St. Benedict enjoined the monks to read and provided that, among their personal belongings, there would be a *graphium* and the *tabulae,* the tablets and the stylus; he equipped them, therefore, with the means to write and get books at a time when the production of books was neither large nor easy.

The art of writing was therefore a necessity in the monastery; those who were unable to break the sod with a plow could trace the letters of the codices, an art no less noble than the others destined to glorify God and his house and no less wearisome. If in fact, «tria digita scribunt», notes the Cassinese writer, «totum corpus laborat» *. And only «qui scribere nescit putat nullum esse laborem» **, while «sicut qui navigat desiderat portum, ita scriptor novissum versum» *** (Cod. Cas. 5). The work was made lighter, however, by the thought that the fruits would bring spiritual gifts for the fellow monks and would be useful for the divine service. The scribe Savinus asks, therefore, «Omnes qui legitis, oro vos orate pro me peccatore» ****, and another prays, «suscipe completi laudes, o Christe, laboris, quas cordis laeti vox subdita reddit amoris. Sit merces operis oratio sacra legendis, quae jungat superis nos toto robore mentis (Cod. Cas. 7)» *****.

---

   * «Only three fingers do the writing... but the whole body works».
  ** «only those who do not know how to write believe that there is no toil in it».
 *** «The sailor longs for port like the writer for the last line».
**** «All you who read this, I pray that you pray for me a sinner».
***** Accept. O Christ, for the completed work the praises that come to you from the humble and loving voice of a contented heart». The compensation for this work will be the sacred prayer of the reader who joins us to heaven with all the strength of the soul».

Indeed the pious transcriber does not seek human praise; often he does not give his name, «meum nomen non pono, quia me laudare nolo» * (Cod. Cas. 7). Thus writing skill is a means for the edification of the monks.

In the large rooms located around the cloisters, the monks, generally in groups of twelve, bent over the parchment membranes in calm silence, work steadily under the direction of a senior monk, the *armarius*.

Through the centuries their diligent and assiduous work gave life to the tradition of the Cassinese *Scriptorium*. Like the intellectual and the artistic activity to which it participated, the life of the *scriptorium* was tightly connected with the historical happenings at the monastery and showed the effects of its alternating turns of fortune. Its range of activities extended to all the delicate operations necessary to the making of a book, from the preparation of the papyrus pages or the white parchment, to the choice of inks and colors to the making of the precious bindings, and above all, to the writing and the miniatures which had their own well-defined characteristics.

The typical script, used not only for the codices but also, in an essentially equal form, for the documents, was the one currently called «beneventan» to indicate the area where it was especially used, that is, in the territory of the ancient duchy of Benevento. It was also called, however, «Lombard-Cassinese» from its main center, and this not improperly, because it took root only where there were monasteries, of *lictera longobarda monastica*.

In its formative stage it begins to appear in the last decades of the eighth century; it reaches the summit of perfection during the abbacy of Desiderius. The codices of that epoch are real works of art. It declined in the succeding centuries, until at the end of the thirteenth century it was replaced by the gothic minuscule and only resurfaces exceptionally a few times during the fourteenth century. In the minor centers its progress was slower and did not always reach the perfection of the Cassinese exemplars. In some

---

* «I am not signing my name because I desire no personal praise».

place, like Bari and Dalmatia, it also assumed variant forms.

When this script was no longer used, others were employed, as we have already hinted, in the Cassinese *scriptorium,* which continued its activity until the fifteenth century, when the diffusion of the printing art facilitated the supplying of books.

For some time, however, even printed books were provided with rubrics by the calligraphers and were illuminated, that is, adorned with miniatures in the initials and the margins.

The codices were, in fact, embellished by the miniaturists with their wonderful artistic skill. The miniature like the script took on in the Cassinese *scriptorium* a character of its own. Its development naturally is related to that of the script, but it also felt influxes from various areas which operated on Cassinese art; thus it was not altogether original in all of its elements.

Few are the names of the clerks and copyists which are well known. The greatest of all was Leo in the eleventh century; the rest were Giaquinto at the time of Aligernus, Savinus, Paul the deacon, Turbo, John, another subdeacon, Alboin, Grimoald the deacon, Carsus, John the priest, Boniface the deacon, Simeon the deacon, Ferro, and Gauthier the binder. Later to the same is added the indication of the country or of the father; thus in the thirteenth century we find Pietro d'Atina; in the fourteenth, Antonio di Mario of Florence, John the Hungarian, master Giovanni of Calabria, and others among which one finds not only monks but also laymen.

To the latter, one must credit the last manuscripts at Monte Cassino that were decorated with miniatures. By request of the Abbot Squarcialupi, between 1507 and 1523, the Florentine master, Giovanni Boccardo, with his son Francesco and the disciples master Matteo and Loise completed the splendid books of the choir. In spite of their origin, the work of the artists was closely related to the ambiance from which they drew their inspiration and whose artistic tradition it followed. The harmony and the fusion of the colors, the play of light and shade provides a worthy frame of splendid peace and solemn wealth for the sacred text. «Even today the turquoise imperceptibly turns into the ultramarine blue of the nobler miniatures and under shadows of golden hair a fresh fluttering of a Botticelli's spring makes one feel a poetry higher than love, a beauty which dreaming and praying seems divine» [31].

Of particular interest is the ornamentation of the liturgical rolls, the famous *Exultet* used for the singing of the Easter proclamations until the fourteenth century, according to the custom prevalent in southern Italy.

Miniature art once again gained a place of honor in the Cassinese cloister during the last century through the support of d. Oderisio Piscicelli-Taeggi, mentioned above. In our own days, this art has once again come alive through the splendid work of d. Eusebio Grossetti. This young artist, cut down by the storm just before the extreme desolation while he was still very young has left behind besides some other minor compositions, an *Exultet* and an unfortunately unfinished evangelistary *ad usum Ecclesiae Casinensis,* in which the pages seem to smile at the reader through the splendor of the art. Clearly, to Grossetti had been revealed both the secrets and the enchantment of the ancient tradition.

One of the principal contributions of the Cassinese *scriptorium,* and the one that is of particular interest to future generations, was the conservation of ancient culture. Monte Cassino was one of the chief workshops for the preservation and the transmission of those works.

The oldest work on grammar that has come down to us, the *De Lingua Latina* of Varro, which contains also fragments of preceding authors, is in the Codex Flor. Laur. 51.10, written at Monte Cassino, at the time of Abbot Desiderius. From it, which is also the most complete, all the other known codices depend. Moreover, even those older fragments which are contained in the codex Paris. 7350 of about the end of the eighth century, originate from Monte Cassino. In the same Parisian codex, one finds the treatise *De metris horatianis* by Servius. To this codex, together with another from Benevento, Casan. 1086 of the ninth century, we owe the *Scholia* to the tragedy *Thyestes* by L. Varius. In the same codex Flor. Laur. 51.10 a special tradition of Cicero's

Pro Cluentio is also found.

Another codex Flor. Laur. 68.2 of the eleventh century, which Boccaccio took away from Monte Cassino, contains books I-V of the *Historiae* and books XI-XVI of the *Annales* by Tacitus. This same codex is also the only source for the *Metamorphoses* or the *Golden Ass* of Apuleius and for a collection of selected passages called the *Florida,* taken from the essays of the same author.

The well-known treatise by Frontinus, *De aquaeductu Urbis Romae,* so important for the study of the topography of ancient Rome, is in the codex Cass. 361, which was written in the twelfth century by Peter the Deacon. For the *Dialogi* of Seneca the most important manuscript is a Cassinese codex of the eleventh century, the Ambros. C. 90. The best text of Cicero's *Somnium Scipionis* is found in another codex written at Monte Cassino at the beginning of the twelfth century, the Vat. Lat. 2337, which is very important also for the text of the *Philippics*.

Very important for the texts of Ovid's *Fasti* is the codex Vat. Lat. 3262 and the 118 of the library of the University of Leiden for the *De legibus, De natura deorum* and *De Divinatione* of Cicero; both were of Cassinese origin and were written in the eleventh century. Also to the age of Desiderius belonged the most ancient text of Corippus's work *Iohannis seu de bellis Libicis,* which, however, has been lost since the sixteenth century. The sixty missing lines of Juvenal's sixth satire were also found at Monte Cassino and, one must add also, that it was Paul the Deacon in the eighth century who composed an important compendium to Festus, which is all we have from that author.

Besides these works of classical authors, there are also those of the Fathers and of Christian antiquity. These include *De mysteriis* of St. Hilaire and the famous *Peregrinatio,* which are in the codex that from Monte Cassino was brought to Arezzo and is now kept at S. Maria della Fraternità (VI, 3); the commentary on Job by Julian of Eclana; the treatise against Origen by St. Jerome; a very ancient version of the *Psaltery*; and various sermons and homilies by St. Augustine, St. Jerome and other

Fathers of the church. Some lives of saints are all works which we owe exclusively to the work of the Cassinese copyists.

To them we owe moreover, some historical and literary monuments of the Middle Ages: The oldest papal *Register,* that of John VIII (Arc. Vat. R. 1), the oldest text of the *Decretum* of Gratian (Cod. Cas. 385), one of the oldest codex of the *Micrologo* of Guido d'Arezzo (Cod. Cas. 318), and the *De curatione aegritudinum partium totius corporis,* which was edited on the basis of Cod. Cas. 351. Here also we find the translation of the medical works made by Constantinus Africanus, an unknown article from St. Thomas' *Summa Theologica* (Cod. Cas 138), the last doctrinal writing of the same holy doctor in his letter to abbot Bernard (Cod. Cas. 82), and the *Ambrosiaster* (Cod. Cas. 150, the oldest at Monte Cassino, dating back to the sixth century). Besides the oldest medieval texts of the *Psalterium iuxta Hebraeos* of St. Jerome (Co. Cas. 434), there are the *Libri Rerum gestarum saxonicarum Widukindi* (Cod. Cas. 208, of the eleventh century). Of the eleventh century also is the Cod. Cas. 494, which, besides being one of the earliest containing the life of St. Remigius of Incmar, has great importance for the study of the Gregorian chant; it is, in fact, one of only four which present the so-called *notazione comasca,* while the very ancient fragment of the *Sacramentario Gregoriano,* in Cod. Cas. 271, shows the primitive stage of that very important liturgical text. Also the famous medieval hymn, *O Roma nobilis,* has been preserved exclusively in Cod Cas. 318 and in Cod Cas. 3227, which also had belonged to Monte Cassino.

The Cod. Cas. 459, although not written at Monte Cassino, is the one that has preserved for us the *Summula statutorum Floridorum Venediarum* by the doge Andrea Dandolo.

At the end of this arid but fruitful enumeration, we can fully justify the statements of Traube and Loew, who see in Monte Cassino «a veritable center for the transmission of the Latin classics». Were this the only merit, it would suffice to earn for the monks the gratitude of posterity. They prevented, in the normal evolution of the human spirit, a sudden and total fracture with the past, such that could have set civilization back for many centuries.

3. The library and the archives.

«Claustrum sine armario sicut castrum sine armamentario: a monastery without a library is like a fortress without an armory».

The Cassinese militia, which in its long history had to fight so many harsh battles and accomplish so many glorious missions, had a well-furnished armory at its disposal. The *scriptorium,* of which we have admired the providential activity, had the task to provide in fact, these weapons: the library was the natural recipient of its production.

That it existed from the very first times, there can be no doubt; the Rule itself mentions it: «Accipiant singuli codices de bibliotheca» * (Chapt. 48), and the expression keeps its original force, even if here «bibliotheca» literally has another meaning. At any rate, it was required for the demands of the daily conobitic life, which must have codices for private and common reading, the latter, for example, during meals and before compline, for the divine service and for the needs of the school for the young oblates.

The precepts of the Legislator often, through the course of the centuries, were confirmed with special dispositions which watched over the safekeeping of this patrimony of the abbey, which was indispensable and connected with the very nature of monasticism. While the medieval copyists implored: «quisquis quem tetigerit lota sit ei manus» **, they also had serious threats for eventual thieves: «si quis hunc librum quolibet obtentu ex hoc sacro loco auferre praesumpserit, cum illis mansionem sortiatur aeternam, quibus in extremo judicio dicturus est Christus: ite

---

* «Let everyone take a book from the library».
** «Whoever touches it, let him first wash his hands».

maledicti in ignem aeternum» *. While the constitutions in later centuries forbade to everybody, even the abbots, to take out of the library or the archives, for any reason: «privilegia, litteras, instrumenta... libros» and even more strongly to alienate or give away, among other goods of the abbey, also «... libros», Sixtus V threatened excommunication for whomsoever, of any rank, under any pretext, who should take out, even for a short time, books either handwritten or printed. One cannot claim that, especially after the later judicial dispositions, such penalties were still in effect, but the copy of the Brief of Sixtus V of April 5, 1588, *ad perpetuam rei memoriam,* remained affixed to the splendidly carved entrance door, artistically written on a tablet with miniatures and designs until the tragic day of the Allies' bombing.

Still even all that care and vigilance could not prevent, in the course of over fourteen centuries, dispersions and destructions. The sad events in Cassinese history had their painful reflexes also on the library.

In the beginning, the collections were mostly on papyrus. This was the written material of the time; even the Rule was written on papyrus and in the thirteenth century some codices were still kept of this material. The papyrus was followed by the parchment and then the paper.

At the first restoration of the monastery, among the gifts offered by pope Zacharias were books of Sacred Scriptures, and in the same century Anselm was able to take several codices from Monte Cassino to his newly established monastery of Nonantola.

In the ninth century Abbot Autpert (834-837) was said to have appreciably increased the collections of the library. Abbot Bertharius in the same century extended his activities also to this field: in the great Cassinese solemnity of Tuesday after Easter «domnus abbas illum ante pectus deferat codicem quem mirifice Bertharius Christo beatoque construxit Benedicto» **.

---

* «If anybody, under whatever pretext, will carry this book away from this sacred place, let him go to stay forever with those to whom in the final judgement Christ will say: Go, you accursed, into the eternal fire».
** «Let the Abbot carry on his chest that codex which Bertharius had beautifully

Other codices were written at Capua, and from them we have some that are truly valuable, as for instance the 175. Also to be remembered are a missal «cum tabulis argenteis deuratis» and an «evangelium quoque simili opere» *.

Upon his return to Monte Cassino, Aligernus gives a great deal of attention to the library and besides a «textum evangelii undique contextum argento inaurato cum smaltis ac gemmis», provides also «codices plurimos ac diversos» **. John II furnished also codices «magnos et pulchros»; his successor Atenolf adds twenty more. There were, of course, depredations and dispersions: some codices were turned over to the dependent houses. Thus, for instance, Liuzio, when establishing the convent of Albaneta, took with him various codices; he also received a good supply of them from Guaimarius, the prince of Salerno. One could say that for these reasons there were not enough books at Monte Cassino. This situation was remedied by abbot Teobald who, as we have seen, started a new cultural era for southern Italy. He had already collected many codices through his travels, but the others, the greater part, he had them written at Monte Cassino and a list of them has been preserved. Moreover, some of those codices have come down to us.

From then on, the increases proceeded at an accelarated pace. Frederick of Lorraine donated an antiphonary and a small evangelistary adorned with gems and gold, and the empress, Agnes gave another evangelistary bound between silver tablets etched in gold. Obviously, as in other similar cases, those precious gifts were destined to the liturgical services, but they still went to increase the collection of the library, which was also obtaining materials of more current use.

It was Desiderius who gave the largest increase to the collection and put up a small building on the eastern side to house it, which then became the library. Among the codices that he had

---

adorned in honor of Christ and blessed Benedict».
   * «With gilded plates of silver and a Gospel of the same kind».
   ** «A text of the Gospel all covered with gilded silver with enamels and gems», provides «several codices of various kind».

copied were treatises on music, calculus, and astronomy, Vitruvius's work *De Architectura*, the works of Esculapius and Ippocrates, that of Pliny on the natural sciences of Apuleius on Quadrupeds; others on precious stones, many in history, classical writers, law and ecclesiastical sciences. Some of these volumes, covered with miniatures, bound in gold, silver, and ivory and studded with gems and enamels, were veritable masterpieces. To understand fully the work of Desiderius in this field, it is sufficient to remember what with good reason, has been said about him: «for his love of the arts and his desire to collect codices... he must be considered as the earliest forerunner of the humanistic movement, also because he shared with the humanists the characteristic versatility of mind and the variety of cultural interests» [32].

His example was followed also in this case by his successor Oderisius.

Even at the conclusion of this golden century, the workshop of the library continued its activities in spite of the many misfortunes that befell the abbey. The library was thus endowed with other codices; in fact, to the twelfth century belong, among others, the *Regesto* of S. Angelo in Formis and an *Exultet,* although it was not possible to save from the depredations of the following century the rich and precious bindings, prey of the vandalism of the soldiers that occupied the abbey.

The library was left untouched by the terrible earthquake of 1349. Still, we have the testimony of Urban V that later, within the tottering walls of the abbey and the plunderings of that century, it incurred serious damages and costly depredations. Urban, the Pope who helped so much in the restoration, lamented in a Bull of 1367 to the bishops of Aquino, Sora, and Veroli the ruin of the books among the other sacrilegious devastations. Gregory XI, a decade later, also reported and deplored the removal and theft of volumes.

Should one put among these the celebrated one by Boccaccio? He certainly removed the Tacitus and Apuleius codex, now in the Laurenziana library in Florence. The conditions of the time are sufficient to explain the facility with which he succeeded in the enterprise and to throw light on that act which Benvenuto da Imola describes with hyperbolic irony, amplifying and exaggerating the importance of what the man from Certaldo narrated *jocose* (in jest). Besides, has not one seen worse in our own days? Fortunately there were no longer any codices at Monte Cassino at the time of the bombing, but parchments, books, art objects, and marbles were stolen, and horrible to say, pieces were broken off from the marvelous stalls of the choir, taken away as souvenirs by persons evading the vigilance of the few custodians or paying no attention to unarmed imploring protests [33].

Urban V had already destined the considerable amount of 300 gold florins to aquire new books, and the codices of that century were numerous, 22 just Biblical ones, and quite beautiful. They, together with those salvaged from the preceding centuries, testify to the fact that, although the terrible conditions of that era were the cause of some negligence, the occurences were sporadic. At any rate, we have already seen that even in the fifteenth century the Cassinese continued their studies, maintained a school for the «oblates», wrote books, and did miniatures.

The fifteenth century brought new spoliations. While the abbots Enrico and Pirro Tomacelli at the beginning of the century donated a considerable number of codices, the forced abandonments and the tragic events encouraged the humanists to repeat Boccaccio's exploit. It was then that Poggio Bracciolini removed the *De lingua Latina* of Varro and Frontinus, and some codices of Cicero were taken away by Pontano. Searches were also conducted by Bruni, Niccoli, Traversari, Ciriaco d'Ancona, and Sulpizio Verolano.

Another cause of the dispersion was Pope Paul II who, as commendatary of the abbey, requested an inventory of all the codices. This was obviously not done for the purpose of consultation, because many of those codices found their way into the Vatican Library.

The invention of printing did not bring an improvement in the collections, because its beginnings coincided with the era of the commendataries at the abbey, and they had quite different priorities than books. Wars and fires in the following century were other negative factors.

With the strong recovery of the sixteenth century, however, the whole abbey began to be animated by the humanistic spirit. Lost manuscripts were recovered and new books were acquired.

In the planning of the central part of the buildings, Abbot Angelo de Faggis made allowance for the needs of the library. He kept the old orientation of the building but made it larger between the halls of the Chapter and that of the Common Fire. Thus, that very large hall, that maintained that function until the last destruction, took form. It had then, as described by Petrucci, the appearance and the organization of the Renaissance libraries: ample, beautifully designed shelves held the most important works, which were made secure by chains. The new building, which attracted students even from abroad, is remembered by Sixtus V, in the brief that he wrote on its behalf. To avoid, as it had been ordered in the papal disposition, that volumes be taken out of the main library, other smaller libraries were then formed to serve particular needs as, for example, the novitiate.

A century later, Abbot d. Sebastiano Biancardi (1681-1687) decided to renovate the interior according to contemporary artistic tastes. The sixteenth century shelves were removed, and in their place, at a cost of 2000,00 ducats, new monumental shelves were installed designed by the Roman architect G.B. Contini. Richly carved in walnut, they were a work of art worthy to be compared with the magnificent choir. The shelves rose up to the small pediments of the lunettes of the vault, while over the richly adorned cornice at the height of the corinthian columns, which acted as dividers between the shelves, in the guise of watchful custodians stood the busts of the fourteen most celebrated Cassinese savants carved in wood. A heavy door, carved in solid walnut with elegant foliage in full relief and suitable decorative motifs like an inkwell, pens and a book, all beautifully intertwined, gave access to the vast room, in the center of which there were four massive walnut tables. All in all, the room was a masterpiece of that type of art.

Around the same period all the volumes, both handwritten and printed, were bound uniformly in parchment; thus many coverings typical of preceding eras were lost, while fragments of ancient codices that today would be priceless were used as coverings for the inside leaves at the front and at the end of the volumes.

The new setting was barely in place when, in 1685, Mabillon visited the library and described it with admiration.

Later on, to make room for new acquisitions (quite notable those made by disposition of Abbot D. Arcangelo Brancaccio 1722-1725, and through the loving care of the bibiophile d. Giustino Capece and the librarian d. G. B. Federici) the manuscripts were transferred to the new location which Abbot d. Angelo de Grassi had prepared for the archives (1631).

The treasure trove of old charters and other documents on parchment dealing with the monastery, its possessions and rights, had been arranged at the time of the great works done in the sixteenth century in the last room of the lower eastern hall named after St. Ann. Abbot de Grassi prepared a much more dignified setting, furnished with shelves and chests for the protection of the documents. This area was located under the abbot's apartments, which, still in the old tower, found itself now between the two trunks of the great halls. The rooms of the archives turned out to be somewhat higher than the adjacent ones and communicated with the Abbot's quarters. A third room was added by Abbot Brancaccio, who through the use of special chests made of walnut, cypress, and pine, tried to keep the greedy woodworms away from the precious documents.

The result was that magnificent complex with the pleasant southern exposure which guarded the precious patrimony of Cassinese tradition until that tragic October 17, 1943. A few years before, it had been carefully restored and provided with marble and wooden floors. Other rooms were almost ready to be added to take care of the growing number of documents that needed storage. The new rooms were under the attached reference library, called Paolina in honor of Paul the Deacon (1899), and were located in the rooms that originally served as living quarters for the archivist, but then had been used as storage. The direct communication with the Abbot's rooms was cut with the building of the new entrance and reception gate in 1880.

The codices placed in the second room above the chests with the charters were catalogued with tireless diligence when the two Federici were prefects of the archives and by their successors, d. Ottavio Fraja-Frangipane and d. Andrea Caravita. The cataloguing was then perfected with the printing, partial up to now, of the *Bibliotheca Casinensis* (Codd. 1-358) and the *Catalogus* by Inguanez (1-600).

Among the most eminent students of history the world over, there was hardly one that did not feel the singular fascination that emanated from these austere rooms. Among the codices, the oldest went back to the sixth century, and among the documents on parchment, the one from Taranto, was of 809. Among the registers and the notarial protocols, the countless charters of the ancient feudal jurisdiction and of the ancestral patrimony, the place seemed to evoke the memorable events of the past and, with the eyes of the mind, one could see, as if projected against a magic screen, the millenary course of European history, of the papacy and the empire, of the kingdoms and the nations. Up above, the solemn paintings reminded one of the ancient privileges and the eminent personages who had spent most of their lives there, while looking downward through the windows one could see the sun drenched valley of the Liri river.

The library of printed materials remained in the traditional place and, in spite of the fact that during the terrible storm of 1712 a lightening hit its vault, it suffered no damages and there were no changes until almost the end of the eighteenth century. Then it had to suffer through the destructive fury of the French republican militia. The soldiers ransacked the whole library hoping to find money hidden there. Many books were scattered all over the monastery, some were torn, others soiled, burned and thrown out of the windows, and thus many collections were then found missing or useless [34]. Besides all this, drunk soldiers, seeking a place to rest, also used the great counters of the library, where laughing and shouting, they even set fires that the few monks left as custodians were, fortunately, soon able to put out.

A few years afterwards the suppression decree was passed; as we have seen, however, the monks were allowed to stay in their ancient house, chiefly to watch over the artistic and cultural patrimony accumulated through the centuries old tradition.

When the abbey was once again restored to their own ownership during the works of restoration, care was taken also of the library. In 1825 the vaulted ceiling was decorated, and sketches and technical plans were drawn for an expansion that was needed because of the increase in the number of volumes. The project which would have added to the library the adjacent «hall of the common fire», which was of the same size, would have very beautifully doubled the size of the library, but it was not carried out because of the new decree of suppression. In fact, the changed local needs also brought to an end the work of renovation already started. It was then to find shelving space for the books, that standing shelves were placed in the middle of the hall, which cluttered it and made it look ugly. No other modifications were made except the repairing of the vault which was damaged on the left outside wall by the 1915 earthquake and by the collocation of a large sculptured counter, which from the pharmacy had been carried to the sacristy and left there for several years.

Not much time went by before the continuous increase of the collections required new provisions. It was no longer possible to add the new acquisitions to the old holdings, both because the space next to the library had been assigned and also because it was not possible to add new titles to the catalogue. Thus the old library of the sixteenth-eighteenth century was kept unchanged. It contained twenty thousand volumes, carefully catalogued by authors, which were mostly bibliographical rareties, from the incunabula, which in 1929 received their own printed catalogue, to the books that Card. Mai assigned in his will, to those of the attorney general office of the Maurini, to the editions of the Fathers by a grant of Mabillon, to the documents of French history turned over by De Salvandy.

On the same level of the archives, however, and as a continuation, although separate, of the Paolina, a new library was established which soon reached and surpassed sixty thousand volumes. Some important collections were part of it; the famous musical archives with very precious autographs of Pergolesi (the original of the celebrated *Stabat Mater*), of Scarlatti, of Jommelli, of Leo, and of other Neapolitan masters of the eighteenth century. Then there were the collections of the *Imitation of Christ,* that of Dante and the rich Neapolitan one, that of the sixteenth century chorales of Monte Cassino and S. Severino of Naples, which were in deposit from that church; there were also various archival holdings, the most important being the one from Pomposa with over two thousand parchments. There were also several incunabula.

With this, and counting the smaller libraries like those of the novitiate, the college and the seminary, the abbey had more than one hundred thousand printed volumes. To this one must add also several tens of thousands of documents written on parchment, the registers, the incunabula, and the collection of the central account books, etc. One can thus form an idea of the holdings, most of them exceptional and of irreplaceable value.

This collection, without any doubt one of the oldest and most precious in the world, which up to the present in its entirety had offered the most in-depth documentation of the monastic activity, «should have secured for the Cassinese the perennial gratitude of mankind» [35]. Even today, among so many disasters so many destructions, although partially swept away and destroyed by the last absurd bombings, with its best part barely escaping to the safety of Rome, it remains a witness to the continuity of the monastic family. Gone were the buildings, the art treasures and that precious jewel, the basilica, but the library alone, with the tomb of St. Benedict, came out miraculously unscathed from that avalanche of fire and steel hurled against them, as a witness and a pledge of the vitality of the family of the

Patriarch, which through fourteen centuries of greatness and sorrows has not been enclosed within nor consisted of the material buildings but must be found in the spiritual continuity and the strength of the tradition of the house.

N O T E S

[1] A. LENTINI, *op. cit.,* 105.

[2] I. HERWEGEN, *op. cit.,* 87-88.

[3] R. MORGHEN, *Paolo Diacono,* in «Enciclopedia Treccani», s.v.

[4] *Ibid.*

[5] G. MANACORDA, *Storia della scuola in Italia,* Palermo, Sandon 1914, 102.

[6] G. MINOZZI, *op. cit.,* 3 ff.

[7] A. LENTINI, *Ilderico e la sua «Ars Grammatica»,* Miscellanea Cassinese n. 39, Montecassino 1975.

[8] F. NOVATI - A. MONTEVERDI, *op. cit.,* 144.

[9] G. FALCO, *op. cit.,* 533.

[10] G. MINOZZI, *ibid.,* 10.

[11] U. BALZANI, *op. cit.,* 161.

[12] *Chronicon,* Prologus.

[13] PH. SCHMITZ, *op. cit.,* II, 132.

[14] W. GIESEBRECHT, *De litterarum studiis apud Italos primis medii aevi saeculis,* Berlin, Gaertner, 1845, 33.

[15] M. INGUANEZ, *Un dramma della passione del secolo XII°,* Montecassino 1939, Miscellanea Cassinese n. 18. According to L. SPITER in *Studi Medievali,* (1952), p. 48: «The *Ritmo* should be from now on studied as the first, perfect poem of Italian literature».

[16] *Op. cit.,* 404-409.

[17] PH. SCHMITZ, *op. cit.,* II, 133.

[18] GATTOLA, *op. cit.,* 103.

[19] *Op. cit.,* 61 About another monk, named L. da Montenero, we know that around 1225 he was studying literature, see, T. Leccisotti, *I Regesti dell'Archivio,* I, 39, n. 35.

[20] Cfr. T. LECCISOTTI, *S. Tommaso d'Aquino, cit.*

[21] G. MINOZZI, *op. cit.,* 400.

[22] *Ibid.,* 294.

[23] *Ibid.,* 429.

[24] *Ibid.,* 477. Unfortunately the cod. Cass. 709 which contained the autographs was lost in the last destruction.

[25] In *Museum Italicum,* I, Paris, 1687, 126, and he adds that the monks «eo in loco quam laudabiliter viventes, divina officia, si uspiam alibi in Italia, rectissime celebrant».

[26] L. TOSTI, *Storia,* IV, 3.

[27] A. LENTINI, *Versi inediti o poco noti di Vincenzo Monti,* in «Giornale storico della letteratura italiana», 56 (1938), vol. 112, p. 223-244.

[28] In an audience of July 7, 1908 he had brought with him to Pius X the old follower of Garibaldi, Fazzari, with conciliatory proposals. See, P. ROMANO (E. Martire), *Il*

garibaldino che portò la profezia della Conciliazione e Carteggio Amelli Fazzari, in «Rassegna Romana», VI (1934), 217-230.

[29] C. L. TORELLI, *op. cit.,* 40.

[30] During this same century, in 1281, Charles of Anjou had the monk John come from Monte Cassino to Naples to apply miniatures to eight volumes of parchment. During his stay in the capital, d. John had quarters at the Archbishop's palace who was the brother of his abbot, Bernard.

[31] G. MINOZZI, *op. cit.,* 550.

[32] C. SCACCIA-SCARAFONI, *Vicende storiche,* 315.

[33] According to the testimony of Pier Paolo Vergerio, the Roman painters used to destroy the codices to prepare pictures of the shroud for the pilgrims. Cfr. P. PASCHINI, *Roma nel Rinascimento,* Bologna, Cappelli, 1940, 6. T. LECCISOTTI, *Ancora a proposito del viaggio di Boccaccio a Montecassino,* in «Benedictina», 15 (1968), 143-145.

[34] See CARAVITA, *op. cit.,* III, 569.

[35] C. SCACCIA-SCARAFONI, *op. cit.,* 328.

BIBLIOGRAPHY

In relation to the importance and variety of the topics, the bibliography of this and the following chapter is, necessarily, quite short and limited to general works. For more in-depth study the reader should turn to monographs dealing with the various scientific branches and, as for the individual writers mentioned, to the customary bibliographic studies, the most useful, for the entries already published, the *Dizionario Biografico degli Italiani,* edited by the Institute of the Enciclopedia Italiana. The memories of many monks have been preserved by H. HOFFMANN in his edition of *Der Kalendar von Leo Marsicanus* in «Deutsches Archiv», 21 (1965), 128-149.

For a study on the Rule of St. Benedict, see A. LENTINI, *Il ritmo prosaico nella Regola di S. Benedetto,* Montecassino 1942 (Miscellanea Cassinese n. 23).

Peter the Deacon gives us the oldest listing of the Cassinese writers up to the eleventh century in *De viris illustribus Casinensis conenobii* in MIGNE P. L., CLXXIII, 1009-1062. The same subject has been treated in an interesting and competent manner by F. NOVATI - A. MONTEVERDI, *Le origini,* Milano, Vallardi 1926, (in a history of Italian literature written by a group of professors). One can say the same of A. VISCARDI, who has continued the series under the same title.

For the *Chronica Casinensis* and the studies on it, see the introduction to Hoffmann's edition. New light on the Cassinese culture of the eighth century has been made by L. HOLTZ, *Le Parisinus Latinus 7530, synthèse cassinienne des arts libéraux,* in «Studi Medievali», 3 Serie, XVI (1975), pp. 97-152.

On the Cassinese school see: G. B. GROSSI, *La scuola e la biblioteca di Montecassino,* Napoli 1826, a work, that in spite of serious shortcomings and omissions, should be read by students of the subject; T. LECCISOTTI, *Un centro di coltura italiana nell'alto medioevo,* in «Vita e Pensiero», XIV (1929), 479-487, 541-550, which is a summary of Cassinese cultural history from the sixth to the twelfth century, concluded, for the thirteenth century, by the study already mentioned on *S. Tommaso d'Aquino,* etc. Of great interest for the Cassinese school in the High Middle Ages is the study of D. LOHRMANN, *Das Register Papst Johannes, VIII.*

For the historians in particular, on should note the excellent book of U. BALZANI, *Le* cronache italiane nel Medio Evo [3], Milano Hoepli, 1914; for the poets, the work of A. MIRRA, *La poesia di Montecassino,* Napoli, Federico e Ardia, 1929.

For the monastic *scriptorium,* see: A. CARAVITA, *I codici e le arti a Montecassino,* 3 vols., Montecassino 1869-1870 and M. INGUANEZ, *L'opera conservatrice degli amanuensi Cassinesi,* Montecassino, 1928.

The Cassinese script, studied already with great competence by O. PISCICELLI-TAEGGI in the works mentioned above, has had its greatest student in E. A. LOEW, *The Beneventan Script,* Oxford Clarendon Press, 1914 and *Scriptura Beneventana; facsimiles,* Oxford, Clarendon Press, 1929, 2 vols.

For the *Exultet,* in such large part of origin or Cassinese influence, the classical study is that of M. AVERY, *The Exultet Rolls of South Italy,* Princeton, London. The Hague, 1936. Concerning the origins of the iconographic cycle of the Cassinese Exultet, see: P. BALDASS, *Die Miniaturen Zweier Exultet-Rollen, London, add. 30337, Vat. Barb. lat. 592,* in «Scriptorium», VIII 61954), 75-88, 205-219. A superb exemplar of the Desiderian era is presented by J. P. GILSON, *An Exultet Roll illuminated in the XI century at the Abbey of Montecassino,* London, 1929.

Besides the works already mentioned of Tosti and Caravita, the history of the library has been the subject of a formal study by C. SCACCIA-SCARAFONI, *Vicende storiche della biblioteca Cassinese,* in «Accademie e biblioteche d'Italia», III (1929), 307-328. On the humanists searches for codices see: R. SABBADINI, *Le scoperte dei codici latini e greci nei secoli XIV e XV,* Firenze Sansoni, 1914. For new and intersting views on the history of the library see: G. BILLANOVICH, *I primi umanisti e le tradizioni dei classici latini,* Freiburg, 1953.

The ancient wealth of the library is documented by *M. Inguanez, Catalogi codicum Casinensium antiqui,* Montecassino, 1941, Miscellanea Cassinese n. 21. The same author edited the *Codicum Casinensium catalogus,* Montecassino, the first three columes of which have been published, 1915-1941. The war has interrupted the continuation, in part already in printed form. The catalogue of the incunabula has been done, however, by I. SANTINELLI and C. SCACCIA-SCARAFONI, *Gli incunabuli di Montecassino,* Montecassino 1929, Miscellanea Cassinese n. 6. An inventory-guide of the archives has been published, with some inaccuracies, by A. GALLO, *L'archivio di Montecassino,* in «Bullettino dell'Istituto Storico Italiano, 45 (1929), 117-159. The Regesti of the archives are in course of publication now, with a grant from the Ministry of the Interior; to the present, 11 volumes have been published, edited by T. LECCISOTTI. In these volumes historical events affecting the archives are commemorated and biographic notes on the archivists are given. The late E. DAGNINO described *L'archivio musicale di Monte Cassino,* in «Casinensia», I, 273-296. He († 1944) had also almost completed the very interesting catalogue. A special treatment id offered by P. FERRETTI, *I manoscritti musicali gregoriani dell'archivio di Monte Cassino,* in «Casinensia», 187-203.

The cultural activity of the years preceding the last war is described by A. SABA, *Storici e artisti a Montecassino,* in «Convivium», 10 (1938), 637-642.

III.

THE ARTISTIC ACTIVITY

«*Quis meliora, Casine, tuis*
Moenia porticibus statuit?
Aurea non domus ipsa Cyri
Non Salomonis opus valuit
Sedibus his rutilare magis» *.

(ALPHANUS)

1. THE EARLY ARTISTIC TRADITION.

When St. Benedict first came to Monte Cassino, he found the top of the mountain covered with the huge structures of the ancient fortress. The temples of Apollo and Jove, and perhaps also that of Venus, were surrounded by small groves and almost certainly by other buildings, among which a portico which probably surrounded the whole sacred area. All these were enclosed within the ancient walls, which showed various construction types and times. One can still see today a small surviving section of them; they had been restored the last time by the Romans.

To this Roman defensive system belonged also the tower that St. Benedict chose for his lodgings. The two stories were joined by an interior staircase, and from its windows one could dominate the whole plain below, and its height and solidity made it better than all surrounding buildings: «Quae turris in eodem loco constituta super totius cellae habitaculum eminebat **» [1]. Other structures had, in fact, been added. The Patriarch himself had overseen their construction as well as the adaptation of the pre-existing buildings. In the *Dialogi* of St. Gregory the Great, we see

---

* «Who has ever built structures more beautiful than your cloisters, Cassino? Not even the golden house of Cyrus nor the temple of Solomon were more splendid that this house of ours».

** «This tower erected in that same place, dominated all the constructions».

him direct, with meticulous care one may add, the building of the monastery of Terracina according to the plan and the requirements of his monastic ideal. Here also, he acted as a *sapiens architectus,* taking into consideration the existing plant, amplifying it, and modifying it.

Thus to symbolize the new orientation and the two-fold aspect of his mission, he established the oratory of St. Martin, the monk bishop and apostle of Gaul, in the temple of Apollo, and that of St. John, the father of the monks of the New Testament and forerunner of the Gospel, in the place where the altar of the divinity had once stood. At the same time, the Gregorian narrative shows us the monks as builders, busy raising new structures [2], but utilizing as well pre-existing materials [3].

In this way the monastery took form on the mountain: a house that Benedict offered to his children as a shelter for their earthly life and a laboratory for the life of the spirit. It was built as the Rule prescribed, answering fully its ideal, providing everything necessary to the cenobitic way of life. Like the ancient patrician houses and villas by which, perhaps, it might have been inspired, this citadel had to be self-sufficient, including therefore all the necessities like workshops, a library, a mill, a vegetable garden, guest-house, vestiary, the novitiate, and a school for oblates offered by their parents, still in very young age, according to the custom of the time.

Thus the father was able to repeat: «Omne hoc monasterium quod construxi» [4].

The indications given in the Gregorian narrative, as well as the few remains, allow us even today to determine the position of some of the main buildings of that first monastic foundation, which followed the model of Eastern monasteries which at that time had spread as far as Umbria.

After the monastic community was established by Petronax once again on the sacred mountain, the monastery entered into relations with flowering cultural centers, even some outside Italy, as for instance the Carolingian court. It was then that the famous scientific school was formed there, with definite characteristics of its own, as we have already seen; indeed, even from the artistic point of view, Monte Cassino acquired a character of its own.

One of the first tasks of Abbot Petronax had been the restoration and enlargement of the ancient structures which the Lombard invaders had been able to destroy only partially, thanks to the solidity of the materials used in the construction.

Soon, however, the monks stopped limiting their activity to rough and humble dwellings, and, enlarging the field of their work, they also extended the range of their influence. Thus, during the reign of Poto (771-778), they built a church in honor of St. Benedict on the lowest slope of the mountain; they dedicated another one to St. Michael at the foothill of the Aquilone, one of the mountains which limits from the east the large plain from which Monte Cassino rises. They adorned them with paintings illustrated with verses and praised as outstanding by Leo of Ostia. A third church was built, probably making use of pre-existing Roman structures, near that of Benedict. It was decorated by abbot Teodemar (778-797) in honor of the Virgin Mary. It had a Greek cross design, and with a large circular tower in the middle surrounded by four small ones, it anticipated the style so largely used by the Byzantines since the ninth century. It survived right up to the present time under the name of the «church of the five towers». The paintings and the decorations which once embellished it have long disappeared and only the naked structure of the building with its monolithic Corinthian style-columns survives. This does not mean, of course, that this venerable building, which was also destroyed by the war fury, does not deserve a prominent place in the history of art of this epoch [5].

These were the first artistic attempts at Monte Cassino in the same century of the restoration, the eighth; the following century, the ninth, witnessed, however, more admirable ones. The resurrection of the cloister on the Benedictine mountain received strong, unselfish help from a neighboring monastery recently established (ca. 702) by three Beneventan noblemen at the direction of the great abbot of Farfa, Tommaso di Moriana. Only a small chain of mountains separated Monte Cassino from S.

Vincenzo *ad fontes Volturni*, and the two cloisters lived for many years a parallel and prosperous life, tied in continuous, mutual relations. Thus at the beginning of the ninth century, while Joshua (793-818) was abbot of S. Vincenzo, Gisulf (797-817) ruled at Monte Cassino; they were both of noble birth, abbots at the same period of time, and both worked with great eagerness on the building and decoration of their monastic plants. The church at Monte Cassino was replaced by a larger one with the roof made of cypress wood covered with lead, which from the interior showed varied and rich ornamentation. The altar on the tomb of St. Benedict had a silver ciborium decorated with gold and enamel, and all the other altars were covered with silver tablets. With the restoration, the ancient oratory of St. John, where the Patriarch rested, had become the main church, and most monastic buildings were now erected in the vicinity of the glorious tomb.

At the foot of the mountain, after the difficulties posed by the swampy terrain were resolved, Gisulf himself, in place of the small church that Poto had dedicated to St. Benedict, built a large basilica dedicated to the Saviour. The work of Carioaldus, monk, architect, and vicar of the monastery below, it was divided into three naves by twelve marble columns. It was 110,33 feet long, 58,22 wide, 37,80 high, and covered with a roof of richly decorated beams and cypress planks. The floor was arranged in squares decorated with multicolored stones. The choir, placed in the middle of the church and in front of the presbitery, was adorned with tables of splendid marble, and the walls were covered with artistic paintings and sacred inscriptions. In the middle apse, which was reached by seven steps, there rose the altar of the Saviour, while in the other two, which closed the side naves, were the altars to St. Benedict on the right and to St. Martin on the left. Conforming to the classical tradition, the basilica was preceded by an open court of the same width but much longer whose side porticoes were supported by marble columns and which had a system of canals for the drainage of rain water. In this court, across from the church entrance, that is on the east side, there was a semicircular apse containing the altar of St.

Michael with the bell tower resting on eight big columns in the middle.

On both sides of the church were lined the ample and decorous buildings of the monastery, which offered the abbot and the numerous monks suitable quarters. The greater part of the monks had to move down the plain because the top of the mountain was too narrow before the great works launched by Desiderius in the eleventh century to enlarge and level it. The great volume of water in the subsoil had required special provisions; in fact, the whole surface of the new large monastery had to be filled with sand and stones and then covered with large plates of marble.

The basilica that abbot Joshua had built at S. Vincenzo was similar to that of the Saviour, and Bertaux rightly saw in them the reproduction of the type of Roman basilica like St Clement's. The monks who built them were probably led to the imitation, not only by the necessity to make use of the rich elements scattered in the ruins of ancient structures but, perhaps also, by the direct influence of Roman art.

As we have seen, an urban center soon formed around the monastery of the Saviour, especially through the efforts of Abbot Bertharius; a similar development took place also around the monastery of S. Vincenzo.

The activities of the Cassinese spread even further, following the colonization of their vast patrimony. At Valleluce, Gisulf directed the building of a church to St. Michael in the locality then named Albiano, which later took the saint's name. Other traces of this expansion are found at Benevento in the famous monastery of St. Sophia, originally a dependence of Monte Cassino.

The relations of Monte Cassino extended, however, way beyond this area: they became cosmopolitan, stretching to France, Germany, and the East. It is no wonder that currents of mutual influence, even in the field of the arts, were established.

Without any doubt, Kraus exaggerated in affirming, without any reservations whatsoever, that the origins of German art in the

ninth and tenth centuries must be traced back to the summit of
Monte Cassino; on the other hand, «among the Benedictines of
southern Italy, a pictorial (and one may add also architectonic)
tradition was forming, rich with Latin, Campanian, Byzantine,
and·German motifs». This tradition, although based on contemporary Roman art, which in the cosmopolitan city fused the most
diverse elements, in its development at Monte Cassino took on
elements of its own and was able to make its influence felt far
away.

Contemporary criticism aims rather at limiting the concept
of Benedictine-Cassinese art, trying to force it into the general
panorama of Campanian and southern art, in spite of the fact
that the most celebrated exemplars of eleventh century painting
are to be found right in the middle of the area of direct Cassinese
influence, like S. Angelo in Formis [6].

Still, even without considering that such critical positions are
always susceptible to revisions and modifications, the artistic
penetration of Monte Cassino into the surrounding regions remains a valid fact, and, to quote an illustrious student of
Cassinese art, one can even now speak «of a Benedictine κοινὴ
well-defined in time and space» [7].

Almost nothing has survived of this artistic activity of
medieval Benedictines in southern Italy, and even what little remained would have gone unnoticed if d. Oderisio Piscicelli
(1840-1917) had not made known an ancient oratory discovered
by chance. Decorated with paintings, it is a remain of the
destroyed abbey of the Volturno and goes certainly back to the
times of abbot Epiphanius (826-847). Only this oratory can give
us an actual idea of the ancient monastic art which had its main
centers at Monte Cassino and S. Vincenzo.

Once again, however, the natural development of this artistic
activity was violently arrested by the Saracenic raids that, as we
have already seen, destroyed the two great abbeys at brief intervals from one another.

Even if the artistic production was greatly limited to the cities
of Teano and Capua, where the Cassinese fugitives had withdrawn,

and marked a period of regress, the ancient tradition still grew gradually richer, more varied, and more complex. Samples and proof of this are the paintings of the Grotta dei Santi e delle Fornelle near the town of Calvi Risorta, of the cave of S. Biagio near Castellammare di Stabia, of Maiori, and the miniatures of some codices.·

2. THE EAGER AND DILIGENT WORK THROUGH THE CENTURIES.

With the recovery, the artistic tradition also gained new life. Leo and John, abbots at the time of the exile, already had taken to heart the conditions of the buildings which had been abandoned at Monte Cassino, although difficulties and the great distance prevented a complete restoration.

With Aligernus, however, the roof of the church was replaced, the walls were decorated with paintings, the altar of St. Benedict was covered with silver tablets, and the surrounding floor was done over in polychromic marbles in various designs. The front part of the altar of St. John was also covered with silver. Besides this, the church was furnished with a rich collection of artistic objects, like a large cross of gilt silver, and an evangelary held in a gilt silver binding with gems and enamels. The monastery of Capua was also the object of Aligernus' cares: the church was enriched with a tabernacle and enlarged with a longer transept. It was also decorated with paintings, bells, precious objects and provided with many codices. Of all these riches gathered by Aligernus, nothing is left except, perhaps, a small chest, which, according to Caravita's conjecture [8], was brought over from Capua at that time.

Abbot John III (997-1010) gave his attention to the fortification of the buildings, although he did not stop enriching the collection of liturgical objects. He built also a church in honor of St. Nicholas in the locality called «Monticelli» close to S. Germano, where the ancient *Thermae* of *Casinum* were.

He was followed in this work by his vicar Teobald, who transformed a Roman sepulcher of ancient Casinum into a church to the miracle worker of Bari. This, with the name of the church of the Crucifix, was still in existence until the latest destruction. It had a Greek cross plan and was built with large square blocks of local stone placed one over the other with lead-filled seams without any cement or plaster covering; its upper part ended in a circular dome. In a small lateral chapel, a later addition, there were various remains of ancient paintings, mostly dating, however, from the later Desiderian period.

Already as vicar of S. Liberatore alla Maiella, Teobald had given proof of his abilities and love for the arts. That important Cassinese dependency had been rebuilt by him, with particular care for the church, which was enlarged and decorated with frescoes. The main altar, dedicated to Christ the Saviour, the liberator from death who gave the name to the monastery, had the front part covered with a plate of silver of marvellous beauty, decorated with gilt, while above the same altar there was a table in relief of the Virgin Mary carved in ivory, with figures of saints on the sides. Silk cloths from Constantinople or from the Arabs of Spain or Africa covered the altars; enamels and precious decorations adorned the church, which was also well stocked with codices nicely bound. When he became abbot, Teobald showed no less interest in favor of the mother house. He had two excellent bells cast, covered the altar of St. Gregory with engraved silver tablets; he also had reliquary in silver made for the wood of the Holy Cross and a pastoral and a processional cross made of the same material. In addition, he devoted great energy to the improvement of the buildings, and among other things he enclosed the front court of the church in the form of a cloister ending in two towers, realizing perhaps the project of his predecessor, Atenulf, who had been brought up in a monastery in Germany. Moreover, Teobald established, or better renewed, in S. Germano a *mansio abbatis,* i.e., the Abbot's house.

Thus began the golden century of the Cassinese abbey. It arrived, indeed, with the smile of art upon it, but amidst the strife of wars and political turbulences, so that «within the whole abbatial domain the building of new churches and the establishments of new settlements were accompanied by great works of fortification» [9].

Even Richer, tenaciously preparing for the future, did not neglect beautification and the improvement of the buildings of the monastery. He covered the basilica with lead plates brought from Sardinia, embellished the front court with arches springing from small columns, and started to build a residence for the Abbot on the north side. His work, however, pales compared to the grand scale constructions carried out by his successors.

Among these «the superior man who, becoming Pope took the name of Victor III, owes his renown less to the predominant role that he had in the history of the Normans of Italy and to the papal crown that he wore than to the impulse he gave to the sciences, literature, and the great works of art that he sponsored during his rule at Monte Cassino under the name of Desiderius» [10].

And in his building program, lyrically sung by Alphanus, «one is at a loss whether to admire more the boldness of the plan than the rapidity of the execution». The first concern of Desiderius was to bring order and light in the ruinous chaos of monastic structures. As first test, he completed the palace started about eight years before by Richer, then «as inspired by a superior force» he had some of the buildings not yet a hundred years old torn down and began to build successively a small library, an apartment for the Abbot, a dormitory for the monks, and a hall for the chapter. Finally, he had no hesitation in trying the undertaking from which all his predecessors had backed away: the building of a church the size of a Roman basilica.

The difficulties that the task posed seemed unsurmountable. It was necessary to transport heavy materials and precious monoliths up the steep slopes of a mountain about two thousand feet high. The unevenness of the summit had forced the early builders to group structures of mediocre importance among the rocks, trying to avoid ditches and high points. Desiderius levelled out an area almost two hundred yards long, where, «using fire», the foundations for a very large edifice were excavated. The work, started in March 1066, was completed in five years, and on the first of October, 1071, the basilica was consecrated by pope Alexander II» [11]. In tearing down the old church, Desiderius even kept the presbitery intact, in order to leave undisturbed the sepulcher of the Saint, and he lowered the level of the nave.

In place of the old oratory of St. John rose one of the masterpieces of medieval art, a statement of the power of the Cassinese abbey and of the intense spiritual life which was led there.

As at present, a great stairway led to the front courtyard of the church. Since then, in fact, Cassinese topography has remained unchanged in its main lines. Then also the churchyard was preceded by a portico, at both ends of which, two chapels, dedicated to St. Michel and St. Peter, whose traces were still visible until the last destruction, raised their slender towers towards heaven. In the court «quod nos (according to the *Chronicon* [12]) Romana consuetudine Paradysum vocitamus *», on the east side, the waters of the large well served as a remainder of the duty of purification, and all around on the walls there were frescoes with episodes from the Old and New Testaments. The side of the portico adjacent to the church was decorated with mosaics and carried metrical inscription written in gold letters, and at one side stood the solid bell tower. One entered the basilica through the bronze doors, inlaid with silver, which had been made in the imperial workshops of Constantinople. On their panels also in silver letters, there was a listing of all the multitude of churches which were dependencies of the mother church at Monte Cassino. The narrow band of marble mosaics led from the portico to the inside of the church, where it widened to form the floor of the three naves. The paintings which decorated the walls and the wooden roof gave way at end of the basilica to richer and more brilliant mosaics. In the apse there was Christ in triumph, surrounded

---

* «which we, so says the Chronicon, accordin to Roman use, call Paradise».

by the saints, among whom the two Johns were clearly recognizable. While from the top of the arch the devout dedicatory inscription of Desiderius shone brightly in its golden letters. In the apse at the feet of the Saints a warning inscription glowed: «Haec domus est similis Synai... lex inde exivit, mentes quae ducit ab imis... *».

A splendid display of marbles set in metal framing completed in the center of the church the polychromatic decoration of the walls and the floor. Above all, the eyes were attracted by the choir enclosure formed of great plates of marble of various shapes and in the middle a column of gilt silver rising from a base of porphyry to form the candelabrum for the Easter candle. The sanctuary was all alive with beautiful works of jewelry placed on various lines. At the entrance of the choir, the first pergola was a source of admiration and veneration. Six silver columns rose to support a beam of painted and gilded wood, over which several bronze arms held up a second beam of the same metal. Under the wood beam, among the columns, five, round, painted images, were suspended in carved silver frames, while above one could see thirteen other rectangular icons, in gilt silver, with figures in relief. While the wooden beam was a support for the icons, the bronze one was for the lamps. It had, in fact, small hooks from which thirty-six lamps could hang, and it supported fifty holders for candles. Other lamps and candles were held by a great crown of solid silver which hung from the ceiling by a chain. It was surrounded by twelve small towers and weighed over a hundred pounds. Behind the iconostasis, four bronze railings marked a second separation, while closer to the altar, four more columns of silver, among which there were two great crosses of the same metal on marble bases held up another beam of silver. The ciborium of the altar, rising above steps covered with oriental marbles, was also made up of silver lintels resting on columns of the same precious material, which held hanging from the front

* «This house is like Mount Sinai... from where came the law that led minds from the depth...»

and rear sides some round icons, also of silver, with engraving in relief on both sides. Through these arches of precious metals, one could finally see the altar itself, which was decorated with very fine chasings and most delicate miniatures in pure gold and enamel; they were all small portraits representing scenes from the Gospels and the life of St. Benedict.

This was the everyday decoration that the sanctuary offered to the eyes of spectators, but much greater was the pomp of the feast days. Then between the two iconostasis, shining with gold and light, seven bronze candelabra and six silver ones were placed, and the vases adorned with gems and enamels and the evangelaries bound in ivory and gold were brought out of the Treasure room. The evangelaries had been the gift of Agnes, empress of Germany, who, drawn by the renown of the new temple, had hurried as a new queen of Sheba and had stopped there six months. Other gifts came from Romanus, the Byzantine emperor, and from Amalfitan merchants. The oriental carpets used as tapestries behind the choir had been given by Robert Guiscard. One really has to conclude with Bertaux, whose narrative has been followed here, that «in the time of Desiderius there was not in western Christendom anything comparable to the Cassinese basilica.»

Splendid in its ornaments and enriched by the inestimable treasure of the sacred relics, which were even placed in the capitals of the columns, the marvelous basilica must have appeared like a vision of peace to those who came for the memorable consecration.

«Later, in January 1075, the church of St. Bartholomew, built to the west of the great basilica, was consecrated. And still eight months later, the bishops of Aquino and Sora came to dedicate the two chapels placed at the end of the portico. At the same time the leveling of the mountain top was completed and a completely new monastery was built, with a refectory, a dormitory decorated with paintings, and a cloister which had one hundred and ten marble columns.

Desiderius, however, did not live long enough to see the completion of the basilica of St. Martin, which he had wanted to rebuild on the site of the oratory that St. Benedict had built where the ancient temple to Apollo had stood. It was finished three years after his death and was consecrated under his worthy successor, Oderisius I (1087-1105), in August 1098. The new Abbot then built, among others, the church of St. Andrew, consecrated in June 1098, attached to which there was a hospital with great works of art and excellent hygienic facilities.

All the structures which had not been rebuilt during the governance of Desiderius were all completed before the end of the eleventh century; thus in fifty years the aspect of Monte Cassino was completely renewed» [13].

One must regret, of course, that Desiderius, in his fervor for renewal, destroyed every trace of the pre-existing buildings, venerable for antiquity and memories. This is the only criticism that one can move against such an otherwise noble enterprise. To Desiderius the memory of St. Benedict was indissolubly attached to the whole place more than to any material structures.

«Also in the "Land of St. Benedict" and nearby areas all the old Benedictine churches were rebuilt. Thus, on the model of the Cassinese basilica of St. Martin, Oderisius built a new church near Alife, S. Maria in Cingla, and in 1108 Pope Pascal II solemnly consecrated the church of St. Benedict in Capua, which had been already rebuilt by Desiderius.

To this gigantic building program, one must add the unbelievable wealth of the polychromic decorations, of the churches' furnishings, of the objects in precious metals and exotic and rare cloths, and, as we see them glitter in the descriptions of the chroniclers, our own imagination remains dazed. Such prodigality, while it presupposes an almost limitless source of wealth, unceasingly renewed by the offerings of the faithful, presumes also, in the man who has assumed the initiative for such undertakings, an absolute certainty about the future and a strong conviction about what the times made possible for his order. Rightly, Desiderius' historian has seen in the multitude of these towers and these colonnades, the enamels and the gold, almost a material image of Benedictine power» [14].

Of all the riches gathered on top of the mountain, almost nothing has come down to our days. The centuries, through the destructions caused by earthquakes and the repeated devastations of men, have seen everything disappear; what is still left, besides the numerous codices which are still unharmed today, and the paintings of the already mentioned church of the Crucifix near Cassino, are a few mosaics and the door of the Desiderian basilica [15].

The artistic school of Monte Cassino had extended its range of influence more than ever at that time. The artists that came from Byzantium, perhaps, were able to teach the monks unknown technical secrets, but they must also have found local elements that had survived the times and which, recalling Roman, German, Irish, and Arabic motifs, were tied to the Cassinese school of the ninth century. This new direction, perhaps better, artistic rebirth (new flowering of the perennial Romanity of our art... remote harbinger of the Renaissance» [16]) made its influence felt, besides in painting and architecture, in the enamels, the mosaics, and miniatures. It ranged very far, more or less directly or effectively, in various forms. S. Angelo in Formis, Ausonia, Foro Claudio, among the localities closer to Monte Cassino, have kept until the present the impress of Cassinese art of the eleventh century. Minuto, Bussi, Pianella, and the Abruzzi region in general, Rome with the church of S. Sebastianello al Palatino, Salerno with its cathedral, Aquino with S. Maria della Libera, S. Agata dei Goti and other localities more far away, even outside Italy, received their origin or artistic influence from Monte Cassino.

Due to the changed condition in the twelfth century, however, circumstances did not prove favorable to a further development of the artistic activity. Artistically, the activity consisted of imitating, more or less well, the works of predecessors; politically, the new century brought the beginning of those continuous depredations which resulted in the total disappearance of the old precious works.

The state of political confusion, in which for various reasons the region of Campania found itself long involved, caused many losses to the «Land of St. Benedict». To meet the ever-growing difficulties, abbot Nicholas I (1126-1127) sought the alliance with Robert of Capua, but he had to pay such a high price for it that a large part of the treasure had to be used. In this way, the gold and silver objects donated by King Theodoric of Saxony, by the Emperor Otto, by Guy the Marquis of Tuscany, by Henry II, Robert Guiscard, Pope Stephen IX, etc., all disappeared. Such damages, unfortunately, were not compensated by other princely donations, because these became few and of modest value, as, for instance, the two silver candelabra offered by Pope Celestin II and a few other offerings by Emperor Lothair and his wife Richiza. Instead, the depredations continued. King Roger, to sustain the war in favor of the anti-pope Anacletus, helped himself repeatedly to the treasure of Monte Cassino, which suffered even more serious losses when all the monks were driven out by Ascletin and the monastery was occupied by his soldiers.

We have already seen how the struggles between Frederick II and the popes became fatal to Monte Cassino. While Arab bands at the service of the Emperor devasted the vicinities, Cardinal Pelagius, the legate of the papal army, struck coins out of the silver and goldplate of the abbey. When the monastery then fell into the hands of the imperial troops, whatever was left over was also lost. It was then that a silver table from the altar of the Virgin Mary, an icon covered with precious stones from that of St. Benedict, evangeliares and codices covered with valuable bindings, and the gold piece from the altar of St. Benedict were taken away. Abbot Stephen was later able to ransom the altar piece, but it disappeared once more later, never to be recovered again. At that time, however, between 1251 and 1260, the Abbot and Cardinal Riccardo had the basilica decorated with paintings on glass, the work of master Bartolomeo from S. Germano.

Among the places that gained almost new life through the work of restoration of Bernardo Ayglerio, one must remember S. Liberatore alla Maiella, whose church was decorated with frescoes, the work, it is believed, of the monk painter Todinus. The church was also enriched with a new mosaic floor. Of that same period are some paintings still existing in the church of St. Nicholas at S. Vittore in Latium.

The era of the Abbot-bishops was unfavorable indeed to the development of the arts, all the more because it was saddened by depredations like the one by Iacopo Papone and above all, the great earthquake of 1349 which destroyed all the splendid structures built by Desiderius.

The work of restoration began under the rule of Urban V (1362-1370). The basilica was rebuilt on the pre-existing foundations [17], the monks' dormitory and the workshops were repaired, and the colonnaded cloister was restored; three hundred florins were spent for various acquisitions, including codices.

The abbot Andrea da Faenza (1369-1373) renewed along noble lines the chapel of St. Agatha in front of the entrance of the monastery. Pietro de Tartaris (1374-1395), from Rome, devoted great care to the church. As he had with the Lateran basilica, he had the roof covered with lead and decorated the interior with paintings, the work of masters who came from Rome, among whom there were also some from Flanders and France. This Abbot had the choir fitted with a double row of sculpted seats, carved at intaglio with foliage and figures.

Of the two Tomacelli abbots, the second, Pirro (1414-1442), was more well-deserving for his interest in the arts and the work of reorganization, the first, Enrico (1396-1413), built for the monks the sepulchral chapel dedicated to St. Ann. Abbot Carafa (1446-1454) is remembered even today for the second gate of the main entrance to the monastery, which was done in travertine with a lunette in marble in 1433, the work of Brother Celsus from S. Germano, author of other works of not negligible interest.

A memorial of this epoch, which fortunately survived the destruction, has come down to us: three large figures of the Crucifix and the SS. Peter and Paul painted on wooden boards. The first, which perhaps decorated the arch of the presbitery of the Cassinese basilica, is an excellent work, probably from the beginning of the fifteenth century.

These years, from the earthquake on, except for a few during the restoration at the end of the fourteenth century, were certainly the most agitated and miserable in Cassinese history. In spite of all these disasters caused by external factors, which had unfavorable results for life at the abbey, one must note that the monks always sought to carry on with their program of prayer and work. In every era one can see them busy in restoring the ruins that piled up around them, in embellishing the house, and in transcribing codices. And even if the rapid and destructive course of time has always managed to destroy and scatter the fruits of their sacrifices, the memory of their work, tenacious and full of hope, confirmed by the documents and the surviving remains, is enough to command our admiration.

The same must be said of the work of the commendataries, who, however, did not neglect the buildings altogether. Among them were the Cardinal Trevisan, Pope Paul II, who rebuilt from the foundations the guest-house, and in a special way Cardinal Giovanni d'Aragona. This latter, besides endowing the church with sacred furnishings and other gifts of extraordinary value without paying attention to the cost, had master Bartolomeo of Florence carve new choir stalls which turned out as a most wonderful work of this kind, with intaglios and inlays of great beauty and artistic excellence. Later, a book-stand, believed to be inspired by the same style, was added to the choir to hold the magnificent liturgical books that abbot Squarcialupi had made. This stand has survived to the present and has the date of 1514. Though badly damaged, the gracefulness of its slender form, the design and execution of the intaglios and sculptures, and the harmonious beauty of the parts and the whole makes it a precious memory of the Renaissance.

As a memory instead of Cardinal Giovanni de' Medici, Cassinese commendatary for eighteen years and then Pope under the name of Leo X, who right or wrong gave his name to the century, from the artistic side there only remains a small shrine which in 1497 was placed close to the old entrance to the monastery to house a more ancient statue of St. Benedict.

With him, as we know, the series of commendataries ended. Then began an era of peace and prosperity for the abbey, not only comparable to the most luminous periods of its history, but longer lasting, stretching uninterruptedly for three centuries. All forms of art contributed to the splendor of the monastery. The newly restored wealth and the refined taste of the Renaissance era were placed completely at their service. Thus the abbey in its renewed dress of candid marbles florished again on the mountain «as a lily» which opens «to the dawn» [18]. The building program of the sixteenth century respected the pre-existing plan which Desiderius had set for centuries to come, but completed it by uniting all the structures with a line of three great cloisters.

The great work of reconstruction was initiated by Abbot Ignazio Squarcialupi, who came to Monte Cassino from the Florence of the Medici, resplendent in the classical beauty of the Renaissance. One must credit to him, besides other minor works, the court in front of the church and the solemn stairway leading to it, also the restoration of the great southern dormitory (the lower dormitory) which, as already seen, was in very poor condition. «Among the magnificent porticoes of the lower cloisters, crowned by the lovely "Loggia del Paradiso" and the baroque church with a splendid series of marble inlays and luminous frescoes, the court of the basilica is a pause» [19]. And the decorative elements added later did not take away from this cloister its atmosphere of solitary meditation, which the same author with convincing arguments attributes to Antonio da San Gallo the younger. Maintaining «still intact the elegance of a Brunelleschi's model» [20] the court was then completed at the time of Abbot Crisostomo d'Alessandro (1527-1531), who had the well dug out and completed with a beautiful octagonal cup designed by Solosmeo. The same Abbot d'Alessandro furnished the sacristy with beautiful sculptured cupboards.

The activity begun by abbot Squarcialupi had no more interruptions except delays imposed for economic reasons. Almost all abbots followed the same line; stirred by noble fervor, they tried to attract the best artists to the house of St. Benedict to make it more beautiful. «Coenobii aedificia auxit» is the praise that the historian Gattola repeats for almost all of them.

The one, however, who can be considered as the personification of the «*cinquecento Cassinese*» in the artistic fields was d. Angelo de Faggis. Pious, authoritarian, and pragmatic as a ruler, as a humanist he put all his outstanding gifts into the service of the monastery. A new Desiderius, he kept on with unflagging energy to the task that he began. When, with the title of prior, he held the governance of the abbey in 1539 while the abbatial chair was empty, «he had so many masons, stone-cutters, fitters and other workers come to the abbey that one could have built a town. And with great fervor he had work done in the southern dormitories and then he started the dormitory down at S. Germano» [21].

Thus began that building cycle that led to the definitive arrangement of the central complex of buildings at Monte Cassino. From 1531 to 1570 the southern dormitories with twenty-four cells were completed, and the eastern one with fourteen cells was built from the ground up next to the funeral chapel of St. Ann. The last rooms of this lower dormitory were used as the archive. Close to the church, on the eastern side, three great halls were now on the site formerly occupied by the old chapter. They were going to be used as the new chapter, the library and the room of the common fire.

In 1543 Abbot d. Girolamo Sclocchetto ordered the construction of a new choir, of the chapels flanking the presbitery and a bell-tower. He also had the crypt excavated, the walls of which later, at the time of Abbot d. Ignazio Vicani (1556-1559), were decorated with paintings done by Marco Pino da Siena and the vault was done then in the *grottesco* style.

Abbot d. Mattia Mattaleia rearranged the great refectory, the kitchen and the cellars between 1570 and 1572.

In that year, Sangrino returned for the third time to the governance of the abbey and, besides completing the halls of the chapter, the library and the room of the common fire, «he began the construction of the middle cloister». The site of the medieval cloisters «which must have represented one of the most unique piece of decorative art, among the most beautiful and interesting in southern Italy» [22], was taken over by the cloister of the Prior, with nine arcades in the longitudinal line and five in the other. The building was entrusted to Giovanni M. Bassano and Giuliano da Cremona.

Abbot d. Girolamo Brugia (1590-1595) built a wall around the vegetable garden that surrounded the monastery. His name, though he was a great mathematician, is connected especially to the building of the grandiose cloister, later on inexactly called of Bramante, which with the monumental doric covered gallery of the «Loggia del Paradiso» and «the overhanging balustrades divided by acroteria produced a fantastic pictorial effect» [23]. He also placed the guest-house in a building overlooking it, with the infirmary for the monks on the lower floor and the hospital on the ground floor.

It is true, of course, that through such a great and continuous building program the medieval character of Monte Cassino disappeared, but the abbey acquired a diverse one «admirable in the sober harmony of the lines and the architectonic decorations... Monte Cassino (as Giovannoni wrote in 1929) as it appears to a contemporary observer or student, is in its complex a great monument of the monastic architecture of the «cinquecento»... in which perennially lived what one may call the spirit of the monument, the collective feeling which dominates the individual one.

Three interesting aspects, which complement each other, soon become evident to the student of this great architectonic monument. First, the almost total absence of personal vanities expressed by names, dates, and coats of arms; the other consists of... a delay in stylistic forms... The third aspect is revealed by the continuity of lines and forms which repeat previous schemes» [24].

This is the character and the aspect that Monte Cassino has offered to the admiration and wonder of successive generations.

«Except for the great transformation of the Church, the successive centuries have added little to the Renaissance aspect of the abbey, and what has been added... harmonizes, with a magnificent sense of stylistic continuity, with the pre-existing architecture» [25].

Minozzi, in his lively description of the abbey as it then appeared, says, «From the second entrance tower, massive and powerful, which gave it the aspect of a redoubtable fortress, one came upon a flight of cloisters soaring in the purest blue sky. The quiet and solemn harmony of the complex immediately struck and lifted up the soul. Beyond the heavy, iron-studded gate one felt the firm and complete detachment from the world of sound outside. The silent peace gave one a feeling of intoxication which made the most inner fibres tremble. The first court appeared so large, powerful and slender at the same time, that the names of Bramante and San Gallo came to mind. Only their genius or that of their best disciples could have extracted such pictorial effects from line so simple and chastened, from arches so austere, from the wise use of the diverse masses. The Renaissance began its triumph right at the gate of the abbey.

From there one moved to the splendid central cloister, in the center of which there opened a narrow well above a polygonal cup flanked by two small columns, slender and gay in their elegant grooves, raising like lovely stems to delightful capitals supporting an architrave shadowed by a triumphant cross. All around seemed to smile lovingly, in the kindly peace, to the murmuring of the small chain that the light pulley kept replunging from time to time, bejewling it with rainbows escaping through the cool lobes... By the luminous stairway one mounted to the glory of the major basilica, feeling with each step a gradual release from the weight of the flesh, entering a world of serene joy only offered to the spirit and...

An extraordinary stream of artists had continuously invaded the abbey, leaving behind proof of ineffable love. The larger part passed on unknown, veiled in monastic humility like the silent illuminators.

Some appear timidly on paybooks or through the crumpled pages of laconic chronicles: Chima of Florence, Girolamo e Riccio from Carrara, Tommaso and his brother Andrea from Milan, Gaspare from Venafro, Nicola from Brescia... Every year of the golden century had left its gem in the joy of the divine house...

Andrea from Salerno (1518-1530)... brought there from Rome... the smile of Raphael's school, and his great compatriot, Giovanni Merliano, had composed for their eternal rest the sepulchral urn of the Fieramoscas before the Sangallos prepared the resting place for Pietro de' Medici.

Master Zucca from Gaeta (1534-1538) had decorated the sacristy with white intaglios... twenty years later Marco Pino da Siena (1557-1558) covered (the walls of the crypt) with historical portraits in strong colors... for which Benvenuto da Brescia, called the Lombard, carved in 1558 a walnut choir, a masterpiece of austere beauty...

There was a royal profusion everywhere. Miters, pyx, pastorals, and reliquaries brightened all the chapels in large number, engraved by Iannuccio di Antonio from Ferrara (1516-1530), by Mariano da Sulmona (1558?), and by the unpredictable Cellini, who bowed as well to Benedict's call...

Marco Mazzaroppi from Cassino, a disciple of the abbey, was the leader of that great band of artists which covered with luminous colors the palace of prayer and work. Towards 1590 he completed the crypt, which had been left unfinished by Marco Pino, and before and after, with the love of a son, he filled the monastery with Madonnas so sweet in the diaphanous, virginal pallor of their faces, which besides the Flemish school, reminded clearly of Raphael and anticipated Reni, who soon after also came up the sacred mountain to work for the Saint of Nursia, preceding Spagnoletto and especially Giordano, who in the seventeenth century will fill with tranquil beauties the restful house... The refectory, refurbished by abbot Ruscelli in 1590, also received then a delightful and sacred atmosphere. It was made as large and solemn as any church by the da Bassano brothers, who completed for it a grandiose canvas in their typical style, (which loved rural scenes). The canvas was large, full of movement, with trees full of leaves, and was festive in the warm reflections of a pictorial bravura, in which, Paolo Veronese would have undoubtedly found something of himself» [26].

Access to the abbey was also made easier with the new road, the construction of which, though many times interrupted and completed only in 1720, had begun in 1590.

The dependent houses, meanwhile, had not been neglected, D. Desiderio from Brescia (1580-1585) built the greater part of the new edifice at Albaneta, for which he himself had laid the first stone; d. Basilio, also from Brescia (1595-1596), renovated almost from the ground up the magnificent church of S. Liberatore alla Maiella.

While the sixteenth century had given Monte Cassino its definitive architectonic aspect, the pomp and magnificence of the decorations were the work of the seventeenth and eighteenth centuries. This can be said especially for the church, which at that time received the greatest attention. The result was a structure marvelous for the opulence of its marbles, engravings, gold decorations and paintings, which according to Corrado Ricci, was one of the most beautiful examples of the baroque style. The abbots used mostly, especially for the decorations, Neapolitan artists whose works, perfectly in tune to the luminous blue of the southern sky, excelled among all other schools. The architectonic lines were in the major part preserved, but as we have seen, already before the first half of the preceding century, abbot Sclocchetto had considerably modified the ancient structure, adding the new choir behind the apse and excavating the underground crypt down to the live rock.

At the beginning of the following century, in 1613, the dome was raised, on a design by Orazio Torriani built by the masters Niccolo de Giorgio from Milan, Pierantonio from Lugano, and his son G. Giambattista. At the beginning, some thought was given to decorating the interior with mosaics for which the Hon. d'Arpino would have furnished the designs. It was decided, however, to initiate instead contract discussions with Domenichino and Lanfranco to cover the dome with their paintings. In the end, the work was entrusted to Belisario Cerenzo and carried out during the rule of d. Simplicio Caffarelli (1625-1628). Continuing the work of his predecessor, d. Bernardino Saivedra (1621-1624), completed the covering of the choir and the new arrangement of the presbytery, the floor of which he had lowered by about 12 inches.

It was only later, under abbot d. Desiderio Petronio, that the ancient basilica was torn down, with the exception of the presbytery which went back to the eighth century and the choir which he had decorated with paintings by Charles Mellin from Lorraine. D. Domenico Quesada (1650-1653) finally undertook the new construction, for which the architect Cosimo Fanzago in the preceding years had already arranged the presbytery. Abbot Quesada alone spent more than twenty-five thousand ducats for the building of the church, without taking into account the work of men and animals used for the task. The work proceeded so quickly that abbot d. Severino Pepe (1675-1680) was able to entrust to Luca Giordano the task of covering with frescoes the whole central nave, which was already beautifully decorated with gildings and plaster decorations.

«One year was enough for the tempestuous Giordano (who one may add, began his work to the well-wishing ring of all the bells of the abbey) to start and finish the many frescoes which were in the central nave, a feat hard to believe, unless one knows that he was a man who did not waste any time between the conception and the execution of the work. That oil painting on the wall, eighteen feet high and thirty-two wide, representing the scene of the consecration of the church, is a monument not only to his own glory but to that of the whole Neapolitan school; I dare say that one can see in it, in perspective, all that fervid imagination and that animating fire which are characteristic of the Neapolitan genius in the arts. It would be a very long task indeed to discuss all the details of this great painting; I will say only that Giordano's hand did not fail his imaginative genius. All those people, in fact, which with marvelous naturalness crowd into the basilica of Desiderius, that impudence of the multitude to see at close quarters the Pontiff consecrating the altar, pressing against the immobility of the papal guards, the free access of the princes of Capua, Salerno, and Naples right up to the altar, the various feelings of devotion, curiosity, thoughtlessness which appear in crowds hastening to church for a solemn ceremony were masterfully expressed in various groups which create the illusion of reality of the happening. These scenes were not fantasies produced in successive frame but a powerful outburst of imagination which conceived the whole in all its parts at once, and were represented by a very skilled hand». This is how Tosti [27] described the painting full of life and rich in colors which covered the whole wall of the church behind the entrance door.

At the same time the organ was built by Catarinozzi at a cost of ten thousand ducats, and Solimena completed the four great paintings of the choir. Later on, abbot d. Andrea Deodati (1680-1681; 1687-1692) commissioned Paolo de Mattheis for the decoration of the vaults of the side naves; each of the ten divisions had an episode drawn from the life of the abbey.

Luca Giordano, meanwhile, continued his work in some of the eight lateral chapels and also in the crypt. At that time also, on a design of Alessandro Scappi from Senigallia and with the cooperation of Domenicantonio Colicci, to whom the rich appearance of the organ must also be credited, the marvelous choir was sculpted which «for difficulty and excellence of sculpture, Tosti wrote [28], I do not think there is anything to equal it... it must be seen because words cannot describe the subject».

This is how Caravita [29] faithfully describes it: «beautiful is the entablature supported by slender columns half grooved and half at intaglio in relief with their Corinthian capitals, and an array of foliage with little angels and animals, which in a thousand capricious ways adorn the backs of the seats and the entablature. It has a double row of seats, forty-eight above and thirty-four below. Those above have high backs in which, with superb craftmanship, there are engraved in relief foliage with flowers, fruits, animals, and, in the middle in small niches, the half figures of all

the Saints of the Benedictine order; in the lower and upper arms
there are figures of small children all sculpted in full relief, laying
in different poses; each arm is supported by other full figures,
some symbolic, some even drawn from the fables of paganism.
The capitals of the slender columns are surmounted by the heads
of cherubims who appear as supporting the entablature and participating in the monks' psalmodies. The two first chairs on the
left and the right have larger sculptures representing the glory of
St. Benedict and St. Scholastica. The stand in the middle of the
choir is of the same style, octagonal in shape, with flowers and
groups of little angels».

The enlargement of the hospice or Abbot's palace in S. Germano, which had been built by d. Sebastiano Biancardi
(1681-1687) was also the work of abbot Deodati, who was as well
responsible for the laying of the foundation of the wing of the
monastery adjacent to the entrance near the great stairway, for
this he availed himself of G. B. Contini, who at Monte Cassino
built many structures».

The monastery, meanwhile, became more and more com-
plete and rich in details: in the cloister of the benefactors, for instance, all the plaster statues placed there by abbot della Noce
were gradually replaced with marble ones, and the church acquired more rich furnishings, like the great silver piece for the
main altar, on which the last supper of the Savior was sculpted.

The eighteenth century received and made its own, with
perfect identity of views and goals, a glorious inheritance.

In this century Abbot d. Ippolito della Penna (1697-1704)
completed the series of the lower cloisters in the right wing, while
d. Gregorio Galisio (1704-1717) entrusted architect Arcangelo
Guglielmelli with the task of building the powerful structure with
the other courtyard on the left wing, a solid building which
originally was to be a guest-house first, the seminary and then
later the newly established college. Thus «that scenographic complex of solemn and royal pomp» [30], which forms the most notable
characteristic of Monte Cassino, was completed with the three
main cloisters. During his abbacy, De Matteis continued his work

in the church, and later he was also asked to decorate the Abbot's chapel in the palace of S. Germano.

A few years later the church was consecrated by pope Benedict XIII, «completed in all its parts, rich and resplendent in gold and the brightest of marbles, decorated as if it was a perpetual feast day, whoever crosses its threshold... will be greatly impressed and will be taken by great pleasure» [31].

Two other areas, (the sacristy and the chapter), were splendidly decorated during the first half of the century. The first, with its sixteenth century architectonic style (1512), kept the floor, which was composed in the same century (1544) with the remains of the other ancient ones. The design for the renewal was furnished by Domenico Simonetti from Astano; Gennaro Franzese, from sketches by Paolo De Maio, carved the magificent dorsals of the benches, with scenes drawn from the Scriptures symbolizing the Eucharistic sacrifice. Pietro Nittolo, using designs by Maini, was the author of the statues placed between the bas-reliefs, with small spiral columns and festoons of flowers done in gilt copper to increase the air of opulence. The vault, like the walls, richly decorated in plaster and gold, had in the middle a great painting by Conca, «the washing of the feet». Other paintings of the Evangelists and the Prophets lined the walls, and other scenes of the Passion were in the entrance hall, which at the end of the sacristy led into the chapel of the relics. The complex, in the style of Louis XV, was sumptuous and artistically pleasing.

The chapter as well was decorated at this time (1745) in plaster and gold, with three paintings of De Maio in the vault and with ten great canvasses of De Matteis and De Maura along the walls showing Biblical episodes symbolical of the conventual events to which the hall was destined; a painting of Andrea da Salerno was placed between the windows in the rear, but was replaced in the nineteenth century with another by Mazzaroppi representing the Madonna between the SS. Benedict and Scholastica; these works were done during the abbacy of d. Antonio Capece, who also renovated the great hall.

At the same time, many buildings, especially churches,

parochial houses, and farm houses, were being renovated throughout the towns of the Cassinese jurisdiction, especially by Abbot d. Gregorio Galisio.

The access road to Monte Cassino was finally finished, with some variations in the design, by d. Nicola Ruggi (1717-1722), while his successor d. Arcangelo Brancaccio in 1723 also opened the one for Albaneta. D. Sebastiano Gadaleta (1725-1731; 1739-1745) restored the monastery and the church of S. Liberatore, and the monk d. Prospero Pagano (β 1702) rebuilt the chapel of the Colloquy.

The devastating storm that raged on Monte Cassino at the end of the eighteenth century caused great losses of furnishings, art objects, paintings and silver plate; it left, however, the architectonic complex almost intact.

When peace was restored, however, it became necessary to take particular care against the damages caused by the passing years. Naturally, great attention was bestowed on the church, which was restored on the outside, later, received a new roof, partly in lead and partly in tiles and asphalt. In the interior, Gioacchino Scognamiglio from Naples restored the paintings, and the Venetian Pietro Paoletti between 1830-1833 renovated some of the frescoes of the cupola and three in the vault of the choir. He also painted the canvas of St. John the Baptist, which took the place, in the chapel dedicated to him, of the original one by Solimena, which was taken to the church of St. Antony in Cassino. In the chapel of St. Bertharius, the altarpiece was changed, and in place of that of Francesco de Mura, which itself had taken the place of an older one by Vanni, a canvas by the Hon. Sessa, greatly praised by all contemporaries, was hung. It remained there until 1929, when it was moved to the ambulatory, and the altarpiece of the De Mura was restored to its original place.

At the same epoch, the restoration of the magnificent sixteenth century choir of the crypt, which had been gravely damaged, was begun. The Hon. Luigi Ottaviano from Naples, a true master of intaglio work, was able to repair only four stalls before the suppression of 1868 put an end to the work.

In exchange for the twenty-four canvases which in 1811 had been brought to Naples by royal order, the Bourbons sent back others from royal galleries.

Monte Cassino, therefore, was able to appear in the twentieth century in the preserved and sumptuous dress which Ferdinand I of Bourbon had once described as a monastic royal house. In spite of the changes imposed by the new conditions, one could still write that, «From afar, in its complex... it appears as a large citadel, crowning the top of the mountain with its solid walls, from which only the cupola of the church barely emerges... The present general plan is simple, masterly, leading through successive degrees of wealth and elegance to the culminating point, the church which like an ancient acropolis dominates from the top of the rock the enormous pedestal formed by the whole complex of court, porticoes, and cloisters. Even in its grandiosity, however, the plan is exquisitely simple. The greater axis crosses the church, dividing then into two symmetrical parts the cloisters and the buildings, ending on the great loggia which surmounts the main terrace.

From the loggia, open to the countryside, the inner perspective has extraordinary grandeur. The vast cloister is closed on three sides by majestic porticoes open on both sides as walk-through galleries which link the main courtyard and two others of similar design but of lesser importance. In front, a magnificent stairway cuts its way through the buildings with five large landings and leads to a portico located on the summit, through which one enters the open court directly in front of the church».

This is how a writer [32] of the end of the last century described the plant of Monte Cassino. We have quoted him not only because his synthesis gives an exact description of that marvelous monument, as it still was on the day of its infamous destruction, but because that plan, developed through the centuries according to the very nature of the site, inspired of necessity the reconstruction, now happily accomplished.

3. THE WORKS OF THE CONTEMPORARY EPOCH.

The suppression of 1868 also marked a pause in the field of the arts. It was brief, however, and the recovery was vigorous. Naturally, given the great monumental and artistic inheritance, the recovery was concentrated, first of all, in works of preservation and restoration. There were, nevertheless, new works and, even in maintainance work, important renewals and adaptations were made.

Among the initiatives realized totally *ex novo*, one must count those of the Benedictine school of Beuron, whose major works were the sanctuary of the Tower of St. Benedict, commonly called «La Torretta», and the crypt of the basilica.

The memorable centenary of 1880 was approaching. To leave a perennial and monumental memory of the event which was going to be a solemn occasion pregnant with beneficial fruits, thought was given to restore and place in greater relief what was left of the ancient house of St. Benedict. The area of the monastery where the centuries old tradition placed the habitation of the Patriarch and his early disciples — the sites of such memorable places like the cell of the Saint, the window from which he had the miraculous visions of the deaths of the Bishop S. Germano from Capua and of his sister, the gate that witnessed various prodigies — were all explored with great care under the direction of d. Giuseppe Quandel. The work gave rich results and, although incomplete, formed the basis of further studies. The decoration of those rooms,. some newly brought to light after centuries, was entrusted to the school which recently d. Desiderio Lenz had established in the monastery of Beuron. In that corner of Hohenzollern not many years before, two Cassinese monks of the abbey of St. Paul in Rome, the brothers Mauro and Placido Wolter, had begun the restoration of Benedictine monasticism in Germany. The result of their work was a complex of chapels and rooms disposed in two stories, which formed a religious and artistic sanctuary among the most suggestive in the catholic world, which the Cardinal Legate Pitra consecrated as a church.

On the walls of the upper floor, the life of the Patriarch was illustrated in the various episodes of the Gregorian narrative, so that to the cycle in the basilica captured by the magic brush of Luca Giordano this other one was now added, delicately portrayed by the filial love of the monks of Beuron. The chapels of the lower floor still had paintings with stories of the Saints, allegories, and events related to the life lived there fourteen centuries before; only the cell, which according to the tradition had belonged to St. Benedict, kept its severe, majestic nudity. In that place where the Rule had been written and where so many prodigies had taken place, in the sight of the bronze statue of the legislator and incomparable Father and in the light of those perennial votive lamps, the soul was filled with reverence and love. In that mystical atmosphere even the smallest details — the furniture, the sacred furnishings — conformed to the hieratic style of that school, so that in leaving the sanctuary, the visitor was strongly moved by the memory of the great father who was filled with the spirit of all just men.

Besides Quandel, great credit for this realization goes to d. Bonifacio Krug, who never spared himself to see to it that it would be worthy of St. Benedict. To meet all necessary expenses, he received large support from Benedictine monasteries and from the faithful all over the world; he went also to America to ask for contributions from those generous Catholics.

He returned again, in 1900, when he was already Abbot of Monte Cassino, to raise funds for another great work: the crypt. Many times the restoration of that outstanding monument of the «cinquecento» had been discussed. The suppression had stopped the execution of the project, for which the Hon. Francesco Fontana had prepared the plan on the original design by Tosti. Still in 1880, lack of money had prevented the realization of the work. When he was elected abbot, Krug revived the idea and proposed to «honor St. Benedict in Monte Cassino with a monument that could vie with the most beautiful and famous works in Christendom and would make in our age a new statement of catholic thought in religious art» [33].

The execution was entrusted to the same monks from Beuron who had so suggestively decorated the «Torretta» and who here translated the beautiful project of Fontana into the characteristic lines of the art. No longer painting, as in the other monumental work, but sculpture and mosaic were used to glorify St. Benedict. The priceless materials, the sparkle of the mosaics, the vivacious polychromatic richness gave to it an harmonically solemn unity and exalted, around that life-giving sepulcher, the work and the Benedictine spirit.

The central chapel with the large statues of cedar wood and those in bronze, the side chapels dedicated to the famous disciples Maurus and Placidus, the marble frieze with its meaningful figures, the decorations always in the style of the school, and the whole animated by mystical inscriptions, exalted the Cassinese Patriarch «in medio populi sui, in loco ubi pullulant ossa eius» *.

Although there was no lack of criticism of this new religious art, it was impossible not to feel «full of respect before this artistic school so personal and noble in its intentions and aims: before this enormous choral display of colors and plastic forms... an art essentially latreutic, an hymn of faith, an act of adoration, a praise to God sung in the language of art» [34].

To give the «Torretta» its new decor, all the paintings which had been placed there to decorate the walls had to be removed. Together with others scattered in various places throughout the monastery, a collection was formed which was placed in the sixteenth century hall adjacent to the library, which had been used for the common fire. There too, because of the restoration of the crypt, was taken the choir of Benvenuto da Brescia, and to make room for it, the monumental stone fireplace, a magnificent work of the sixteenth century, was deposited in the small courtyard next to the bell tower.

After the restoration of the crypt, abbot Diamare turned his attention to the buildings of the monastery, which during his long govern were almost completely renovated, provided with electric

---

* «In the midst of his people, where his bones are sprouting forth to a new life».

Our Lady of the Assumption

Frescoes of the dome
by P. Annigoni

The death of St. Benedict

St. Scolastica's Burial

St. Benedict's vision

S. GVLIELMVS ABB.
FVND. ORD. MONTIS VIRGINIS

St. Romuald Abbot

Medaillons of the dome

St. Alferio Abbot

The Steadiness

The Poverty

The Obedience

The Chastity

The Glory of St. Benedict. Fresco by P. Annigoni

St. Benedict gives the Rule and the Crosier to Abbot Desiderius

Ivory crucifix of the high altar

Cassinese Codex of the 11th cent. - St. Benedict and St. Teobald Abbot

St. Benedict gives the Rule to his disciples
Illuminated choir-book of the Florentine School

omnes uj do mi no

die festi celebrites sub

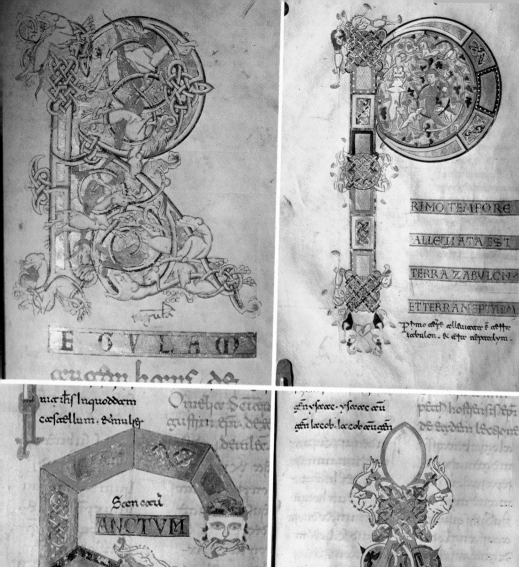

EGVLAM

cuozin hanc de

Scdm catil
ANCTVM

euangeliu
EVANGELIVM

RIMO TEMPORE

ALLEUIATA EST

TERRA ZABVLON

ET TERRA NEPTALIM

Primo ote alleuiata e terra
zabulon. & ostr neptalim.

V   DISTIS

ERS   KMI

One of the vitrines in the museum

Illuminated initials of the 11th cent.

power, a pipeline for drinking water, and, in parts, a heating system. A special series of works was required because of the damages caused by the 1915 earthquake. The church, the sacresty, the great refectory, the old library, the cloisters, especially that of the Benefactors, all underwent considerable restorations; the great corridor of the novitiate was radically restored, with all the rooms attached. This area which had been used after the suppression as the diocesan seminary was now returned to its original purpose.

Another important cycle of construction was carried out on the occasion of the centenary of 1929. In the church, all the plaster work and the gildings of the cupola and the presbytery were renovated and a new system of indirect lighting was installed to add suggestive relief to the rich decoration of the basilica. To avoid disturbance to the quiet serenity of the abbey by the ever growing crowds of visitors exploring the various areas of the monastery, a show of the main relics was established in the hall which formerly had been used as a picture gallery while the *antiquarium,* located next to the archives, was settled mainly in the rooms that gave access to the loggia del «Paradiso», on the left side, and the inscriptions were placed as decorations for the great entrance stairway.

In the last few years, the whole covering of the church and all the roofs, the plaster and the gildings of the vault of the choir, the right side of the nave, and the chapels of the same nave were renovated; the restoration of the chapels on the left side from which the painting had already disappeared for quite a while, was begun, and the chapel of St. John once again recovered its glittering appearance, while in the others the paintings were restored to the original brightness of their colors. This work was supervised, with a love equal to his skill, by the Hon. Giuseppe Anzino, an old alumnus of the college and d. Eusebio Gossetti also lavished on it all his versatile genius. Another old alumnus, Arduino Scaccia-Scarafoni, painted a canvass with the image of St. Thomas Aquinas for the altar of the chapel of the Relics, which on 1924 was dedicated to the Holy Doctor.

A great part of the paving of the abbey was done over; the whole upper floor of the entrance cloister as well as the roofs of that of the Benefactors were also done over; a new floor was added on the eastern side in the halls of the chapter, the old library and in the exposition rooms; the rooms of the archives were completely restored and a new location was prepared for it. The renovation of the roofs of the great corridor and other works were well along, while others were anticipated and planned, especially for the coming centenary of the death of St. Benedict.

At the same time efforts were made to replenish the furnishings of the house — the sacred vestments, the precious objects for the sacred service — for all of which there was a great dearth on account of the vicissitudes of the last centuries.

Outside the monastery, considerable works were carried out in Cassino at the abbatial palace, which was largely renewed, and also to give a decorous location to the catholic associations. Further renovations were undertaken at the monastery of the Benedictine nuns, and the church of the Carmen, which was decorated by d. Eusebio Gossetti, who painted a large canvas of the Crucifixion for the rear wall. At this time the orphanage added to it was built, and the house of the Sisters of Charity was renovated and its oratory was rearranged and decorated by d. Eusebio Gossetti. In the depending parishes, many works of restoration were carried out and new kindergartens were opened.

Thus, even from the point of view of artistic activity, Monte Cassino not only preserved its ancestral traditions, but was well along in worthily emulating the best periods of its millenary history when it was crushed by the destructive storm of 1944.

What has been done to rebuild it and restore its artistic beauty has already been seen in a concise manner in chapter IX of Part I of this volume.

NOTES

[1] GREGORII, *Dialogi,* c. 35. Of the polygonal walls large remains, that had been hidden by the structures of the monastery, have returned to light during the rebuilding, both below the archives and in the area of the «Torretta».

[2] The expression of St. Gregory are, in fact, quite meaningful: «... habitacula eiusdem cellae construerent» (c. 9), (while they were building the monastic londgings); «in eodem loco foderent», (while they are effecting an excavation): «coquinae aedificium» (c. 10), (the fabric of the kitchen); «dum fratres parietes, quia res ita exigebat, paulo altius aedificarent», (while the monks raised somewhat the wall, as the job required); «parietem cum fratribus perficeret» (c. 11), (he completed the wall with the brothers). The reconstruction work has allowed to trace the ground plan of the ancient oratory of St. Martin, traces which have been reproduced at the ground level of the entrance cloister. Also under the presbytery of the church, ancient walls of Roman and Benedictine construction have appeared. These last venerable remains have been made into an oratory and a lamp, alimented by the generosity of the Hon. Moretti, burns perennially in the immediate vicinity of the urn.

[3] «Lapis in medium jacebat quem in aedificium levare decreverunt» (c. 9), (there in the middle was a stone that they decided to use in the construction).

[4] *Ibid.,* c. 17. Pius XII, elevating St. Benedict to the heavenly patronage of architects and engineers, with the brief *Technicarum artium momentum* of Nov. 19, 1957, explains the choice reminding that «aedium at artificiorum auctor fuit et fabrilia cum precatione conjunxit».

[5] The study of E. SCACCIA-SCARAFONI, *S. Maria delle Cinque Torri, op. cit.,* advances the hypothesis that the church derived from a preexisting temple or pagan Nynpheum.

[6] Among such critics F. BOLOGNA, *La pittura delle origini,* Rome, Editori riuniti, 1962.

[7] O. MORISANI, *Gli affreschi di S. Angelo in Formis,* Cava dei Tirreni, Di Mauro, 1962-1965. In this volume the pictorial cycle of the well known Campanian church is presented complete for the first time. The study, appearing at the same time as the one by Bologna, is a luminous answer to the many critical positions assumed by the latter.

[8] *Op. cit.,* I, 45.

[9] E. BERTAUX, *op. cit.,* 156.

[10] *Ibid.,* 157.

[11] *Ibid.,* 158.

[12] *Chronicon Casinense,* III, 28.

[13] E. BERTAUX, *ibid.,* 159.

[14] *Ibid.*

[15] The doors, the panels of which had been damaged and disarranged by the war, have been recomposed and restored by the Central Restoration Institute. In their oldest parts at least, they go back to the age of Desiderius. Blessed and placed back in their original place on Feb. 15, 1963, they represent the most direct tie of the resurrected basilica to the past centuries.

[16] E. SCACCIA-SCARAFONI, *Note su fabbriche,* 108.

[17] «... praefatam ecclesiam et monasterium super suis fundamentis, quae illesa consistunt» (... the above mentioned church and monastery on their fundations, which remain intact), are the words of Urban V in the bull already cited, *Monasterium Casinense.*

The restoration of the monastery in its whole extension was, at that time, blocked by the successive happenings. Notable, in the same bull, the phrase with which it is asserted: «tam celebre monasterium, quod aliorum fuit inicium ac forma... et unde... constructionis aliorum monasterium forma processit». The thinking of the old Abbot of St. Victor does not seem in doubt: Monte Cassino had been the prototype also materially, of western coenobia. And undoubtedly the identity in planimetry that it has with other monasteries is extraordinary. A planimetry, one may add, which was part of the medieval Cassinese cloister, and one can surmise that it could have been there since the earliest years. It is also useful to remember here the narrative of St. Gregory about the establishment of Terracina. St. Benedict himself, however, has repeated, adapting them to local conditions, the traditional schemes of his native Umbria, which had come from the East. See Pirri, *loc. cit.*

[18] G. Minozzi, *op. cit.*, 546.

[19] E. Scaccia Scarafoni, *L'atrio*, 22.

[20] Id., *Note su fabbriche*, 98.

[21] O. Medici, *Annali*, III, codd. Cass. 674, 682, Ad. a.

[22] G. Giovannoni, *Relievi*, 327-328.

[23] A. Venturi, *Storia dell'arte italiana, XI. Architettura del Cinquecento*, p. I, Milan, Hoepli, 1938, 613-614. He attributes, wrongly, however, the architecture to Antonio da Sangallo the young.

[24] G. Giovannoni, *op. cit.*, 334.

[25] *Ibid.*, 333-334.

[26] G. Minozzi, *op. cit.*, 546, ff.

[27] L. Tosti, *Storia* III, 264-265.

[28] *Ibid.*, 265.

[29] A. Caravita, *op. cit.*, III, 392-393.

[30] E. Scaccia-Scarafoni, *Architetture cinquecentesche*, 18.

[31] L. Tosti, *Storia*, III, 226.

[32] G. Clausse, *Les origines bénédictines*, Paris, Leroux, 115, 116, 148.

[33] A. Capecelatro, *Commemorazione di D. Bonifacio Krug, Abbot of Monte Cassino*, Rome, Desclée, 1914, 4. The «cell of St. Benedict», which was spared by the bombardment, has been given, however, a new pictorial decoration by Agostino Pegrassi and the adjacent chapel of the Holy Monks as well. The other chapels have been replaced by the «oratory of St. Martin» built on designs by d. Angelo Pantoni, while d. Francesco Vignanelli has sculpted the lunette placed on the entrance door and also the sketches for the altarpieces of the three altars.

[34] C. Constantini, *Il Crocifisso nell'arte*, Firenze, Salesiana, 1911, 157.

BIBLIOGRAPHY

For this chapter also one should consult the works already mentioned and those that deal with art history. Mention is made here only of some special studies.

A complete history of Cassinese architecture, which gathers information from various sources, especially from the archives of Monte Cassino, was prepared by G. Quandel, 1878-1879, 3 vols., has not been published.

For the polygonal walls, the oldest of which are the exterior ones (fourth century) while those embossed reach their perfection only in the third century B.C., see G. Lugli,

La tecnica edilizia romana, Roma, Bardi, 1957, 99.

For the early times, besides the quoted CARETTONI, E. SCACCIA-SCARAFONI and PAN-TONI, let us remember: G. MORIN, *Pour la topographie ancienne du Mont-Casin*, in «Revue Bénédictine», 25 (1908), 277-303, 457-486; A. ALINARI, *Il primitivo monastero*, in *Conv. storico di Montecassino*, 51-81; A. PANTONI, *Su di una antica chiesa del monastero cassinese*, in «Rivista Arch. Cristiana», 13 (1936), 305-330. By the same, *Problemi archeologici cassinesi*, in «Riv. Arch. Crist.» 16 (1939), 271-288.

The artistic school of the eighth century has been studied especially by P. TOESCA, *Reliquie d'arte di S. Vincenzo al Volturno* in «Bull. Istituto storico italiano», 25, (1904), SCACCIA-SCARAFONI, *S. Maria delle Cinque Torri*, in «Riv. Arch. Crist.», 22 (1946), 139-189 and *Sulla traccia del battistero paleocristiano di Cassino, ibid.*, 40 (1964), 73-90. A. PANTONI, *S. Maria delle Cinque Torri di Cassino*, in «Riv. Arch. Crist.», 51 (1975), 243-280. A. PANTONI, *La basilica di Gisulfo e tracce di onomastica longobarda a Montecassino*, in *Atti I congresso internazionale studi longobardi*, Spoleto, Accademia Spoletina, 1952, 433-442, gives the first informations on the excavation of this ancient monument.

For the basilica of Abbot Joshua at S. Vincenzo al Volturno, see Pantoni, *Due iscrizioni di S. Vincenzo al Volturno e il loro contributo alla storia del cenobio*, in «Samnium 35 (1962), 64-79. To the brief monograph, *San Vincenzo al Volturno e la cripta all'abbate Epifanio*, Montecassino 1970, one must add now the great work of A. PANTONI, *Le chiese e gli edificii del monastero di San Vincenzo al Volturno*, Montecassino 1980, (Miscellanea Cassinese, 40), where he gives a relation on the works done and the results obtained.

The activity of Teobald at S. Liberatore alla Maiella has been illustrated by I. C. GAVINI, *Storia dell'architettura in Abruzzo*, Milan-Rome 1927, 27-69.

An attempt at reconstruction of the Desiderian monastery was made by H. M. WILLARD and K. J. CONANT, *A Project for the Graphic Reconstruction of the Romanesque Abbey at Monte Cassino*, in «Speculum», 10 (1935), 144-146. Another iconographic reconstruction was the work by SCACCIA, *La torre di San Benedetto, op. cit.*, N. ACOCELLA, *La decorazione pittorica di Montecassino dalle didascalie di Alfano I*, Salerno, Di Giacomo, 1966, has written on it with insight and great competence. The frescoes of the church of the Crucifix in Cassino, placed in greater relief by the war events, and those of S. Maria di Trocchio have been illustrated by A. PANTONI, *Un insigne monumento di arte benedettina: le pitture della chiesa del Crocifisso a Cassino*, in «Benedictina», III (1949), 239-248 and *S. Maria del Trocchio e le sue pitture*, in «Bollettino d'arte», 1953, 14-29. The above frescoes were detached under the supervision of the Superintendence of medieval monuments in Latium and taken to Monte Cassino.

The connexions between the cathedral of Salerno and the basilica of Monte Cassino have been studied by A. PANTONI, *La basilica di Monte Cassino e quella di Salerno ai tempi di San Gregorio VII*, in «Benedictina», 10 (1958), 35-44, with accompanying bibliography. A study of the Libera of Aquino was made by M. CAGIANO D'AZEVEDO, *La chiesa di S. Maria della Libera in Aquino*, in «Rivista del R. Istit. di Archeologia e Storia dell'arte», 8 (1941), 189-200.

For the more recent centuries, important contributions were made by: E. SCACCIA-SCARAFONI, *Note su fabriche e opere d'arte medievale a Montecassino*, in «Boll. d'arte», 30 (1936), 397-421; G. GIOVANNONI, *Rilievi e opere architettoniche del Cinquecento a Montecassino*, in *Casinensia*, 305-355; E. SCACCIA-SCARAFONI, *L'atrio della chiesa di Montecassino*, in «Boll. d'arte», 26 (1932), 22-33; IDEM, *Architetture cinquecentesche in Montecassino*, in «Boll. d'arte», 32 (1938), 9-24; G. GIOVANNONI, *Architettura cin-*

quecentesca in Montecassino, in «Palladio», 2 (1938), 192-194; E. Scaccia-Scarafoni, *Ancora del Sangallo a Montecassino,* in «Boll. d'arte del ministero Pubbl. Istruz.», 1962, 69-74. The work of Contini has been illustrated by H. Hager, *Giov. Batt. Contini e la loggia del Paradiso della abbazia di Montecassino,* in «Commentari», 21 (1970), 92-118.

For the buildings of Monte Cassino during the sixteenth century and their transformations, besides the already mentioned study by Leccisotti, *Montecassino agli inizi del Cinquecento,* see also A. Pantoni, *Una descrizione inedita di Montecassino del tardo Cinquecento,* in «Asprenas», 11 (1964), 341-357.

One must note also: A. Pantoni, *Opere e avanzi trecenteschi a Montecassino,* in «Arte cristiana», 30 (1942), 45-51; Idem, *Opere quattrocentesche a Montecassino,* in «Arte Cristiana», 26 (1938), 201-208, which gather the memories of the surviving monuments of those centuries at Monte Cassino, now, unfortunately, for the most part disappeared. The same author has examined with greater care the *Crocifisso sagomato con le immagini dei principi degli Apostoli,* in «Benedictina», 14 (1967), 225-233.

The splendid study of P. Fogaccia, *Cosimo Fanzago,* Bergamo, Arti Grafiche, 1945, deals also with the activity of this artist in the basilica of Monte Cassino.

The door of the Desiderian basilica has been studied by T. Preston, *The bronze doors of the abbey of Monte Cassino and of St. Paul's in Rome,* Princeton, 1915, and, on the occasion of the restoration by M. Cagiano De Azevedo, *La porta di Desiderio a Montecassino,* in «Bollettino dell'Istituto Centrale del restauro», 1951, n. 5-6, 93-97. Also dealing with them, G. Matthiae, *Le porte bronzee bizantine in Italia,* Rome, Officina Edizioni, 1971. They will be considered again and more thoroughly in the forthcoming work by H. Bloch, announced in the general bibliography.

A general survey of Cassinese art was given by T. Leccisotti, *L'operosità artistica del Montecassino medievale,* in «Vita e Pensiero», 20 (1929), 137-143; 632-642.

For a thorough examination of the questions concerning the characteristics of Benedictine art and the influence exercised by Monte Cassino in this field, besides a general bibliography on the topic, we refer the reader to the complete and lucid synthesis, *Opinioni, valutazioni critiche e dati di fatto sull'arte benedettina in Italia,* in «Benedictina», 13 (1959), 111-158 by A. Pantoni, whom this author wishes to thank for his considerable help in the improvement of this chapter. Particular importance has also the opinion expressed on Benedictine art by N. Cilento, *Sant'Angelo in Formis nel suo significato storico (1072-1087),* in «Studi Medievali», 1963, 899-912 and in *Italia Meridionale Longobarda,* Milan-Naples, Ricciardi, 1966, 225-239.

More recent in the work of H. Belting, *Studien zur beneventanischen Malerei,* Wiesbaden, 1968, (Forschungen zur Kunstgeschichte und christlichen Archälogie, 7).

Fundamental is the work, mentioned already many times, of A. Pantoni, *Le vicende della basilica di Montecassino attraverso la documentazione archeologica,* Montecassino, 1973 (Miscellanea Cassinese, 36).

The same author gathered the *Descrizioni di Montecassino attraverso i secoli,* in «Benedictina», 19 (1972), 539-586.

For the paintings of Annigoni, see *Annigoni a Montecassino,* Rome, Ed. La Gradiva, s.a. (1979).

IV.

THE «LAND OF SAINT BENEDICT»

«Ut in omnibus glorificetur Deus» *.

1. THE FORMATION.

These words of the apostle Peter [1], quoted by St. Benedict in the Rule about the material activity of the monks destined to the arts and crafts, became then the distinctive motto and the universal aspiration of all his children. If in fact the whole creation, if, above all, every human life has for its end the glorification of God, monastic life must be even more a sacrifice of praise.

Monastic activity then, even when it must turn for the material necessities of its existence to earthly things, can never lose sight of the supreme end: «quaerite primum regnum Dei» [2]. And, according to the promise, everything else has been bestowed in the measure of the faithfulness to this evangelical principle. The history of monastic institutions demonstrates this: the abundance of earthly goods is always tied to the fervor of their spiritual life.

Monastic patrimonies, however, are not accumulated to form a sterile wealth and to provide material goodbeing; on the contrary, after the necessary sustenance and the administrative expenses are provided for, the rest was destined to works of charity and for the embellishment of the house of God.

We do not know what the patrimony of the house of St. Benedict was at the beginning of its existence. As it has already been mentioned, a late and corrupted tradition speaks of large donations made by the Patrician Tertullus, even in Sicily. Still, in spite of the false amplifications, one must bear in mind that this legendary tradition contains a kernel of truth. At any rate, with

---

* «Let God be glorified in all things».

the Lombard invasion everything was lost, and, as it appears from later events, even the mountain and its surroundings became part of the fisc of the dukes of Benevento.

The reconstruction of the patrimony at the restoration of the community early in the eighth century had to be done *ex novo,* but it was rapid. Princes and kings, who came to the holy mountain as devout pilgrims or to pursue political aspirations, left rich gifts and diplomas granting large territorial concessions. The series was begun by the duke or Benevento, Gisulf II, and continued by, among others, Desiderius, the King of the Lombards and Carloman, the new Roman Emperor, setting an example to other powerful people who, in the course of the centuries, followed them in the political control of the region.

The donation of Gisulf, which in a sense was a form of compensation for the destruction and the damages caused by his ancestors, gave to the abbey a stable and independent position within the Beneventan duchy. Of the largesses of King Desiderius, about which there are no doubts, we do not know the entity, because the diploma that has reached us is obviously a falsification.

With Charlemagne, the relationship between Monte Cassino and the western Emperors began. This continued not only with the Carolingian successors, but also with the Ottos of Germany, who in persuance of their Italian policy, granted large concessions to the abbey. Monte Cassino was declared an imperial abbey, exempt and immune, thus becoming one of the great fiefs of the empire. From the top of his mountain, the Abbot «like a small Jove» [3] managed the small state entrusted to his care and often played a role in Italian and European politics.

At this time the donations from private citizens were numerous and continuous. These donations while constituting a clear indication of the religious rebirth, after the deep shadows and the destructive cycle of the Lombard invasion, and a sign of the growing renown of the monastery and of an increase in the devotion for St. Benedict, also tended to have practical goals. The donors, in fact, often were trying to save properties from confiscations, reserving the income from the lands for themselves, and on other occasions they were simply placing capital to useful work for themselves.

In this way especially, a large monastic patrimony was formed, which became one of the more important in Italy and the largest in the South. The rhythm of its growth was extraordinarily rapid through the whole age of Abbot Desiderius, when it experienced its largest increase; it then declined and stopped almost altogether in the thirteenth century.

Within this domain the Cassinese Abbots had no superiors except the two supreme medieval authorities, the Pope and the Emperor; thus they freely exercised both spiritual and temporal jurisdiction.

In virtue of this last power, they could build and tear down cities, raise armies (in which their subjects had to serve for the first three days at their own expense), employ a constable, declare war or contract alliances, grant fiefs and enjoy the right of liege homage. They could, moreover, exchange territories with other princes, grant titles of nobility and military rank, put down rebels and nominate notaries, judges, and lawyers from whom they received the oath of loyalty. Besides this, the monastery, as an independent house under imperial protection, could not be granted as a fief and could enjoy many privileges like port and beach rights, the determination of weight and measures, jurisdiction in civil and criminal cases, and many others. Criminal jurisdiction, the *jus sanguinis,* solemnly confirmed and, perhaps, even granted by Emperor Henry VI (1195), was revoked by King Charles of Anjou (1282) for the «Land of St. Benedict». The territories that were not part of the «Land of St. Benedict», were not affected, however, by this revocation of criminal jurisdiction. The motives, or better still, the pretexts adduced were futile; in reality the King wished to vent his peevishness against Abbot Bernard, once his good friend, because, as papal ambassador to Constantinople, he had promoted the restoration of peace between the churches, which was contrary to the political interests of the Angevins. As seen above, this criminal jurisdiction was won back only in 1669, at a very high price.

The spiritual jurisdiction was also very extensive. St. Benedict and his successors soon assumed, without conflict, the place of the old bishops of Cassino. There is no doubt, in fact, that the holy Patriarch exercised from his first arrival among those people, who had been long without a shepherd, some of the duties of a bishop. Such unchallenged activities lead one to believe that the Saint had received explicit permission from the superior authorities.

When Monte Cassino resumed then its life after the destruction by the Lombards, the situation had changed. Not only was there no longer any trace of the old episcopate, but the population had also almost completely disappeared; it began then to form again around the villas and the monastic cells. The lands, as already seen above, had passed from the ducal fisc to the full and free ownership of the monastery. And since ecclesiastical exemption was also soon extended to these lands, the original nucleus of the ancient diocese became much larger. The tradition, accepted for many years, traced back to pope Zacharias, that is to the beginning of the restoration, holds that it was a wide and complete exemption. To be sure the relative bull, as we have it today, is a quite evident falsification, but it cannot be completely excluded that there is in it some small element of the original truth.

It is indicative, however, that while the Abbots exercised a real and effective jurisdiction, there does not appear any trace of the old authority or any episcopal opposition in the «Land of St. Benedict».

At any rate, the exemption was fully recognized at the times of John VIII (882) and probably earlier during the pontificate of Nicholas I (859). The Cassinese Abbot then administered the sacraments of confirmation and minor orders and could ask any bishop to confer the majors orders; he judged those who violated ecclesiastical immunity, he sponsored parochial competitions, was named in the canon of the Mass after the Pope, could excommunicate usurpers of monastic goods, summon synods, of which we have memories and documents from the thirteenth century, sat on the high throne in the Cassinese basilica, was assisted in the pontifical masses by seventeen servers besides the lower clerics, and used all the insignia and episcopal vestments.

We must remember that the abbey had been elevated into a bishopric by John XXII, a concession that pope Urban V then revoked, only to do away with the inconveniences that had resulted. On the other hand, there were some bishops, even an archbishop of Naples, who did not find the office of General Vicar of the Abbot of Monte Cassino demeaning.

Even now, after the events of the past centuries, the spiritual jurisdiction remains at Monte Cassino, which exercises it over parts of its ancient patrimony. Thus parishes in Campania, Lazio, Abruzzi, Molise, and a sanctuary in Tropea (Calabria) are under the jurisdiction of the Abbot of Monte Cassino.

Not the whole patrimony, however, maintained the same ties of dependence. Directly subject and firmly tied with the life of the monastery was the «Land of St. Benedict», an homogeneous and compact complex between the counties of Teano, Comino, Venafro and the duchy of Gaeta. It underwent, of course, some border changes, but it remained until the seventeenth century the fundamental nucleus of Cassinese power; it was called even in recent centuries from the sixteenth to the eighteenth century the «State of S. Germano».

Besides this state, there were four other units, more or less large, with their own administrations which were part of the Cassinese jurisdiction: Cetraro in Calabria, S. Liberatore alla Maiella, S. Pietro Avellana, and S. Vincenzo al Volturno.

In the rest of the patrimony, in the possessions that were farther away and detached, control was less direct; the abbey only nominated the vicars and collected the dues.

These dependencies scattered throughout Italy, even in the North, had an important function from the religious and social aspect. Together with similar establishments of other great abbeys, they kept religious life in close contact with the people: the monks acted as evangelical heralds, as messengers from Rome, and they constituted a powerful weapon for the preservation of the Christian spirit not at all inferior to the future mendicant orders.

2. The organization.

As the extent varied in the course of time so did the organization of the Cassinese patrimony.

From the restoration of the eighth century to the destruction by the Arabs, economic activity was based on the *curtis* system. The population, whose increase was encouraged in every way by the monks, was in large part gathered around a «corte», where there was a church or an oratory with a *xenodochium* and, sometimes a monastery. A vicar in charge of the enterprise lived there; in the vicinity there were the lands cultivated directly by the monks and their dependents, who were mostly freed serfs; farther on there were woods and the lands of the farmers.

This typical organization, which answered well the demands of the Rule, had appeared in a period in which «one can say that the process of transformation from the Roman villa to the medieval *curtis* was effected» [4], and large extensions of land were placed under a uniform system, with considerable advantages not only for agriculture and land reclamation but also for the people who enjoyed the benefits of a paternal and equal control. This was the system with which throughout Europe, as in the Cassinese patrimony and in particular the «Land of St. Benedict», the monks put under culture and colonized the lands, bringing into life new villages and towns. The increase in the economic power of the monasteries acquired, therefore, in a devastated world «a decisive importance for the preservation of what was left of ancient civilization» [5].

While the vital center remained always near the tomb of the Father in the house on top of the mountain, the everyday necessities, which required a place of easier access, were met by the establishment of the *curtis major,* from which all other *curtes* depended, at the foot of the mountain. It was there that the first abbot, after the restoration, had built another monastery and where St. Bertharius later built his Eulogimenopoli. The place had kept its name until our days, as also in some towns the memory of the ancient organization in curtes and abbatial palaces persists [6]. The Vicar General resided in the «*curtis major*»; he was, in modern terminology, the chief administrator. All administrative matters had to be referred to him and once a year, on the last day of August, which since the eighth century marked both for the civil administration and for that of the Roman Church the closing of the financial year, all the vicars of the various dependencies gathered at the «*curtis major*» to give an account of their stewardship and to receive the new assignments.

Besides, these *curtes,* especially the main one, were not only large agricultural enterprises but also manufacturing centers to which the dependents and farmers of the monastery went for their needs in preference to the city merchants.

In fact, under this aspect, the main curtis of S. Salvatore, at least at the time of abbot Bertharius, had, as it appears to us, a special character; it was both a private and a public market. In fact, attached to it was the small capital of the «Land of St. Benedict», Eulogimenopoli, with its «negociantum foro», and the Abbot, besides being the Lord of the curtis, was also the Prince of the fief and, at the same time, the spiritual shepherd with episcopal attributes.

At the return to Monte Cassino from the Capuan exile, things changed. Aligernus called cultivators from all over to repopulate the lands won back but still uninhabited after the great Arab devastations. With these free farmers, to secure the income but even more to provide for the rebuilding of Monte Cassino, he stipulated land leases. These same farmers he gathered in fortified strongholds. The lease system took the place of the «curtis» and this changed the juridical position of the inhabitants.

In this way... «the people, through the work of reclamation of the land, the rebuilding of villages, the safety and the assistance provided, and especially the equitable conditions of work offered by the abbey, gained interest in the direct management and improvement of their own private enterprise, and in this way they were helped, almost pushed on the way to autonomy and freedom. Which thus prepared and supported, flowered then in the mature life of the Communes» [7].

The evolution was, naturally, gradual. The beginnings appeared as a resumption of the ancient system. In the course of one century, the aspect of the «Land of St. Benedict» was changed. The servile element almost completely disappeared and the domain was greatly reduced; most of the agricultural lands were cultivated in the greatest part by free farmers on leased plots. The movement reached its conclusion in the eleventh century. The government of abbot Richer, of whom we have been able to note the influence on the formation of the new era, had also in this field a considerable importance. He had expelled from the lands of the abbey the Normans, who in those early years of their infiltration were rather undesiderable guests. To organize defenses against them, he summoned the peasants to come and live in strong positions which he surrounded with walls, marking thus the beginning of the fortified castles. Thus a military class came into existence, the *consuetudines* of the various localities were formed and guilds were organized; the first example of them had already appeared at S. Angelo in Theodice at the times of Aligernus.

The developement of the communes in southern Italy, however, as it is well known, was arrested by the establishment of Norman centralization, and to it all other minor formations had to yield. Monte Cassino also lost its freedom and political independence, being transformed into a fief within the southern monarchy.

This is the character that the Cassinese domain would have until the end of the eighteenth century. The Swabian emperors restored briefly the ancient immunity, recognizing its dual jurisdiction; the Angevins, in turn, gave back what they had taken away from the Swabians, and so with Bernard I, the patrimony was reconstituted and usages and customs were codified, but the same Charles of Anjou took away the right of criminal justice, the ancient *jus sanguinis*.

Politically the decline of Monte Cassino became more marked. Still, among the new regional units, the «State of S. Germano» was one of the larger fiefs of the kingdom of Naples, dependent from it and part of the royal organization.

The administration experienced also its unavoidable changes. The «Land of St. Benedict», until the time when it was absorbed into the new kingdom of Italy, was governed mostly under Lombard law, according to local customs, and through various legislation enacted Abbots and Popes.

Justice was originally entrusted to the *advocatus Casinensis*. With the increasing amount of business as early as the eleventh century, we find the local judges assisted by the *boni homines*. At the end of the same century and during the following one, we find a central court in full activity; it was an appeals court from the lower authorities and the only competent tribunal for major cases. It was the *curia major*, a name used also to indicate the central administrative organ. Called in older times the *curia abbatis,* it was formed by the Abbot, the *magister iustitiarius* in criminal cases, by the *iudex* and the *advocatus casinensis,* by other judges, and by the castald, that is to say, the officer of the court. Likewise in the other castles there were the *curtes minores,* made up of the *rectores,* bailiffs, judges, and castalds. One of these lower courts had its seat also in S. Germano, in the same palace of the high court, and several served to administer local justice.

After criminal jurisdiction was forfeited to the King in cases of this kind, a judge named by the King sat beside the abbatial judge.

The execution of the sentence was the duty of the *milites*, the armed force under the command of the constable, which resided in S. Germano and by long custom was chosen among the milites of that city.

In most villages there were notaries in residence chosen by the Abbot. Since the twelfth century they were chosen even among laymen. The establishment of the protonotariate goes back instead to the epoch of Abbot Bernard I.

The administration proper was made up of the *curia major,*

the supreme tribunal, which, as already seen, was also the major administrative organ for the whole patrimony, the *rector casinensis* and the *consilium fratrum*. On the other side there was the *camera abbatis* and the *officia* or *oboedientiae:* the hospital, the infirmary, the sacristy, the camerariate, the cellarer, the vestry, the conventual, the treasurer and, in the fourteenth century, the office of the restorer.

The administrative branch of the *curia major* in the old days was composed by the Abbot, the *advocatus,* the dean or, in his place, a monk; later it was made up of the *judex casinensis* and a good number of the major administrators; at the time of Bernard I it was increased even further to include the Abbot, the *advocatus, judex Casinensis, capellani, rector casinensis* (who apparently took the place of the Vicar), other officers of the monastery, some knight of the Abbot's family, and the protonotary. The *consilium fratrum,* called on to give its opinion on all the Abbot's proposals and those of the high officers, was made up of the whole community, the chapter. The high officers mentioned above must render an account of their administration to it two or three times a year. To this consilium also, every five years, the Abbot presented the registers in two original copies with the inventory of the landed estates and the rights which were exacted from the vassals. Of these two registers, a copy went to the archives and the other remained with the Abbot or one of the officers.

Together with the council of the chapter, the Abbot chose two monks, who after they had taken the oath, had charge of receiving the revenues from the *oboedientiae* and of spending them according to the orders of the Abbot and the views of the community. In front of these and the rectors and the bailiffs, who paid up the dues, the monks must, every month, render an account of their management.

As it appears, the administrative power of the Abbot, supported by the small council of the *curia major,* was counterbalanced by the assembly of the monks, which monitored its activities and exercised full judgement on its work. The abbey had arrived at this democratic regime, which was perfected in the thirteenth century, through long experience in the safeguard of the patrimony of the monastery.

The majors offices were autonomous entities with their own patrimony, rents, vassals, and administrative agents.

The local administration originally was based on the *curtis* system, the *advocatus* had mainly judiciary functions and for administrative necessities he took orders from the Vicar. When the castles were organized, a monk as rector represented the monastery. The *curia minor* then was organized around him, with various officers to fill its various needs.

The secular clergy, which was always under the jurisdiction of the Abbot, in the twelfth century was under the control of the Sacrist, who, for the most part, installed the archpriests (every castle then had an archpriest with its chapter) who were elected by the clergy and confirmed by the Abbot.

This was, in its general lines, the bureaucratic machine of the «Land of St. Benedict» and, in general, of all the Cassinese jurisdiction, which worked with so great efficacy, especially during the centuries of its greatest power.

In more recent times, it underwent other changes. In the era of the commendataries, a governor was at the head of the whole domain; at the time he was called a viceroy. In the smaller villages a monk remained as rector, while in some of the more distant territories, especially those out of the «Land of St. Benedict», one even sometimes finds lay governors for the collections of all dues. At the head of all the dependent vicariages there was a monk called the Chief Vicar.

Most recently, in the reorganization of the Italian dioceses under the directives of Vatican II, twenty-eight parishes were taken away from the Cassinese jurisdiction, that is those outside Latium, and four were added from that region.

Undoubtedly, a stronger ethnic unity has resulted, but a moral unity of over a thousand years was shattered.

Still, even thus reduced, the Cassinese diocese, after fifteen centuries, keeps on doing the work of its Patriarch.

3. SOCIAL AND WELFARE WORKS.

This large patrimony which included hundreds of thousand acres of land, with two outlets to the sea, with two ports, with warehouses at Amalfi and Salerno, with a small fleet of ten vessels to trade with Ancona, Ravenna, Dalmatia, Apulia and the mines of Sardinia, was intended mainly for the glorification of God. Not only therefore «fiscal extractions were quite light, compared to other feudal lordships», but it was permeated by the Christian spirit which gave life to all so that, except for the rights of justice and the basic demands of proprietary rights, charity worked silently and unceasingly.

This balm, incomparable and irreplaceable, tried to sooth all human infirmities, all social needs, It was the monastery that made possible for so many men groaning in the bonds of slavery to become free men, by accelerating the redeeming action of the teaching of Christ. It has already been mentioned that the old cultivators of the abbey's possessions were in large part freed serfs. Having acquired their full personal freedom, it did not take long for them to experience the advantages of free farmers. Thus around the monastery a large family grew up, many of whom preferred to remain more intimately connected with the monastery under the tie of *oblates*.

Throughout the decay of all civilian authority, the Church, on its own initiative, had tried to be a remedy within the limits of its possibilities. Thus a network of shelters, called from their Greek name *xenodochia,* was established to offer hospitality to pilgrims and travellers. St. Benedict dedicated an important chapter of his Rule to this, which was then one of the principal social missions of monasticism. Thus, every monastery had its hospital, where if in the guests «one welcomed and adored Christ himself», the poor, orphans and the sick were welcomed in the same spirit. These institutions were kept not only in the great abbeys but also in the dependent houses, some of which were established for this purpose, especially in places like the great main roads and mountain passes and near sanctuaries, wherever the need was greatly felt.

Monte Cassino kept increasing, throughout the towns and the territory of its domain, the number of these foundations, to which many charitable congregations of our epoch trace back their beginnings.

There were several in S. Germano, where they existed at the time of Desiderius, but probably had been there long before. Others existed at St. Peter in Monastero, at S. Angelo in Theodice, at Valleluce, at S. Vittore, at S. Elia, at Barrea, at Vallerotonda, at S. Angelo in Formis, at Lucca close to the monastery of St. George, at Benevento (St. Benedict at Xenodochium), and on Mount Gargano. To these, special houses for the lepers must be added.

The mission was universally recognized and praised by rulers like Robert II of Sicily (1147) and Emperor Frederick II (1221), who proclaimed Monte Cassino: «unicum egenorum solatium peregrinorum et necessitatem habentium portum» *.

Some of these pious foundations had a long life; hospitality, although in different form, remained in honor at Monte Cassino until the last destruction. Obviously one did not wash the feet of the guests any longer, and the whole community did not move «en masse» to meet them as of old. The large numbers, besides the changed social customs, would not allow this any longer. One must remember here that in certain years the number of visitors was over forty thousand, not counting those that came only for the day.

But from the oldest age, of which we have the evidence in a letter attributed to Charlemagne, «In the high mansion of St. Benedict so dear to God, the guest never lacks vegetables, fish and abundant bread» to the age of Desiderius, who welcomed especially the great crowds who came for the consecration of the church, to the eighteenth century, when Abbot Galisio built the huge structure which saved the lives of the poor custodians of the basilica who had taken refuge in its basement during the terrible

---

* «Only support of the needy, harbor that welcomes pilgrims and the unfortunate».

bombardment of 1944, Monte Cassino welcomed all. The French poet Ozanam in 1847 wrote, «Oui vous êtes vraiment les fils de Saint Benoît — L'étranger qui s'assied un jour sous vôtre toit — Y trouve réunis d'une saint alliance — Et le savoir moderne et la vieille croyance; — Et l'hospitalité, vertu des anciens jours. — Que le monde croyait éteinte pour toujours»; until its dying moments in 1944, thousands of exceptional, unfortunate guests sought refuge in the house of St. Benedict. As the Holy Patriarch had foreseen, guests were never missing in his house.

Reading from the sacred books could also no longer be done for all comers; still there were not a few who, like St. Ignatius one day, came alone or in small groups to seek a retreat, to attend to divine things, and to receive words of life.

The Abbots took also to heart the bettering of economic conditions for the villages subject to them; thus they built a paper-mill and a textile factory at S. Elia and another textile mill and a needle and pins factory at S. Germano. Building of roads and other public works were also organized from time to time to alleviate unemployment, while schools were provided to educate the illiterate paesant population; orphanages and kindergartens were open to help children, especially those who were abandoned. Even recently on the grounds of the abbatial palace, a building for the Sisters of Charity who were called at Cassino in 1854, and for their school was put up by Abbot Celesia (1850-1858), who died as Cardinal and Archbishop of Palermo. At the same time, the new orphanage of the Sisters of the Stigmata, who had come to Cassino at the time of Abbot Pappalettere (1858-1863), was built. In both structures the soul and the brush of d. Eusebio Grossetti has brought to the decoration of the places of prayer a high spiritual note.

Through the helpful work of the local pastors, new orphanages were built in the villages, while in Cassino itself a section of the abbatial palace was decorously adapted to house catholic organizations, among which was the active recreation hall for young children away from the dangers of the streets.

Thus the «Land of St. Benedict», all the Cassinese inheritance, in spite of the sometime unavoidable deficiencies, appears through the centuries as a single, great patriarchal family, sharing the same traditions, ideally close around the tomb of St. Benedict and ruled by his successors with the discretion which is characteristic of the Rule and which is an indispensable condition to obtain the final goal: «ut animae salventur» *.

---

* «The salvation of the souls».

NOTES

[1] In the epistle I, cap. IV, 11 with a small variation from the text of the Rule: «ut in omnibus honorificetur Deus...».

[2] «Look above all for the kingdom of God and His justice, and all these things will be added». It is the promise of the Lord in the Gospel of St. Matthew, VI, 33.

[3] F. GREGOROVIUS, *Storia della città di Roma nel Medio Evo,* I, VI, c. IV, Rome 1900, Vol. II, 291.

[4] F. CARLI, *Il mercato nell'alto medio evo,* transl. by Luzzatti, Padua, Cedam, 1934, 174.

[5] A. DOREN, *Storia economica dell'Italia nel medio evo,* Padua, Cedam, 51.

[6] D. ANGELO PIETRA, or as mentioned above, Pria, who died at Monte Cassino, in his classic address *Indirizzo degli economi,* etc. Mantua, Osanna, 1586, which marked an era in the history of accounting, at p. 27 gives a definition of the *Curtis* as: «a place where the ministers of the monastery in charge of the possession have residence». This use of the congregation is not, however, contrary to what has been said above; in fact, it derives from and corroborates it. Let us note here another interesting information by him concerning the fiscal year: «The custom of our whole congregation in Italy is to begin it on June first». Also from him we obtain the explanation of why the fiscal year changed its beginning date: «The custom of our whole congregation in Italy is to begin it on June the first, because at that time, our general chapter has been held and the greater part of the prelates and ministers have moved to other monasteries, everyone knows better what he leaves behind and what he finds himself with». The Curtis of S. Germano was, besides, the seat of the ecclesiastical tribunals and of the civil and criminal courts of the state of S. Germano. Under that name various traditions were joined and several offices and functions were united.

[7] C. CALISSE, *op. cit.,* XXXV.

[8] GATTOLA, *Accessiones,* 4-6, notes that Monte Cassino was not a fief, because it did not hold lands from anybody. Thus in the *Catalogus* of the barons it was not listed; there was only a note that it «obtulit milites». The expression *fief* is to be understood not in its proper but in analogous sense, especially for the «Land of St. Benedict» itself.

[9] Thus L. FABIANI, believed that he could so state at p. 436 of the first edition of his

study already mentioned working out the demonstration in the second, quoting the work of abbot Bernard I: «non decet viros religiosos molestiis et exactionibus subditos suos fatigare, et nobis cor est a gravaminibus illatis vobis abstinere et pacem ac quietem vestram, modis quibus possumus, ampliare».

BIBLIOGRAPHY

For the story of the Cassinese domain see, L. FABIANI, *La terra di San Benedetto, op. cit.*, L. DIAMARE dealt with a particular century in *L'organizzazione del monastero Cassinese nel secolo XIII*, in «Archivio Società Romana di Storia Patria», 68 (1945), 33-61.

For the jurisdiction of Monte Cassino see, T. LECCISOTTI, *Alcune osservazioni sulla giurisdizione cassinese* e *Note sulla giurisdizione cassinese*, in «Bollettino Diocesano», Monte Cassino, 1961, pp. 159-167; 1962, pp. 77-87. About the probability of the donation of Tertullus, see, *ibid.* and by the same author, *I Regesti dell'Archivio*, II, Rome 1965, XLIV-XLV.

For the reclamation of the lands, cfr. I. IMBERCIADORI, *L'idea di S. Benedetto in the history of land reclamation*, in *Studi in onore di Amintore Fanfani*, Milan, Giuffrè, 1962, vol. I, 427-449 and the volume published on the initiative of the Ministery of agriculture, *La bonifica benedettina*, Istituto della Enciclopedia Italiana, 1963, which takes a panoramic view of the works of the monks in this field and adds a rather complete bibliography on the topic. For the work of Monte Cassino in this area see, L. FABIANI, *op. cit.* ·

An example of local ordinances is found in V. FEDERICI, *Gli statuti di Pontecorvo*, Montecassino, 1932 (Miscellanea Cassinese, 10).

The dependent houses in Sardinia have been studied by A. SABA, *Montecassino e la Sardegna medievale*, Monte Cassino 1927, (Miscellanea Cassinese, 4). Those of Capitanata by T. LECCISOTTI, *Le colonie cassinesi in Capitanata*, Montecassino, 1937, 1938, 1939, 1957, (Miscellanea Cassinese, 13, 15, 19, 29, and in «Benedictina», I, 1947), 83-133; III (1949), 203-215. For the medieval expansion of Monte Cassino in Tuscany see: H. M. SCHWARZMAIER, *Das Kloster St. Georg in Lucca und der Ausgriff Montecassino in die Toskana*, in «Quellen und Forschungen aus Italienischen Archiven und Bibliotheken», 49 (1969), 145-184.

ANGELO PANTONI is currently conducting diligent researches on the townships of the Cassinese diocese in *Bollettino Diocesano di Montecassino*, while for the same area T. LECCISOTTI is investigating facts concerning the spiritual jurisdiction.

On the same *Bollettino*, 27 (1972), 321-327, T. LECCISOTTI, has recalled *L'opera ricostruttrice dell'Abate Rea*, for the religious buildings of the «Land of St. Benedict».

Of Monte Cassino as an imperial house, see M. INGUANEZ, in *Atti V Congresso Studi Romani*, 1942.

«MONTE CASSINO IS ST. BENEDICT»

(Pius XI)

Typical creation of his mind and his heart, fruit of so much sweat and tears, intimately connected with the most important events of his life, Monte Cassino identifies itself with the moral and spiritual personality of St. Benedict: «His soul seems to live there more than in any other place on earth» [1].

It is not, therefore, a naked, cold, more or less artistic mass of stones, but the realization of an ideal among the noblest and most fecund in results that humanity ever had.

How this ideal has been kept alive through the vicissitudes of fourteen centuries has been seen. Empires and kingdoms have fallen, philosophic and artistic systems have faded away, people and nations have disappeared, but the ideal of Benedict has survived, hewn from the rock of his mountain, now covered with woods, now barren, now crowned with peaceful silvery olives, now savagely devastated.

A life always in harmony, until our own days, with that of Italy, a companion in tribulations and joys, in mourning and resurrection, almost a symbol of the perennial vitality of the people of Italy, of these Benedict can well be called the father. If one considers, in fact, that not only «in the final catastrophe of the western empire, he personified with rare purity the true Roman spirit, but he was also one of the last executors of the mission that Providence assigned to the spirit of Rome in the history of humanity..., we can indeed say that he was the last of the Romans» [2].

But when we think that he was one of the most eminent architects of European unity, the true father of the new people united in brotherhood in the sacred name of Christ and that of Rome we can also salute him as «the first... of those, that the Roman race grafted onto the plant which was to give to her, in the Italian nation, the glorious daughter... as the one whose name and whose work forms one of the strongest link, around which, from beginning to end, the unity of the national history of Italy was woven» [3].

In his Monte Cassino, the accents of the national life, of these wholesome Italian feelings, were always present even through the Middle Ages. Auxilius, Vulgarius, Amatus, and Alphanus are the most significant expressions of it, but the inner feeling, the obscure but stubborn working of the nameless tradition are especially well expressed by that unknown monk of the eleventh century who, lamenting the fact that, regrettably, the glorious inheritance of Rome had fallen into the hands of barbarians, continued, saying, «as a spark snatched from the fire, as the plankings surviving from a shipwreck, we do what little we know and can do...» The small spark was kept alive here at Monte Cassino throughout the Middle Ages; its light was at times pale and then grew brighter through the various periods of our history; it became a flame in the age of our Risorgimento when on this mountain «which looks from above the beautiful country that surrounds it and seems to invite men to reach for the longed for concord of heaven and earth» (Gioberti), «Luigi Tosti dreamed, hastened, and prepared with his writings and his work Italian unity and peace between the church and the State» [4].

If there is then a place where the great events of our history seem to crowd together, that place is Monte Cassino. How many memories there are of men and times around this mountain where Pontiffs and Emperors came to attempt, most of the times vainly, to establish peace between heaven and earth. The children of St. Benedict, from time to time, saw from the summit of this mountain Goths, Lombards, Arabs, Normans, French, Spaniards, and Germans go by as a devastating storm through the plain watered by the Liri river; they saw the rise and the fall of dynasties. Sometimes they were caught in the storm and swept away, but the tree planted here by St. Benedict always gave forth new shoots. The mountain, a bright beacon and safe harbor among the storms of the centuries, as Vincenzo Gioberti defines it, preserved and handed over to succeeding generations the flame of Italian life, a life renewing itself on the example of the monks, who were associated in the bond of prayer, of work in the fields and in the studies, in the pursuit of poetry and the arts, and in the uplifting of the soul to God» [5].

The task of this Italian nation has been, in the history of the world, that of providing the line of transmission for western civilization. Along this line Monte Cassino is one of the most significant stages. She has been a watchful custodian and a tireless worker not only of ancient literature but of all culture. It was her Rule, the Cassinese Rule, heir and epitome of the preceding founders of monasticism, which civilized and unified Europe; the children of her Patriarch were the first «who rose to snatch the nations from the darkness of paganism and barbarism, to lead them into the light of the Christian faith and the benefits of civilization. It is not an exaggeration to assert that few nations in the world have been converted to Christianity and taught the arts of peace without the dedicated participation of monasticism» [6]. Silent and obscure was the task of these tireless workers: «their names are mostly unknown... History barely asserts that they preached and taught; they lived, worked and died, and this is how the people, among whom they lived, became Christian» [7].

Pius XII then rightly and solemnly declared St. Benedict «Father of Europe» [8]; Paul VI proclaimed him «Patron». And in fact, we shall repeat with I. Giordani that «the ferment scattered by his numerous disciples, God's workers, developed western civilization in which all modern nations were formed. Some, as it happens, paid him back destroying his houses and scattering his children. These children, however, returned from everywhere, full of forgiveness; they rebuilt the house above the ruins, and over the bones of their martyrs erected the altar and resumed God's work» [9].

It is no wonder then that this civilizing mission that Monte Cassino directly or indirectly carried out in the formation of the Christian world, together with all her history, has had a great apologetic function in God's Church. In our own days, Pius X recognized this authoritatively and solemnly: «What the religion of Christ can do is firmly attested by the abbey of Monte Cassino, shining monument of the Christian Faith, ornament and pride of Italy... in times of violence a support of the Church and a bulwark of faith; her glories through a long series of years formed a large part of the history of the Roman Church» [10]. The efficacy of her mission was due especially to the quality of the seed that the monks scattered, to the evangelic *verbum bonum* of which they were the means of diffusion, to the message of that Christian peace which is essentially love.

«May they be one thing only as we also, Father, are one thing only». That was the supreme wish of Christ. Peace then in the unity of love, the opposite of egoism. This is the social aspect of Christianity; the true pacification of men with God and with each other. To spread this love, to fight and arrest adversaries, which, unfortunately, are always active in the world and cause great harm, that is the mission of the Church through the centuries. To make less harmful the effects of egoism, to unite all people, all nations, in a single, solidary family, this is the goal that Christianity tenaciously pursued. Romans and barbarians, poor and rich, all must feel equal in Christ.

If the ideal sometimes seemed close to realization, if the world gradually cast off the ancient form of rampaging egoism, the struggle never ceased between the two cities: that of love and that of hatred.

In the more difficult moments, in the most decisive phases of the struggle, the church of Rome has found this ideal and showed that it was alive in the houses of her faithful servant, Benedict. What was, in fact, the function of Benedictine monasticism from the epoch in which arose, perhaps the most obscure period of the Latin-Christian world, if not that of repeating to the people in despair, to the conquerors and the vanquished, the word of Christ, and to keep repeating it above the contingencies of a passing world, loudly as if strengthened by a powerful amplifier? It was the Christian life in its purity of love, checking and vanquishing individual egoism, that appeared inspired in all the monasteries following the ideal of Monte Cassino. It had been reserved to Benedict, in his fullest adaption of monasticism to the Latin spirit, to form with his Code the monastic unity among the so many, sometime contradictory, pre-existing forms which were strongly pervaded by individualism.

His unity was not external, hierarchic, bureaucratic, almost a unification and centralization, but it was instead inner unity with a moral, familiar tone. The children around the Father in the constant communal life free themselves from all egoisms, and their individual traits seem to disappear. The late descendants of the *Furii* and the *Scipiones,* these heirs of the very famous and illustrious clans, lived side by side with the children of those barbarians, the very name of whom horrified the Romans; often they found themselves behind their ancient slaves. In the humility of the cloister, we have kings of hostile nations, as Carloman and Ratchis, become brothers in the only existing army for peace, tending their sheep and their fields. How many things had to be given up every day! The holy habit of self-denial covered hearts ready to forget themselves at any moment for the common good, for the advantage of others, for love.

It is, however, a voluntary communal life, freely embraced and not a forced levelling, absolute and animal-like. Everybody must avoid, of course, any form of individualism, conforming to the family-like model; everyone must pursue what is more useful to the others; all goods are held in common and what is mine or yours must be absolutely banned. Everyone will receive what he needs from the father, not in a measure absurdly identical for all, but according to individual need, observing a reasonable frugality, without envy or struggle.

At the same time, work, no longer the despised activity of slaves, is a common obligation such as will sanctify and give joy to the soul, so that as true monks, they must not turn away from even the heaviest obligations on which their own sustenance might depend [11]. The efforts of all are absorbed and united in the whole, but no one is forbidden to profit from his own individual attitudes and abilities, provided that this will not lead into a position of exaggerated individualism, which fatally will turn into egoism and arrogance. There is no room for egoism in the house of Benedict, where everyone lives «*alieno iudicio et imperio*»; his program, born in sharp opposition to individualism, is a communal life in the strictest sense of the word, lived within the family nucleus.

The family might well grow, widen its range until it may become almost a *municipium,* transforming itself into a *curtis* or in a true *respublica*, but the pattern does not change, it remains an organization strictly patriarchal in character. The center does not move; the statutes remain the same. The family, even when it becomes very large, is always headed by the father; everyone contributes with his work, ennobled and at the level of prayer, to the common good; everyone expects from the father justice and directives, and the necessities for life and work. The result is a true organization, a communal life, in which as it has been noted, justice and charity complement and vivify each other [12].

This small world was an almost synthetic, typical image of the larger family, the Church. Benedict's unity was formed by returning to the pure, simple, and fundamental principle of Christianity, love, the true and effective spring of pacification.

Love of God: prayer, *ora*; love of neighbor: work, *labora*.

That is why the system was so fecund of beneficial results. Where the eagles of Rome could not arrive, the monks brought the Cross. Their peaceful colonies conquered, more than any army, people still barbarians; continuously during the course of the centuries, they drew with the true *sensus Christi* the souls troubled by struggles and world events.

The message is still the same, the word that St. Benedict repeats from Monte Cassino to our era thirsting, as never before, for a more peaceful and brotherly solidarity; this is the teaching that comes from the history of the house. And if with the destruction of that house, St. Benedict has, perhaps, contributed to avoid some sorrow and larger losses to the Church and to Italy, then let its ruin be the small grain placed in the furrow for the common good, and let its resurrection be a token and an auspice for the renewed life of the people and the Church, in the new open climate and in the perspectives marked by the last Council, which calls all men to a stronger and more conscious brotherhood, to the pursuit of essential values, beyond ephemeral, external forms.

N O T E S

[1] C. BUTLER, op. cit., 209.

[2] I. HERWEGEN, op. cit., 126.

[3] C. CALISSE, S. Benedetto, in «Nuova Antologia», 1929, July-Aug., 27.

[4] P. FEDELE, Accenti d'italianità a Montecassino, in Convegno storico, 16.

[5] Idem, XVII-XVIII.

[6] A. GASQUET, Saggio storico della costituzione monastica, Transl. from English, Rome, Istituto Pio IX, 5.

[7] Ibid.

[8] «Europae pater S. Benedictus est». Homily given in the papal chapel of St. Paul, Sept. 18, 1947. In the same homily, as already in the encyclical Fulgens radiatur, he develops the same motives for such appellation.

[9] I. GIORDANI, Segni di contradizione, Brescia, Marcelliana, 1934, 202.

[10] Archicoenobium Casinens, 1913, February 10.

[13] «When the ancient Romans considered work as a punishment for slaves, when the barbarians scorned it as an occupation unworthy of a nation of warriors, it was St. Benedict that elevated work to the dignity of a religion, consecrating to it the crowds of his disciples... In late centuries, it has been tried to compress the Benedictine program in the two words motto: "Ora et labora"... To be completely exact, however, it is necessary to insert another very important element, pointed out expressly by the biographer; "Ecce labora et noli contristari". Prayer and work go well together, but this is done also by people in jail and sentenced to hard labor. St. Benedict associates with it, especially, a sense of joyful spontaneity, of happy freedom, the only one that preserves the dignity of God's children. Thus in the Rule the Saint prescribes: "Tu nemo perturbetur neque contristetur in domo Dei" »; SCHUSTER, Storia di San Benedetto, 131-132. Let us remember also the beautiful pages of G. BOTTAI, L'ideale romano e cristiano del lavoro in S. Benedetto, in «Roma», 20 (1942), n. 9, 353-367.

[12] SCHUSTER in Storia di San Benedetto, 465, acutely and rightly observes: «Considering the particular Benedictine conception of the "monastery-citadel" on an autarchic plan, with the attached family of farmers, slaves, ordinary workers for various jobs, it was inevitable that once the Roman "polis" was destroyed, it would form again around the abbey of St. Benedict. It is not entirely exact to assert that the Christian democracy in Italy draws its origin exclusively from the Communes of the Franciscan Era.

In fact, long before the twelfth-thirteenth century the Christian proletariat, the workers, and the farmers scattered by the wars and deprived of everything, were gathered and sheltered in *"vici"* or *"loci"* by the efforts of the children and successors of St. Benedict. There is still extant a whole collection of abbatial statutes, in which, from the eleventh century already, we find echoes of the future communal liberties.

It is not difficult to document that almost all the ancient abbatial statutes of Farfa, Monte Cassino etc. draw their origins from monastic work of colonization in territories where centuries old ruins of war had accumulated...

This title ("Land of St. Benedict") from the Cassinese state could be extended to the medieval possessions of our monasteries; it was, in fact, in the name of the Holy Patriarch and according to the instructions set out in his spiritual code, that his children and successors held and governed them. St. Benedict had given to Monte Cassino the organization of a citadel or autonomous state with a monarchic form of government flanked by a double chamber of advisers (Chap. II and III).

Around the rock, there was the ancient diocese of Cassino, with the pagan population that he had converted to the Faith. Over this region the patriarch exercised pastoral jurisdiction, as a kind of "coepiscopus".

When we extend this theocratic system of autonomous government and enlarge it to a hundred, a thousand and more medieval monasteries scattered not only through Italy but in the whole of Europe, one can then see, what decisive influence St. Benedict exercised on the whole life of the Church».

If human events have swept away such monastic units, if by post-conciliar ordinances, the very ecclesial structure of Monte Cassino has been cut down, it still does not mean that all traces of that influence have perished and some regions, like Abruzzi, can be said to have had Monte Cassino as its first capital.

CHRONOLOGICAL LIST
OF THE ABBOTS OF MONTE CASSINO

BY
FAUSTINO AVAGLIANO

Abbots of Monte Cassino

1. ST. BENEDICT	525 (529)	- 547, March 21
2. St. Constantinus	547	- 560?
3. St. Simplicius	560?	- 576?
4. St. Vitalis	576?	- 580?
5. St. Bonitus *	580 c.	
6. Petronax	717 c.	- 750, May 6
7. Optatus	750	- 760, January 4
8. Hermeris	760	- 760, July 18
9. Gratian	760	- 764, August 22
10. Tomichis	764, August	- 771, January 25
11. Poto	771, February	- 777
12. Theodemar	777-78	- 796
13. Gisulf	796	- 817, December 24
14. St. Apollinaris	817	- 828, November 27
15. St. Deusdedit	828	- 834, October 9
16. Hildericus	834	- 834
17. Authpert	834	- 837, February 20
18. Bassacius	837	- 856, March 17
19. St. Bertharius	856, April	- 883, October 22

Cassinese Abbots in St. Benedict in Teano

20. Angelarius	883	- 889, December 5
21. Ragemprandus	890, March	- 899, November 6
22. Leo	899	- 914, August 17

Cassinese Abbots in St. Benedict in Capua

23. John I	914, September	- 934, March 31
24. Adelpertus	934, April 6	- 943?, December 27
25. Baldoinus	943?	- 946, April?
26. Maielpotus	943-944?	- 948, October 24?

---

* According to a late tradition, after the destruction of Monte Cassino, the Lateran monastery was ruled by the following: Valentinian, Gregory, Theodore, John, Leo, Ursus, Agapitus, Leo, John, Romanus, Theophilus, Hadrian.

Abbots in St. Benedict in Monte Cassino

27. Aligernus	948, October 25	- 985, November 23
28. Manso	986	- 996, November 14
		(March 8)
29. John II	996	- 997
30. John III	997, October	- 1010, March 18
Docibilis of Gaeta		
John IV	1010	- 1011
31. Atenulfus	1011	- 1022, March 30
32. Theobaldus	1022, June 29?	- 1035, June 3
33. Basilius	1036, June	- 1038, June?
34. Richerius	1038, June	- 1055, December 11
35. Petrus I	1055, December	- 1057, May 22
36. Fridericus of Lorraine	1057, May 23	- 1058, March 29
37. Desiderius	1058, June?	- 1087, September 16
38. Oderisius I	1087, September	- 1105, December 2
39. Otto	1105, December	- 1107, October 1
40. Bruno	1107, November	- 1111, September
41. Girardus	1111, October	- 1123, January 17
42. Oderisius II	1123, January	- 1126, May
43. Nicholas I	1126, May	- 1127, July
44. Seniorectus	1127, July 12	- 1137, February 4
45. Raynaldus I	1137, February 10	- 1137, Settember 18
46. Guibaldus	1137, September 19	- 1137, November 2
47. Raynaldus II	1137, November 13	- 1166, October 28
48. Theodinus I	1166, October?	- 1167, September 14
49. Egidio	1168	- 1168
(Pietro, Cassinese deacon, admn.)	1168-1171	
50. Domenico I	1171	- 1174, April 25
51. Pietro II	1174, April	- 1186, July 8
52. Roffredo de Insula	1188, July 9	- 1210, May 30
53. Pietro III	1210, June 24	- 1211, January 28
54. Adenolfo	1211, March	- 1215, August
55. Stefano I	1215, September 13	- 1227, July 21
56. Landolfo Sinibaldo	1227, December	- 1236, July 28
(Pandolfo, administr.)	1237, January 8	- 1238, June
57. Stefano II	1238, June	- 1248, January 21
58. Nicola II	1251, March 11	- ?
59. Riccardo	1252, January 26	- 1262, March 1
60. Teodino II	1262, March 1	- 1263, March 29
61. Bernardo I Ayglerio	1263, March 29	- 1282, April 4

62. Tommaso I	1285, September 28	- 1288, September 18
63. Ponzio	1292, March 19	- 1292, September 30
64. Guglielmo eletto	1293, June	- 1294?
65. Angelario II	1294, October	- 1295, April
66. Beraudo	1295, April 18	- 1295, December
(Bernardo, Bishop of Tripoli, admn.	1295, December 14	- 1296, August)
67. Galardo	1296, August 8	- 1301, March 20
68. Tommaso II	1304	- ?
69. Marino	1306	- 1313, December 19
70. Isnardo	?	- ?
(Oddone, Patriarch of Alexandria, admn.	1323	- 1326, July 3)

Abbots Bishops:

71. Raimondo	1326, April 9	- 1340, July 26
72. Guido	1340, November 6	- 1341, August 2
73. Richerio II	1341, October 10	- 1343, February 27
74. Stefano III	1343, March 14	- 1345, February 13
75. Guglielmo	1345, April 7	- 1353, June 20
76. Francesco d'Atti	1353, July 15	- 1355, March
77. Angelo I Acciaiuoli	1355, March 18	- 1357, October 4
78. Angelo II della Posta	1357	- 1362, April 11
79. Angelo III Orsini	1362, August 26	- 1365
(Urban V, Supreme Pontiff)		

Abbots monks:

80. Bartolomeo da Siena	1369, August 31	- 1369
81. Andrea da Faenza	1369, December 5	- 1373, September 18
82. Pietro IV de Tartaris	1374, February 7	- 1395, June 4
83. Enrico Tomacelli	1396, Giugno 22	- 1413, June
84. Pirro Tomacelli	1414, April	- 1442
85. Antonio Carafa	1446, May 26	- 1454, February 1

Abbots Commendataries:

86. Ludovico Trevisan	1454, May 18	- 1465, March 26
87. Paolo II Sommo Pontefice	1465, March 29	- 1471, July 27
88. Giovanni d'Aragona	1471, August 30	- 1485, October 19
89. Giovanni de' Medici	1486, March 14	- 1504, November 15

Abbots of the Congregation:

90. Eusebio Fontana da Modena	1505, January 11	- 1506, May
91. Zaccaria Castagnola da Padova	1506, May	- 1509, May
92. Graziano II da Milano	1509, May	- 1510, August 22
93. Ignazio Squarcialupi da Firenze	1510, October	- 1516, December
94. Vincenzo de Riso da Napoli	1517, January	- 1518, December
95. Teofilo Piacentini da Milano	1519, January	- 1520, May
96. Ignazio Squarcialupi (*2nd time*)	1520, May	- 1521, December
97. Ludovico II Trivulzio da Milano	1522, January	- 1522, May
98. Giustino Harbes, spagnuolo	1522, May	- 1523, December
99. Ignazio Squarcialupi (*3rd time*)	1524, January	- 1526, December
100. Crisostomo de Alessandro da Napoli	1527, January	- 1531, May
101. Agostino Bonfili da Padova	1531, May	- 1533, May
102. Crisostomo de Alessandro (*2nd time*)	1533, May	- 1538, May
103. Girolamo I da Monte Rosso	1538, May	- 1539, May
104. Ignazio II da Genova	1539, May	- 1541, May
105. Girolamo II Sclocchetto da Piacenza	1541, May	- 1546, May
106. Lorenzo Zambelli da Governolo	1546, May	- 1549, May
107. Girolamo II Sclocchetto (*2nd time*)	1549, May	- 1551, May
108. Innocenzo Nicolai da Novara	1551, May	- 1554, May
109. Girolamo III Calcini da Pavia	1554, May	- 1555, May
110. Isidoro Mantegazzi da Piacenza	1555, May	- 1556, May
111. Ignazio III Vicani da Napoli	1556, May	- 1559, May
112. Angelo IV de Faggis da Castel di Sangro	1559, May	- 1564, May
113. Ignazio III Vicani (*2nd time*)	1564, May	- 1565, May
114. Angelo IV de Faggis (*2nd time*)	1565, May	- 1568, May
115. Bernardo III de Adamo da Aversa	1568, May	- 1570, May
116. Mattia Mattaleja da Lignasco	1570, May	- 1572, May
117. Angelo IV de Faggis (*3rd time*)	1572, May	- 1575, May
118. Girolamo IV Sersale da Cosenza	1575, May	- 1577, August

119. Bernardo IV Ferrajolo da Napoli	1577, August 15	- 1580, May
120. Desiderio II da Brescia	1580, May	- 1585, May
121. Bernardo IV Gerrajolo (*2nd time*)	1585, May	- 1587, January
122. Egidio II Sarnicola da Matelica	1587, May	- 1589, May
123. Andrea II da Sessa	1589, May	- 1590, May
124. Girolamo V Brugia da Perugia	1590, May	- 1565, May
125. Basilio II da Brescia	1595, May	- 1596, September
126. Vittorino de Manso da Aversa	1597, January	- 1598, May
127. Zaccaria II Tarasco da Modena	1598, May	- 1599, May
128. Ambrogio Rastellini da Poppi	1599, May	- 1602, December
129. Desiderio III da Monreale	1603, January	- 1604, December
130. Gregorio II Casamata da Castiglione aretino	1605, January	- 1608, August 2
131. Paolo da Cosenza	1608, October 14	- 1609, October 21
132. Onorato Scalisi da Palermo	1609, October 22	- 1614, April 19
133. Isidoro II Agresti da Parma	1614, April 20	- 1617, April 22
134. Paolo II Scotti da Parma	1617, April 23	- 1621, May
135. Bernardino Saivedra da Trani	1621, May	- 1624, December
136. Simplicio II Caffarelli da Tito	1625, January	- 1628, December
137. Paolo II Scotti (*2nd time*)	1629, January	- 1630, December
138. Angelo V Grassi da Fondi	1631, January	- 1631, December 18
139. Paolo Camillo Casati da Piacenza	1632, January	- 1634, December
140. Desiderio IV Petronio da Fratte	1635, January	- 1639, December
141. Severino Fusco da Castelforte	1640, January	- 1645, May
142. Andrea III Arcioni da Parma	1645, May	- 1647, December
143. Desiderio IV Petronio (*2nd time*)	1648, January	- 1649, July 15
144. Domenico II Quesada da Napoli	1650, January	- 1653, December
145. Carlo de Mauro da Aversa	1654, January	- 1657, March
146. Angelo VI della Noce da Napoli	1657, March	- 1661, May
147. Anastasio Perrona da Napoli	1661, May	- 1665, April
148. Angelo VI della Noce (*2nd time*)	1665, May	- 1669, April
149. Mauro Cesarini da Nola	1669, May	- 1675, April
150. Severino II Pepe da Napoli	1675, May	- 1680, May
151. Andrea IV Deodati da Napoli	1680, May	- 1681, May
152. Sebastiano I Biancardi da Milano	1681, May	- 1687, April
153. Andrea IV Deodati (*2nd time*)	1687, May	- 1692, April
154. Severino II Pepe (*2nd time*)	1692, May	- 1697, August 27
155. Ippolito ella Penna da Napoli	1697, November 20	- 1704, April
156. Gregorio III Galisio da Napoli	1704, May	- 1717, April
157. Nicola II Ruggi da Salerno	1717, May	- 1722, August 16
158. Arcangelo Brancaccio da Napoli	1722, September 17	- 1725, April 24
159. Sebastiano II Gadaleta da Molfetta	1725, June	- 1731, April
160. Stefano IV de Stefano da Napoli	1731, April	- 1737, February

161. Ildefonso I del Verme da Napoli	1737, May	- 1739, May
162. Sebastiano II Gadaleta (2nd time)	1739, May	- 1745, May
163. Antonio II Capece da Napoli	1745, May	- 1751, May
164. Giovanni M. Ragosa da Gaeta	1751, May	- 1753, December 3
165. Marino II Migliarese da Pozzuoli	1754	- 1760, April
166. Domenico III Favilla da Napoli	1760, May	- 1766, April
167. Aurelio Parisio da Cosenza	1766, April	- 1772, May
168. Rinaldo Santomango da Salerno	1772, May	- 1778, May
169. Domenico III Favilla (2nd time)	1778, May	- 1780
170. Prospero de Rosa da Napoli	1781, May	- 1787
171. Tommaso III Capomazza da Pozzuoli*	1788, March 21	- 1793, April
172. Prospero de Rosa (2nd time)	1793, May	- 1797
173. Marino III Lucarelli da Aversa	1797, October 4	- 1804, April
174. Aurelio II Visconti Da Taranto	1804, April	- 1816
175. Giuseppe del Balzo da Napoli	1817	- 1821, June 30
176. Luigi III Bovio da Bitonto	1821, November 26	- 1828, May
177. Giacomo Diez da Augusta	1828, June 12	- 1834, May
178. Celestino Gonzaga da Napoli	1834, May	- 1840, May
179. Matteo Morso da Palermo	1840, May	- 1840, November 11
180. Giuseppe II Frisari da Bisceglie	1841	
181. Michelangelo Celesia da Palermo	1850	- 1849
182. Simplicio III Pappalettere da Barletta	1858, April	- 1858, April
183. Carlo II M. De Vera da Napoli	1863	- 1863
184. Nicola IV d'Orgemont da Napoli	1872	- 1871
185. Giuseppe III Quandel da Napoli	1896	- 1896, June 23
186. Bonifacio M. Krug of Huenfeld near Fulda	1897	- 1897, February 27
187. Gregorio IV Diamare da Napoli	1909, July 24	- 1909, July 4
188. Ildefonso II Rea da Arpino	1945, November 21	- 1945, September 6
189. Martino Matronola da Cassino	1971, May 24	- 1983, April 24
190. Bernardo D'Onorio da Veroli	1983, April 25	

---

* The chapter, held in April 1793, had named, as successor to Capomazza, d. Giacomo Andreotti da Cosenza. He died, however, on the following May 1st and, therefore, his name is not listed here.

CONTENTS

CONTENTS

GENERAL BIBLIOGRAPHY

Up to the twelfth century, the principal source, which encompasses and complements all others, is the *Chronica Casinensis*. This works was begun by Leo, later Cardinal of Ostia, and continued and rearranged by others. the last and best edition is the one done by H. HOFFMANN in MGH SS 34, Hannover 1980. The results of long years of preparation and researches in early Cassinese history are included in this edition. The work of E. GAT- TOLA, *Historia Abbatiae Casinensis,* 2 vols. Venice, Coleti, 1733, followed by the *Accessiones*, 2 vols. Venice, Coleti, 1734 is fundamental for the history of Monte Cassino.

L. TOSTI, *Storia della Badia di Montecassino,* 4 vols. Rome, Pasqualucci, 1888-1890 is an outstanging monument of ninteenth century historiography. It carries the story as far as the suppression of 1868. For the late centuries, however, except the episodes of the French devastation of the abbey, the narrative is rather sketchy.

L. FABIANI, *La Terra di S. Benedetto,* 3 vols. Montecassino, 1968-1981 (Miscellanea Cassinese 33, 34, 42) studies in the first two volumes the history of the Cassinese «state» from the eighth to the thirteenth century, especially the juridical and administrative organization. In the third volume he describes its end.

Just recently the eagerly awaited work of H. BLOCH, *Monte Cassino in the Middle Ages,* 3 vols. Rome, Edizioni di Storia e Letteratura, 1986 and Cambridge MA, Harward University, 1986, has finally appeared. This study is the culmination of long years of researches by one of the most distinguished and discriminating Cassinese scholar. It will soon become an indispensable companion to new and old students of Cassinese history for generations to come.

Finito di stampare nel mese di marzo 1987
dalla Tipografia Editrice M. Pisani s.a.s. di Isola del Liri
per conto delle Pubblicazioni Cassinesi di
Montecassino